How to
PLAN & PLANT
YOUR GARDEN

How to
PLAN & PLANT
YOUR GARDEN

Crescent Books

New York

This 1988 edition published by Crescent Books,
Distributed by Crown Publishers, Inc.
225 Park Avenue South
New York, New York 10003.

First published in 1988 by
The Hamlyn Publishing Group Limited,
Michelin House, 81 Fulham Road,
London SW3 6RB, England

Copyright © Hugh Williams, 1988

ISBN 0-517-65519-5

Printed and bound by Mandarin Offset, Hong Kong

h g f e d c b a

Cover photography
FRONT, main picture: Jerry Harpur; left (top to bottom): Photos
Horticultural, Hamlyn Publishing Group Limited, Photos
Horticultural, Harry Smith Horticultural Photographic Collection,
Photos Horticultural; right (top to bottom): Photos Horticultural, Pat
Brindley, Harry Smith Horticultural Photographic Collection, Photos
Horticultural, Hamlyn Publishing Group Limited/W. F. Davidson.
BACK, top row: all by Photos Horticultural; second row: Pat Brindley,
Harry Smith Horticultural Photographic Collection, Octopus Books
Limited/Jerry Harpur; third row: Photos Horticultural, Hamlyn
Publishing Group Limited/Anthony Martin, Harry Smith Horticultural
Photographic Collection; fourth row: Harry Smith Horticultural
Photographic Collection, Harry Smith Horticultural Photographic
Collection, Pat Brindley, Photos Horticultural.

Contents

Introduction   7

Permanent Plants for the Garden   8

Key to the Book   9

Plant Selection Charts   11
     Shrubs and Trees   12
     Herbaceous Perennials and Rock Plants   48

Guidelines for Successful Growing   59

Directory of Plants   73

Glossary   236

Bibliography   236

Index of Common Names   237

Acknowledgements   240

Introduction

This book provides a simple, easy-to-use method of selecting the most suitable plant for a specific situation and set of requirements.

Both the absolute beginner faced with having a garden for the first time and the life-long experienced professional will gain considerable benefit from this selection system, for not only does it offer a quick way of choosing plants to suit a number of separate requirements, but also it will help to find which plants will be complementary to, and associate well with, each other.

For the beginner, it does not matter if you are not familiar with the names of many garden plants – all you need to know are the conditions of the site and your own preferences as to height, colour and plant characteristics.

Professional garden centre assistants who believe in freely giving the best advice to customers are often asked to suggest a plant to suit a particular situation. As a garden centre proprietor, I know how very difficult it is, when under pressure with other customers waiting for attention, to come up with the ideal answer with easy spontaneity.

It is as a direct result of this that I devised the system of plant selection used in this book, originally producing it privately as a small handbook featuring only hardy shrubs for use by my staff and myself. We found it invaluable, and we started lending copies to customers to take with them round our shrub lines. The customers were always delighted that they had managed so easily to locate the right shrub to suit their needs. At the same time the pressure on my staff was reduced.

Landscape gardeners and architects will also find the plant selection system of this book particularly useful when designing customers' or clients' gardens.

It is my hope that it will also prove a valuable handbook to experienced and knowledgeable gardeners, and keen amateurs.

An attractive summer display from hardy herbaceous perennials, roses and lilies ('Cobblers', Crowborough).

Permanent Plants for the Garden

Garden plants, for the purpose of this book, are those of a hardy, permanent or long-term status, and no mention, therefore will be made of bulbs, summer annuals for bedding, of biennials, or of perennials of such a tender constitution as to necessitate inside over-wintering. These plants do, however, have a valuable place as seasonal fillers.

The hardy garden plants that form the permanent planting framework of the garden as described here are divided into three sections.

Hardy shrubs, climbing plants and ornamental trees

These grow either on a short stem, or directly from the surface of the soil. They have woody stems, and may be either deciduous – those that lose their leaves in autumn – or evergreen – those that are in leaf all year round. In fact evergreens lose leaves throughout the year, but produce new ones at the same time.

A small group of shrubs are known as semi-evergreen, as they are prone to leaf loss in hard winters, but retain most of their leaves during mild ones.

The size of hardy shrubs can vary greatly, from low-growing, ground-covering ones to those of 4 or 5 m (13 or 16 ft). Similarly, they can vary greatly in spread.

There is tremendous variety to be had in leaf colour, size and shape and in flower colour, size, shape and season. Some shrubs have gloriously fragrant flowers while others provide startlingly beautiful autumn tints.

Ornamental trees are obtainable as full standards, growing on a single stem of at least 1.5 m (5 ft), or as half-standards, 1.2 to 1.5 m (4 to 5 ft). They are ornamental, either by virtue of their decorative flowers or their foliage, or a combination of both.

Some, such as *Prunus sargentii* and *Amelanchier lamarckii* are renowned for their exquisite autumn colour whilst also producing an impressive display of flowers in the spring.

Care must be taken when selecting a tree, for, though it may look charming and suitable when seen in the garden centre, it may quickly become too big for the garden. The golden weeping willow (*Salix × chrysocoma*) is a good example, often purchased on impulse to be regretted later.

Conifers

This term comes from the Latin, meaning 'cone bearing'. While the majority of conifers are evergreen, there are some, such as the larches, which are deciduous. There is a tremendous variation in height and spread from some of the dwarfs growing to no more than 30 cm (1 ft) to the massive redwoods of California which achieve the amazing height of 108 m (360 ft) in their natural habitat.

Generally speaking, conifers are not too choosy as to soil requirements, and many, especially the dwarf forms, will grow well on quite poor soils and in pots. Junipers (*Juniperus*) and yews (*Taxus*) will thrive on extremely chalky or lime soils.

However, it is my opinion that an extra brightness is always apparent, particularly in the case of gold and blue cultivers of Lawson cypresses (*Chamaecyparis lawsoniana*) when they are growing in neutral or acid soil.

Hardy herbaceous perennials and rock plants

These are soft-stemmed plants which, in general, require cutting back each autumn and lifting and dividing every few years. This means that there is usually nothing to look at in the winter and they do entail a fair amount of work.

However, a well planned and well maintained herbaceous border is enormously rewarding. A mixed border also works very well if carefully selected herbaceous perennials are used together with shrubs and conifers. Alpines are dwarf and compact plants which, in their natural habitats, spend a long rest-period, cosily protected from winds and kept dry under a blanket of snow. They do not always take kindly to wet and cold, but snowless, winters.

Above: *Skimmia japonica* 'Rubella'
Above, right: A formal double cultivar of *Camellia japonica*

Opposite, left: *Lupinus* 'Russell Hybrids'
Opposite, right: *Nyssa sinensis*

Key to the Book

This guide to plant selection consists of two main sections. First, there is a series of easy-to-follow charts, listing well over 1100 plants in a computer-sorted order of category seniority. It is divided into two sub-sections, firstly shrubs and conifers including climbing and wall shrubs and some ornamental trees, and secondly herbaceous and rock garden perennials. A key to the symbols can be found on page 11.

Part two of the book is an illustrated dictionary of the plants with full descriptive and cultural details.

Most people consider plant height to be of paramount importance, so five height groups head the categorization list. These are followed by five categories of flower colour, being second only to height as a main consideration. Thereafter follows leaf colour, then berry, fruit or cone colour, and then general environmental requirements such as light, soil type, moisture requirements and other essential information.

All the items have been sorted into an order which provides a unique plant selection system of unprecedented simplicity. It is not necessary to know the name of a plant or to have any particular one in mind. All you need to know are the basic requirements, that is, those that satisfy your own wishes, plus those that are determined by the conditions and situation of the area to be planted. Usually there are no more than five or six conditions that are of vital importance, plus perhaps one or two desirable ones, such as fragrance or autumn colour.

Since all plants of each height group are placed together, there is no need to look beyond the height group of your choice in order to find a plant to fit in with the other requirements.

By the nature of things, among the necessarily limited number of plants mentioned, there are bound to be occasions when it will not be possible to find a plant that will suit *all* your requirements and you may have to delete one or two of the least important ones. With certain plants, for example, height can be reduced by pruning, trimming or training and where this is possible, a higher height group might be chosen in the selection process.

Having found a plant name that seems to satisfy all your requirements, just turn to the page in the second part of the book (shown in the extreme right-hand column) for an illustration (most but not all plants are illustrated) as well as more information about the plant.

Using the charts

The charts are divided into two sections: Shrubs and Trees, which includes climbers and conifers (pages 12–47), and Herbaceous and Rock Plants (pages 48–57). Each section is subdivided into height categories. These are: Up to 60 cm (2 ft); 60 cm to 1.2 m (2 to 4 ft); 1.2 m to 2.5 m (4 ft to 8 ft); 2.5 m to 6 m (8 to 20 ft); over 6 m (20 ft).

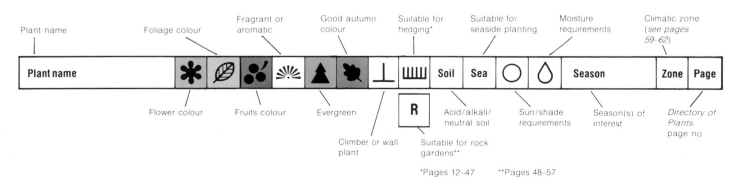

Plant Selection Charts

The charts are divided into two sections: Shrubs and Trees, which includes climbers and conifers (pages 12–47), and Herbaceous and Rock Plants (pages 48–57). Each section is sub-divided into height categories. These are: Up to 60 cm (2 ft); 60 cm to 1.2 m (2 to 4 ft); 1.2 m to 2.5 m (4 ft to 8 ft); 2.5 m to 6 m (8 to 20 ft); over 6 m (20 ft).

KEY TO THE SYMBOLS

✳	FLOWERS (including catkins)	🍒	FRUIT
✳	Flowers in shades of red	🍒	Berries, fruits, cones or seed heads in shades of red, orange or brown
✳	Flowers in shades of pink	🍒	Berries, fruits, cones or seed heads in shades of yellow or gold
✳	Flowers in shades of yellow, yellow/green, gold or orange	🍒	White or cream berries, fruits, cones or seed heads
✳	Flowers in shades of white or cream	🍒	Berries, fruits, cones or seed heads in shades of blue, purple or black
✳	Flowers in shades of blue or purple	🍒	Plant produces berries in various colours (sample shows red or yellow)
✳	Bi-colour flowers (sample shows pink/white)		No symbol indicates non-fruiting plant, or plant with non-decorative cones
	No symbol indicates insignificant flowers or non-flowering plant	Acid	Requires acid soil
🍃	FOLIAGE	Alkali	Requires alkaline soil
🍃	Silver or white foliage	T	Neutral soil or soil tolerant
🍃	Foliage in shades of red or purple-red	Sea	Suitable for seaside planting
🍃	Foliage in shades of yellow or gold	○	Full sun
🍃	Blue or glaucous foliage	●	Full shade
🍃	Foliage in shades of green	◑	Sun or light shade
🍃	Variegated foliage (sample shows green/white)	Ⓣ	Sun or shade tolerant
☀	Fragrant or aromatic flowers or foliage	○	Dry conditions
▲	Evergreen	●	Moist conditions
🍂	Good autumn colour	◖	Semi-moist conditions
⊥	Climber or wall plant or plant requiring the protection of a wall	Season	Season(s) of interest (No entry indicates plant has year-round interest)
⊔⊔⊔	Suitable for hedging	△5	Climatic zone (*see pages 59–62 for more detailed information.*)
R	Suitable for rock gardens	Page	Page reference to *Directory of Plants* for more details

A beautiful garden of mixed herbaceous perennials (Ablington Manor).

SHRUBS AND TREES: up to 60 cm (2 ft)

SHRUBS AND TREES

Plant name	✳	leaf	berries	fan	tree	leaf	⊥	||||	Soil	Sea	○	◊	Season	Zone	Page
Daboecia cantabrica 'Bicolor'	✳	leaf			tree				Acid		◑	◐	Summer/Autumn	5	128
Fuchsia 'Golden Treasure'	✳	leaf	●						T	Sea	○	●	Summer/Autumn	7	144
Fuchsia 'Tom Thumb'	✳	leaf	●						Acid	Sea	◑	●	Summer/Autumn	6	145
Fuchsia magellanica 'Pumila'	✳	leaf	●						T	Sea	◑	●	Summer/Autumn	6	145
Coriaria japonica	✳	leaf	●			leaf			T		○	◐	Summer	9	118
Fuchsia 'Display'	✳	leaf	●						T	Sea	◑	●	Summer/Autumn	7	144
Erica herbacea 'Vivellii'	✳	leaf			tree				T		○	◐	Winter/Spring	5	137
Philesia magellanica	✳	leaf			tree				Acid		◑	●	Summer/Autumn	9	190
Daboecia cantabrica 'Atropurpurea'	✳	leaf			tree				Acid		○	◐	Summer/Autumn	5	128
Calluna vulgaris 'Allportii Praecox'	✳	leaf			tree				Acid		○	◐	Summer	4	99
Erica cinerea 'Atrosanguinea Smith's Var.'	✳	leaf			tree				Acid		○	◐	Summer	5	136
Mitraria coccinea	✳	leaf			tree				T		◑	◐	Summer	9	182
Spiraea japonica 'Shirobana'	✳	leaf							T		◑	◐	Summer	5	221
Erica tetralix 'Pink Star'	✳	leaf			tree				Acid		○	●	Summer/Autumn	5	137
Calluna vulgaris 'Silver Queen'	✳	leaf			tree				Acid		○	◐	Summer	4	99
Erica cinerea 'Golden Drop'	✳	leaf			tree				Acid		○	◐	Summer	5	136
Erica herbacea 'Aurea'	✳	leaf			tree				T		○	◐	Winter/Spring	5	137
Calluna vulgaris 'Orange Queen'	✳	leaf			tree				Acid		○	◐	Summer	4	99
Spiraea japonica 'Golden Princess'	✳	leaf							T		◑	◐	Summer	5	221
Daphne retusa	✳	leaf	●	fan	tree				Alkali		◑	◐	Spring	4	129
Fuchsia 'Alice Hoffman'	✳	leaf	●						T	Sea	◑	●	Summer	6	144
Erica × darleyensis 'Darley Dale'	✳	leaf			tree				T		○	◐	Winter/Spring	5	136
Erica herbacea 'King George'	✳	leaf			tree				T		○	◐	Winter/Spring	5	137
Erica herbacea 'Loughrigg'	✳	leaf			tree				T		○	◐	Winter/Spring	5	137
Erica herbacea 'Atrorubra'	✳	leaf			tree				T		○	◐	Spring	5	137
Daphne cneorum	✳	leaf		fan	tree				T		◑	◐	Spring	5	129
Andromeda polifolia 'Compacta'	✳	leaf			tree	leaf			Acid		◑	●	Spring	3	83

Plant name	✳	🍃	●	✺	▲	🍂	⊥	|||||	Soil	Sea	○	💧	Season	Zone	Page
Spiraea japonica 'Alpina'	✳	🍃							T		◑	💧	Summer	4	221
Calluna vulgaris 'H.E. Beale'	✳	🍃			▲				Acid		○	💧	Summer	4	99
Calluna vulgaris 'Elsie Purnell'	✳	🍃			▲				Acid		○	💧	Summer	4	99
Calluna vulgaris 'County Wicklow'	✳	🍃			▲				Acid		○	💧	Summer	4	99
Calluna vulgaris 'Peter Sparkes'	✳	🍃			▲				Acid		○	💧	Summer	4	99
Erica vagans 'St Keverne'	✳	🍃			▲				Acid		○	💧	Summer	5	137
Erica vagans 'Mrs D.F. Maxwell'	✳	🍃			▲				Acid		○	💧	Summer	5	137
Erica cinerea 'Pink Ice'	✳	🍃			▲				Acid		○	💧	Summer	5	136
Erica cinerea 'C.D. Eason'	✳	🍃			▲				Acid		○	💧	Summer	5	136
Santolina chamaecyparissus	✳	🍃		✺	▲				T		○	💧	Summer	6	215
Helichrysum serotinum	✳	🍃			▲				T		○	💧	Summer	7	155
Hypericum × moseranum 'Tricolor'	✳	🍃							Alkali		◑	💧	Summer/Autumn	8	160
Berberis thunbergii 'Atropurpurea Nana'	✳	🍃	●					|||||	T		◑	💧	Spring	5	95
Berberis thunbergii 'Aurea'	✳	🍃	●						T		○	💧	Spring	7	95
Berberis candidula	✳	🍃	●		▲				T		◑	💧	Spring	5	94
Berberis × stenophylla 'Corallina Compacta'	✳	🍃	●		▲				T		◑	💧	Spring	7	95
Cytisus ardoinii	✳	🍃							Acid		○	💧	Spring	5	127
Cytisus × beanii	✳	🍃							T		○	💧	Spring	6	127
Cytisus × kewensis	✳	🍃							T		○	💧	Spring	6	127
Potentilla arbuscula	✳	🍃							T		○	💧	Spring	5	198
Potentilla arbuscula 'Beesii'	✳	🍃							T		○	💧	Summer/Autumn	6	198
Potentilla 'Tangerine'	✳	🍃							T		○	💧	Summer/Autumn	6	199

Key (see also p 9 and p 11)	✳ Flower colour	🍃 Foliage colour	● Berries/fruits/cones/seed heads colour
✺ Fragrant or aromatic	▲ Evergreen	🍂 Good autumn colour	⊥ Climber or wall plant
||||| Suitable for hedging	Soil Acid/alkali/tolerant	Sea Suitable for maritime or seaside conditions	○ Sun/shade requirements
💧 Moisture requirements	Season Season(s) of interest	Zone Climatic zone (see pages 59–62)	Page Page reference to Directory of Plants

SHRUBS AND TREES: up to 60 cm (2 ft)

SHRUBS AND TREES

Plant name	✳	🍃	●●●	☀	▲	🍂	⊥	⸾⸾⸾	Soil	Sea	○	💧	Season	Zone	Page
Hypericum calycinum	✳	🍃			▲				T		ⓣ	💧	Summer	5	160
Genista tinctoria 'Royal Gold'	✳	🍃							T		○	💧	Summer	6	147
Calceolaria integrifolia	✳	🍃			▲				T		○	💧	Summer	9	98
Pachysandra terminalis 'Variegata'	✳	🍃			▲				T		◐	●	Spring	5	186
Calluna vulgaris 'Gold Haze'	✳	🍃			▲				Acid		◐	●	Summer	4	99
Hebe ochracea	✳	🍃			▲				T	Sea	○	💧	Summer	5	153
Hebe albicans	✳	🍃			▲				T	Sea	○	💧	Summer	5	151
Hebe pinguifolia 'Pagei'	✳	🍃			▲				T	Sea	○	💧	Summer	5	153
Cotoneaster dammeri	✳	🍃	●●●		▲				T		ⓣ	💧	Spring	4	123
Gaultheria procumbens	✳	🍃	●●●		▲				Acid		◐	●	Summer	4	146
Vaccinium vitis-idaea	✳	🍃	●●●		▲				Acid		◐	●	Summer	3	230
Cotoneaster microphyllus	✳	🍃	●●●		▲				T		◐	💧	Summer	5	124
Cornus canadensis	✳	🍃	●●●						Acid		◐	💧	Summer	5	119
Sarcococca humilis	✳	🍃	●●●	☀	▲				Alkali		●	💧	Winter	5	215
Erica herbacea 'Springwood White'	✳	🍃			▲				T		○	💧	Winter / Spring	5	137
Erica × darleyensis 'Silberschmelze'	✳	🍃			▲				T		○	💧	Winter / Spring	5	136
Cassiope 'Edinburgh'	✳	🍃			▲				Acid		◐	●	Spring	6	103
Pachysandra procumbens	✳	🍃			▲				T		◐	●	Spring	4	186
Pachysandra terminalis	✳	🍃			▲				T		◐	●	Spring	4	186
Chamaedaphne calyculata 'Nana'	✳	🍃			▲				Acid		◐	💧	Spring	6	110
Potentilla davurica 'Abbotswood'	✳	🍃							T		○	💧	Summer/Autumn	6	198
Potentilla davurica 'Manchu'	✳	🍃							T		○	💧	Summer/Autumn	6	198
Daboecia cantabrica 'Alba'	✳	🍃			▲				Acid		◐	💧	Summer/Autumn	5	128
Erica tetralix 'Alba Mollis'	✳	🍃			▲				Acid		○	●	Summer	5	137
× Halimiocistus 'Ingwersenii'	✳	🍃			▲				T	Sea	○	💧	Summer	7	150
Calluna vulgaris 'Alba Plena'	✳	🍃			▲				Acid		○	💧	Summer	4	99
Hebe buchananii	✳	🍃			▲				T	Sea	○	💧	Summer	6	152

SHRUBS AND TREES: up to 60 cm (2 ft)

Plant name	✳	🍃	🍒	🔆	🌲	🍂	⊥	⊔⊔⊔	Soil	Sea	◐	💧	Season	Zone	Page
Hebe macrantha	✳	🍃			🌲				T	Sea	○	💧	Summer	7	152
Erica vagans 'Lyonesse'	✳	🍃			🌲				Acid		○	💧	Summer	5	137
Leiophyllum buxifolium	✳	🍃			🌲				Acid		◐	💧	Summer	5	171
Lavandula angustifolia 'Hidcote'	✳	🍃		🔆	🌲			⊔⊔⊔	T	Sea	○	💧	Summer	5	170
Lavandula stoechas	✳	🍃		🔆	🌲			⊔⊔⊔	T	Sea	○	💧	Summer	5	170
Calluna vulgaris 'Multicolor'	✳	🍃			🌲	🍂			Acid		○	💧	Summer	4	99
Calluna vulgaris 'Robert Chapman'	✳	🍃			🌲	🍂			Acid		○	💧	Summer	4	99
Calluna vulgaris 'Sister Anne'	✳	🍃			🌲				Acid		○	💧	Summer	4	99
Hebe pimeleoides 'Glaucocaerulea'	✳	🍃			🌲				T	Sea	◐	💧	Summer	5	153
Vinca major	✳	🍃			🌲				T		◐	💧	Spring / Summer	4	233
Vinca minor	✳	🍃			🌲				T		◐	💧	Spring / Summer	4	233
Rosmarinus lavandulaceus	✳	🍃		🔆	🌲				T		○	💧	Spring / Summer	7	212
Ceratostigma plumbaginoides	✳	🍃				🍂			T		○	💧	Summer / Autumn	8	106
Lavandula angustifolia 'Munstead'	✳	🍃		🔆	🌲			⊔⊔⊔	T	Sea	○	💧	Summer	5	170
Calluna vulgaris 'Hammondii Rubrifolia'	✳	🍃			🌲				Acid		◐	💧	Summer	4	99
Hebe 'Carl Teschner'	✳	🍃			🌲				T	Sea	○	💧	Summer	6	152
Erica cinerea 'Purple Beauty'	✳	🍃			🌲				Acid		○	💧	Summer	5	136
Taxus baccata 'Repens Aurea'		🍃			🌲				Alkali		◐	💧		6	226
Calluna vulgaris 'Golden Feather'		🍃			🌲	🍂			Acid		○	💧		4	99
Juniperus horizontalis 'Bar Harbor'		🍃		🔆	🌲				Alkali		○	💧		4	166
Juniperus horizontalis 'Glauca'		🍃		🔆	🌲				Alkali		○	💧		4	166
Juniperus horizontalis 'Montana'		🍃		🔆	🌲				Alkali		○	💧		4	166

Key *(see also p 9 and p 11)*	✳ Flower colour	🍃 Foliage colour	🍒 Berries/fruits/cones/seed heads colour
🔆 Fragrant or aromatic	🌲 Evergreen	🍂 Good autumn colour	⊥ Climber or wall plant
⊔⊔⊔ Suitable for hedging	**Soil** Acid/alkali/tolerant	**Sea** Suitable for maritime or seaside conditions	○ Sun/shade requirements
💧 Moisture requirements	**Season** Season(s) of interest	**Zone** Climatic zone (*see pages 59–62*)	**Page** Page reference to *Directory of Plants*

SHRUBS AND TREES: up to 60 cm (2 ft)

Plant name	✳	🍃	🍒	🌸	🌲	🍁	⊥	⊞	Soil	Sea	○	◊	Season	Zone	Page
Picea mariana 'Nana'		🍃			🌲				T		○	●		2	192
Taxus baccata 'Repandans'		🍃	🍒		🌲				Alkali		Ⓣ	◊		6	226
Juniperus conferta		🍃		🌸	🌲				Alkali		◐	◊		5	166
Juniperus communis 'Repanda'		🍃		🌸	🌲				Alkali		○	◊		4	166
Juniperus horizontalis 'Plumosa'		🍃		🌸	🌲				Alkali		○	◊		4	166
Juniperus horizontalis 'Douglasii'		🍃		🌸	🌲				Alkali		◐	●		4	166
Buxus sempervirens 'Suffruticosa'		🍃		🌸	🌲			⊞	T		Ⓣ	●		5	98
Picea abies 'Gregoryana' Picea abies 'Nidiformis'		🍃			🌲				T		◐	●		4	192
Arundinaria pumila		🍃			🌲				T		○	◊		5	88
Chamaecyparis obtusa 'Nana'		🍃			🌲				T		◐	◊		5	109
Juniperus sabina 'Tamariscifolia'		🍃		🌸	🌲				Alkali		◐	◊		5	167
Juniperus recurva 'Embley Park'		🍃		🌸	🌲				Alkali		◐	◊		4	167
Juniperus procumbens 'Nana'		🍃		🌸	🌲				Alkali		◐	◊		5	167

SHRUBS AND TREES: 60 cm – 1.2 m (2 ft – 4 ft)

Plant name	✳	🍃	🍒	🌸	🌲	🍁	⊥	⊞	Soil	Sea	○	◊	Season	Zone	Page
Fuchsia 'Madame Cornelissen'	✳	🍃							T	Sea	◐	●	Summer/Autumn	6	144
Fuchsia magellanica 'Variegata'	✳	🍃							T	Sea	◐	●	Summer/Autumn	7	145
Chamaecyparis laws. 'Pygmaea Argentea'	✳	🍃			🌲				T		◐	◊	Spring	6	108
Rosa gallica var. officinalis	✳	🍃	🍒	🌸					T		○	◊	Summer	5	210
Rosa gallica 'Versicolor'	✳	🍃	🍒	🌸				⊞	T		○	◊	Summer	5	210
Azalea 'Mother's Day'	✳	🍃			🌲				Acid		◐	●	Spring	5	93
Azalea 'John Cairns'	✳	🍃			🌲				Acid		◐	●	Spring	5	93
Azalea 'Hinodegiri'	✳	🍃			🌲				Acid		◐	●	Spring	5	93
Azalea 'Addy Wery'	✳	🍃			🌲				Acid		◐	●	Spring	5	92
Cytisus scoparius 'Lena'	✳	🍃							T	Sea	○	◊	Spring / Summer	5	128
Prunus tenella 'Firehill'	✳	🍃							Alkali		◐	◊	Spring	5	202
Phygelius capensis	✳	🍃			🌲		⊥		T		○	◊	Summer/Autumn	8	191
Potentilla fruticosa 'Red Ace'	✳	🍃							T		○	◊	Summer/Autumn	6	198

SHRUBS AND TREES

SHRUBS AND TREES: 60 cm – 1.2 m (2 ft – 4 ft)

Plant name	✻	🍃	🍒	🎆	🌲	🍂	⊥	⊔⊔⊔	Soil	Sea	◑	💧	Season	Zone	Page
Kalmia angustifolia 'Rubra'	✻	🍃			🌲				Acid		◑	💧	Summer	3	168
Lavandula angustifolia 'Loddon Pink'	✻	🍃		🎆	🌲			⊔⊔⊔	T	Sea	○	💧	Summer	5	170
Spiraea × bumalda 'Goldflame'	✻	🍃							T		○	💧	Summer	5	221
Rhododendron yakushimanum	✻	🍃			🌲				Acid		◑	💧	Spring/Summer	5	206
Azalea 'Blaauw's Pink'	✻	🍃			🌲				Acid		◑	💧	Spring	5	92
Azalea 'Hinomayo'	✻	🍃			🌲				Acid		◑	💧	Spring	5	93
Azalea 'Johann Strauss'	✻	🍃			🌲				Acid		◑	💧	Spring	5	93
Erica erigena 'Brightness'	✻	🍃			🌲				T		○	💧	Spring	5	137
Potentilla fruticosa 'Princess'	✻	🍃							T		○	💧	Summer/Autumn	6	198
Potentilla fruticosa 'Royal Flush'	✻	🍃							T		○	💧	Summer/Autumn	6	198
Spiraea × bumalda	✻	🍃							T		◑	💧	Summer	4	221
Cistus 'Silver Pink'	✻	🍃			🌲				T	Sea	○	💧	Summer	8	112
Salix lanata	✻	🍃							T		○	💧	Spring	5	214
Artemisia arborescens	✻	🍃							T		◑	💧	Summer	8	87
Senecio 'Sunshine'	✻	🍃			🌲				T	Sea	◑	💧	Summer	5	218
Ruta graveolens	✻	🍃		🎆					T		○	💧	Spring	8	212
Berberis wilsoniae	✻	🍃	🍒			🍂		⊔⊔⊔	T		○	💧	Spring/Autumn	5	96
Berberis × rubrostilla	✻	🍃	🍒			🍂			T		◑	💧	Spring	5	94
Lonicera microphylla	✻	🍃	🍒						T		◑	💧	Spring	5	175
Hypericum × inodorum 'Elstead'	✻	🍃	🍒		🌲				T		○	💧	Summer/Autumn	5	160
Berberis verruculosa	✻	🍃	🍒		🌲				T		◑	💧	Spring	5	96
Lonicera pileata	✻	🍃	🍒		🌲				T		Ⓣ	💧	Spring	5	176

Key (see also p 9 and p 11)	✻	Flower colour		🍃	Foliage colour		🍒	Berries/fruits/cones/seed heads colour
🎆	Fragrant or aromatic	🌲	Evergreen		🍂	Good autumn colour	⊥	Climber or wall plant
⊔⊔⊔	Suitable for hedging	Soil	Acid/alkali/tolerant		Sea	Suitable for maritime or seaside conditions	○	Sun/shade requirements
💧	Moisture requirements	Season	Season(s) of interest	Zone	Climatic zone (see pages 59–62)		Page	Page reference to Directory of Plants

SHRUBS AND TREES: 60 cm – 1.2 m (2 ft – 4 ft)

Plant name	✳	🍃	berries	fan	▲	🍂	⊥	‖‖	Soil	Sea	○	💧	Season	Zone	Page
Genista lydia	✳	🍃							T		○	◇	Spring /Summer	7	147
Potentilla fruticosa 'Goldfinger'	✳	🍃							T		○	◇	Summer/Autumn	6	198
Phlomis fruticosa	✳	🍃			▲				T	Sea	○	◇	Summer	7	190
Halimium lasianthum	✳	🍃			▲				T	Sea	○	◇	Summer	7	150
Artemisia abrotanum	✳	🍃		🌿					T		○	◐	Summer	8	86
Cytisus decumbens	✳	🍃							T		○	◇	Summer	5	127
Coronilla emerus var. emeroides	✳	🍃							T		◑	◇	Summer	7	121
Salix 'Fuiji-Koriangi'	✳	🍃							T		◑	●	Spring	4	213
Olearia mollis	✳	🍃			▲				Alkali	Sea	○	◇	Summer	9	184
Convolvulus cneorum	✳	🍃			▲				T		◑	◇	Summer	9	118
Cotoneaster horizontalis 'Variegatus'	✳	🍃	●●						T		◑	◇	Summer	5	124
Yucca filamentosa 'Variegata'	✳	🍃			▲				T		○	◇	Summer	8	235
Euonymus fortunei 'Silver Queen'	✳	🍃			▲		⊥		T		◑	●	Summer	5	141
Euonymus fortunei 'Emerald 'n' Gold'	✳	🍃			▲				T		◑	◇	Summer	5	140
Pernettya mucronata	✳	🍃	●●	▲					Acid		○	●	Summer/Autumn	5	188
Prunus laurocerasus 'Otto Luyken'	✳	🍃	●●		▲				T		Ⓣ	◇	Spring	6	200
Prunus laurocerasus 'Zabeliana'	✳	🍃	●●		▲				T		Ⓣ	●	Spring	5	200
Skimmia reevesiana	✳	🍃	●●	🌿	▲				Acid	Sea	◑	◇	Spring	5	219
Gaulnettya × wisleyensis 'Wisley Pearl'	✳	🍃	●●		▲				Acid		◑	●	Summer	4	146
Cotoneaster horizontalis	✳	🍃	●●			🍂	⊥		T		Ⓣ	◇	Summer	4	123
Cotoneaster conspicuus 'Decorus'	✳	🍃	●●		▲				T		◑	◇	Summer	4	123
Danae racemosa	✳	🍃	●●		▲				T		◑	●	Summer	6	128
Viburnum davidii	✳	🍃	●●		▲				T		◐	●	Summer	7	231
Sarcococca confusa	✳	🍃	●●	🌿	▲				Alkali		◑	●	Winter	5	215
Sarcococca hookerana var. digyna	✳	🍃	●●	🌿	▲				Alkali		◑	●	Winter	5	215
Azalea 'Palestrina'	✳	🍃			▲				Acid		◐	●	Spring	5	93

SHRUBS AND TREES: 60 cm – 1.2 m (2 ft – 4 ft)

Plant name	Flower colour	Foliage colour	Berries/fruits/cones/seed heads	Fragrant or aromatic	Evergreen	Good autumn colour	Climber or wall plant	Suitable for hedging	Soil	Sea	Sun/shade	Moisture	Season	Zone	Page
Prunus tenella 'Alba'	✳	🍃							Alkali		◑	💧	Spring	5	202
Skimmia japonica 'Rubella'	✳	🍃		☀	▲				T		◑	💧	Spring	5	219
Fothergilla gardenii	✳	🍃		☀		🍂			Acid		◑	💧	Spring	5	143
Ledum palustre	✳	🍃			▲				Acid		◑	💧	Spring	5	170
Yucca filamentosa	✳	🍃			▲				T	Sea	○	💧	Summer	8	235
Spiraea nipponica var. *tosaensis*	✳	🍃							T		◑	💧	Summer	4	221
Deutzia × rosea 'Campanulata'	✳	🍃							T		◑	💧	Summer	4	131
Philadelphus 'Manteau d'Hermine'	✳	🍃		☀					Alkali		◑	💧	Summer	5	189
Philadelphus 'Sybille'	✳	🍃		☀					Alkali		◑	💧	Summer	5	190
Itea virginica	✳	🍃		☀					Acid		◑	💧	Summer	5	163
Ozothamnus ledifolius	✳	🍃		☀	▲				T		○	💧	Summer	8	185
Cistus × corbariensis	✳	🍃			▲				T	Sea	○	💧	Summer	8	112
Abeliophyllum distichum	✳	🍃		☀					T		○	💧	Winter	7	74
Lavandula angustifolia	✳	🍃		☀	▲			⊞	T	Sea	○	💧	Summer	5	170
Lavandula angustifolia 'Vera'	✳	🍃		☀	▲			⊞	T	Sea	○	💧	Summer	5	170
Perovskia atriplicifolia 'Blue Spire'	✳	🍃							Alkali	Sea	○	💧	Summer/Autumn	7	188
Hebe hulkeana	✳	🍃			▲		⊥		Alkali	Sea	○	💧	Spring/Summer	9	152
Azalea 'Blue Danube'	✳	🍃			▲				Acid		◑	💧	Spring	5	92
Cytisus purpureus	✳	🍃							T	Sea	○	💧	Spring	5	128
Hebe 'Autumn Glory'	✳	🍃			▲				T	Sea	○	💧	Summer/Autumn	7	151
Ceratostigma willmottianum	✳	🍃				🍂			T		○	💧	Summer/Autumn	8	106
Hydrangea serrata 'Blue Bird'	✳	🍃							T	Sea	◑	💧	Summer/Autumn	5	159

Key *(see also p 9 and p 11)*	✳ Flower colour		🍃 Foliage colour		🍒 Berries/fruits/cones/seed heads colour
☀ Fragrant or aromatic	▲ Evergreen		🍂 Good autumn colour		⊥ Climber or wall plant
⊞ Suitable for hedging	**Soil** Acid/alkali/tolerant	**Sea**	Suitable for maritime or seaside conditions		○ Sun/shade requirements
💧 Moisture requirements	**Season** Season(s) of interest	**Zone**	Climatic zone *(see pages 59–62)*	**Page**	Page reference to *Directory of Plants*

SHRUBS AND TREES: 60 cm – 1.2 m (2 ft – 4 ft)

Plant name	✱	❦	●●	⁂	▲	✤	⊥	ШШШ	Soil	Sea	○	◇	Season	Zone	Page
Hydrangea serrata 'Grayswood'	✱	❦							T		◑	♦	Summer	5	159
Hebe × franciscana 'Blue Gem'	✱	❦			▲			ШШШ	T	Sea	◑	◈	Summer	6	152
Ceanothus thyrsiflorus var. *repens*	✱	❦			▲				T		○	◈	Summer	7	104
Caryopteris × clandonensis	✱	❦							Alkali		○	◈	Autumn	5	103
Arundinaria variegata		❦			▲				T		○	♦		5	88
Chamaecyparis laws. 'Nana Albospica'		❦			▲				T		◑	◈		5	108
Cryptomeria japonica 'Globosa'		❦			▲				Acid		◑	♦		7	125
Cryptomeria japonica 'Vilmoriniana'		❦			▲				Acid		◑	♦		5	125
Juniperus communis 'Depressa Aurea'		❦		⁂	▲				Alkali		◑	◈		4	165
Juniperus × davurica 'Expansa Aureospicata'		❦		⁂	▲				Alkali		○	◈		5	166
Chamaecyparis lawsoniana 'Minima Aurea'		❦			▲				T		◑	◈		6	108
Chamaecyparis obtusa 'Nana Lutea'		❦			▲				T		○	◈		5	109
Chamaecyparis pisifera 'Plumosa Aurea Nana'		❦			▲				Acid		◑	◈		6	110
Chamaecyparis pisifera 'Plumosa Rogersii'		❦			▲				Acid		◑	◈		6	110
Juniperus communis 'Compressa'		❦		⁂	▲				Alkali		◑	◈		4	165
Picea pungens 'Globosa'		❦			▲				Acid		◑	♦		2	192
Picea pungens 'Procumbens'		❦			▲				Acid		◑	♦		2	192
Chamaecyparis pisifera 'Boulevard'		❦			▲				Acid		◑	◈		5	109
Chamaecyparis lawsoniana 'Gimbornii'		❦			▲				T		◑	◈		5	108
Juniperus squamata 'Blue Star'		❦		⁂	▲				Alkali		◑	◈		5	167
Taxus cuspidata 'Densa'		❦			▲				Alkali		◑	◇		4	226
Thuja occidentalis 'Danica'		❦			▲				Alkali		◑	◈		4	227
Abies balsamea 'Hudsonia'		❦	●●		▲				Acid		◑	♦		3	75
Juniperus sargentii		❦	●●	⁂	▲				Alkali		◑	◈		5	167
Aronia melanocarpa		❦	●●			✤			T		◑	◈	Spring/Autumn	4	86
Buxus microphylla		❦		⁂	▲			ШШШ	T		Ⓣ	◇		5	98
Picea abies 'Clanbrassiliana'		❦			▲				T		◑	♦		4	192

SHRUBS AND TREES: 60 cm – 1.2 m (2 ft – 4 ft)

Plant name	✳	🍃	🫐	🔆	🌲	🍂	⊥	⊔⊔⊔	Soil	Sea	◐	💧	Season	Zone	Page
Chamaecyparis laws. 'Minima Glauca'		🍃			🌲				T		◐	💧		6	108
Chamaecyparis lawsoniana 'Nana'		🍃			🌲				T		◐	💧		6	108
Chamaecyparis obtusa 'Nana Gracilis'		🍃			🌲				T		◐	💧		5	109
Cryptomeria japonica 'Lobbii Nana'		🍃			🌲	🍂			T		◐	💧		5	125
Cryptomeria japonica 'Pygmaea'		🍃			🌲	🍂			T		○	💧		5	125
Chamaecyparis obtusa 'Pygmaea'		🍃			🌲				T		◐	💧		5	109
Podocarpus nivalis		🍃			🌲				T		◐	💧		6	197
Chamaecyparis pisifera 'Pygmaea'		🍃			🌲				Acid		◐	💧		5	110

SHRUBS AND TREES: 1.2 m – 2.5 m (4 ft – 8 ft)

Plant name	✳	🍃	🫐	🔆	🌲	🍂	⊥	⊔⊔⊔	Soil	Sea	◐	💧	Season	Zone	Page
Cytisus scoparius 'Andreanus'	✳	🍃							T	Sea	○	💧	Spring	5	128
Cytisus scoparius 'Firefly'	✳	🍃							T	Sea	○	💧	Spring	5	128
Cytisus scoparius 'Goldfinch'	✳	🍃							T	Sea	○	💧	Spring	5	128
Rosa foetida 'Bicolor'	✳	🍃							T		○	💧	Summer	5	210
Fuchsia 'Mrs Popple'	✳	🍃	🫐						T	Sea	◐	💧	Summer/Autumn	6	145
Fuchsia magellanica var. *gracilis*	✳	🍃	🫐						T	Sea	◐	💧	Summer/Autumn	6	144
Fuchsia magellanica 'Riccartonii'	✳	🍃	🫐					⊔⊔⊔	T	Sea	◐	💧	Summer/Autumn	6	145
Buddleia davidii 'Harlequin'	✳	🍃		🔆					Alkali		○	💧	Summer	5	97
Cytisus scoparius 'Burkwoodii'	✳	🍃							T	Sea	○	💧	Spring	5	128
Daphne mezereum	✳	🍃	🫐	🔆					Alkali		◐	💧	Winter/Spring	4	129
Rosa rugosa 'Roseraie de l'Hay'	✳	🍃	🫐					⊔⊔⊔	T	Sea	○	💧	Summer/Autumn	5	211

Key *(see also p 9 and p 11)*	✳	Flower colour	🍃	Foliage colour	🫐	Berries/fruits/cones/seed heads colour
🔆	Fragrant or aromatic	🌲	Evergreen	🍂	Good autumn colour	⊥ Climber or wall plant
⊔⊔⊔	Suitable for hedging	**Soil**	Acid/alkali/tolerant	**Sea**	Suitable for maritime or seaside conditions	○ Sun/shade requirements
💧	Moisture requirements	**Season**	Season(s) of interest	**Zone**	Climatic zone *(see pages 59–62)*	**Page** Page reference to *Directory of Plants*

SHRUBS AND TREES: 1.2 m – 2.5 m (4 ft – 8 ft)

Plant name	✱	❧	⁂	☀	▲	♣	⊥	ШШ	Soil	Sea	○	◇	Season	Zone	Page
Rosa moyesii 'Geranium'	✱	❧	⁂						T		○	◐	Summer	5	211
Rosa chinensis 'Mutabilis'	✱	❧	⁂	☀					T		○	◐	Summer	5	210
Punica granatum 'Flore Pleno'	✱	❧	⁂				⊥		T		○	◐	Summer	8	203
Chaenomeles japonica	✱	❧	⁂				⊥		T		Ⓣ	◐	Spring	4	107
Chaenomeles × speciosa 'Simonii'	✱	❧	⁂				⊥		T		Ⓣ	◐	Spring	4	107
Chaenomeles × superba 'Crimson and Gold'	✱	❧	⁂				⊥		T		Ⓣ	◐	Spring	4	107
Ribes sanguineum 'King Edward VII'	✱	❧	⁂					ШШ	T		Ⓣ	◇	Spring	5	207
Hibiscus syriacus 'Woodbridge'	✱	❧							T		○	◐	Summer/Autumn	5	156
Weigela 'Bristol Ruby'	✱	❧							T		◐	◐	Spring/Autumn	4	234
Rhododendron cinnabarinum	✱	❧			▲				Acid		◐	●	Spring/Summer	5	205
Azalea 'Balzac'	✱	❧		☀		♣			Acid		◐	●	Spring/Autumn	5	91
Azalea 'Dracula' *Azalea* 'Gibraltar'	✱	❧				♣			Acid		◐	●	Spring/Autumn	5	92
Rosa 'Climbing Etoile de Hollande'	✱	❧		☀			⊥		T		○	◐	Summer/Autumn	5	209
Escallonia 'Crimson Spire'	✱	❧			▲			ШШ	T	Sea	○	◐	Summer/Autumn	5	139
Escallonia 'C.F. Ball'	✱	❧		☀	▲			ШШ	T	Sea	○	◐	Summer/Autumn	5	139
Kalmia latifolia 'Ostbo Red'	✱	❧			▲				Acid		◐	●	Summer	4	168
Callistemon citrinus 'Splendens'	✱	❧			▲				T		○	◐	Summer	8	98
Hebe speciosa 'Simon Deleaux'	✱	❧			▲				T	Sea	○	◐	Summer	8	153
Hebe speciosa 'Purple Queen'	✱	❧			▲				T	Sea	○	◐	Summer	8	153
Hydrangea macrophylla 'Mariesii'	✱	❧							T	Sea	◐	●	Summer	5	158
Weigela florida 'Variegata'	✱	❧							T		◐	◐	Spring/Summer	4	234
Daphne odora 'Aureomarginata'	✱	❧		☀	▲				T		◐	◐	Winter/Spring	6	129
Weigela florida 'Foliis Purpureis'	✱	❧							T		◐	◐	Spring/Summer	5	234
Ribes sanguineum 'Brocklebankii'	✱	❧	⁂						T		◐	◇	Spring	5	207
Camellia × williamsii 'Golden Spangles'	✱	❧			▲				Acid		◐	●	Winter/Spring	7	101
Abelia × grandiflora 'Francis Mason'	✱	❧		☀	▲				T		○	◐	Summer/Autumn	7	74
Rosa rubrifolia	✱	❧	⁂						T	Sea	○	◐	Summer	5	211

SHRUBS AND TREES: 1.2 m – 2.5 m (4 ft – 8 ft)

Plant name	Flower colour	Foliage colour	Berries/fruits/cones/seed heads colour	Fragrant	Evergreen	Good autumn colour	Climber/wall plant	Suitable for hedging	Soil	Sea	Sun/shade	Moisture	Season	Zone	Page
Rosa rugosa 'Frau Dagmar Hastrup'	✳	🍃	●●	☀				⊞	T	Sea	○	◐	Summer	5	211
Symphoricarpos × doorenbosii 'Magic Berry'	✳	🍃	●●					⊞	T		Ⓣ	◐	Summer/Autumn	3	223
Rosa centifolia	✳	🍃	●●	☀					T		○	◐	Summer	5	210
Lycium barbarum	✳	🍃	●●						T	Sea	◑	◐	Summer	6	177
Chaenomeles × speciosa 'Rosea Plena'	✳	🍃	●●				⊥		T		Ⓣ	◐	Spring	4	107
Chaenomeles × superba 'Pink Lady'	✳	🍃	●●				⊥		T		Ⓣ	◐	Spring	4	107
Symphoricarpos rivularis	✳	🍃	●●					⊞	T		Ⓣ	◐	Summer	3	224
Vaccinium corymbosum	✳	🍃	●●			🍂			Acid		○	●	Spring/Summer	3	230
Syringa microphylla 'Superba'	✳	🍃		☀					Alkali		◑	◐	Spring/Summer/Autumn	4	224
Daphne × burkwoodii 'Somerset'	✳	🍃		☀	▲				T		◑	◐	Spring/Summer	4	129
Clematis macropetala 'Markham's Pink'	✳	🍃					⊥		Alkali		◑	◐	Spring/Summer	5	115
Camellia japonica 'Elegans'	✳	🍃			▲				Acid		◑	●	Spring/Winter	7	100
Camellia × williamsii 'Donation'	✳	🍃			▲				Acid		◑	●	Spring/Winter	7	101
Rhododendron 'Temple Belle'	✳	🍃			▲				Acid		◑	●	Spring/Winter	5	205
Rhododendron williamsianum	✳	🍃			▲				Acid		◑	●	Spring	5	206
Azalea 'Comte de Gomer'	✳	🍃				🍂			Acid		◑	●	Spring	5	92
Prunus glandulosa 'Sinensis'	✳	🍃							Alkali		◑	◐	Spring	4	200
Magnolia stellata 'Rubra'	✳	🍃		☀					Acid		◑	◐	Spring	5	180
Hydrangea serrata 'Preziosa'	✳	🍃							T		◑	●	Summer/Autumn	5	159
Indigofera gerardiana	✳	🍃					⊥		T		○	◐	Summer/Autumn	4	161
Escallonia 'Apple Blossom'	✳	🍃		☀	▲			⊞	T	Sea	○	◐	Summer/Autumn	5	139
Escallonia 'Donard Radiance'	✳	🍃			▲			⊞	T	Sea	○	◐	Summer/Autumn	5	139

Key (see also p 9 and p 11)	✳ Flower colour	🍃 Foliage colour	●● Berries/fruits/cones/seed heads colour
☀ Fragrant or aromatic	▲ Evergreen	🍂 Good autumn colour	⊥ Climber or wall plant
⊞ Suitable for hedging	**Soil** Acid/alkali/tolerant	**Sea** Suitable for maritime or seaside conditions	○ Sun/shade requirements
◐ Moisture requirements	**Season** Season(s) of interest	**Zone** Climatic zone (see pages 59–62)	**Page** Page reference to Directory of Plants

SHRUBS AND TREES: 1.2 m – 2.5 m (4 ft – 8 ft)

Plant name	✳	🍃	🍒	☀	🌲	🍂	⊥	⊞	Soil	Sea	○	◊	Season	Zone	Page
Abelia × *grandiflora*	✳	🍃		☀	🌲				T		○	◐	Summer/Autumn	7	74
Kalmia latifolia	✳	🍃			🌲				Acid		◐	●	Summer/Autumn	3	168
Hydrangea macrophylla	✳	🍃							T	Sea	◐	●	Summer	5	158
Kolkwitzia amabilis	✳	🍃							T		○	◊	Summer	4	169
Clerodendrum-bungei	✳	🍃		☀			⊥		T		○	◊	Summer	6	117
Deutzia 'Mont Rose'	✳	🍃							T		◐	◊	Summer	4	130
Spiraea × *billardii* 'Triumphans'	✳	🍃							T		◐	◊	Summer	4	221
Clematis 'Hagley Hybrid'	✳	🍃					⊥		Alkali		◐	◊	Summer	5	116
Syringa velutina	✳	🍃		☀					Alkali		○	◊	Summer	4	224
Menziesia ciliicalyx	✳	🍃							Acid		◐	◊	Summer	8	182
Lonicera syringantha	✳	🍃		☀					T		Ⓣ	◊	Summer	4	176
Cistus × *purpureus*	✳	🍃			🌲				T	Sea	○	◊	Summer	8	112
Hebe speciosa 'Gauntlettii'	✳	🍃			🌲				T	Sea	●	◊	Summer	8	153
Hebe 'Great Orme'	✳	🍃			🌲				Alkali	Sea	○	◊	Summer	7	152
Abelia floribunda	✳	🍃			🌲		⊥		T		○	◊	Summer	9	74
Raphiolepis × *delacourii*	✳	🍃			🌲		⊥		T		○	◊	Summer	▷	204
Lavatera olbia 'Rosea'	✳	🍃							T	Sea	○	◊	Summer	5	170
Lespedeza thunbergii	✳	🍃							T		○	◊	Autumn	5	171
Kerria japonica 'Variegata'	✳	🍃					⊥		T		Ⓣ	◊	Spring	4	168
Berberis thunbergii 'Red Chief'	✳	🍃	🍒						T		◐	◊	Spring	5	95
Berberis thunbergii 'Rose Glow'	✳	🍃	🍒						T		◐	◊	Spring	5	95
Berberis thunbergii 'Helmond Pillar'	✳	🍃	🍒					⊞	T		◐	◊	Spring	5	95
Berberis aggregata 'Barbarossa'	✳	🍃	🍒			🍂			T		◐	◊	Spring	5	94
Chaenomeles × *superba* 'Boule de Feu'	✳	🍃	🍒				⊥		T		Ⓣ	◊	Spring	4	107
Mahonia aquifolium	✳	🍃	🍒		🌲	🍂			Alkali		Ⓣ	◊	Spring	5	180
Berberis sargentiana	✳	🍃	🍒		🌲			⊞	T		◐	◊	Spring	5	94
Berberis gagnepainii 'Lancifolia'	✳	🍃	🍒		🌲			⊞	T	Sea	◐	◊	Spring	5	94

SHRUBS AND TREES: 1.2 m – 2.5 m (4 ft – 8 ft)

Plant name	✳	🍃	🍒	�台	🌲	🍂	⊥	⊔⊔⊔	Soil	Sea	○	◗	Season	Zone	Page
Petteria ramentacea	✳	🍃		�台					T		◑	◗	Spring/ Summer	5	189
Salix moupinensis	✳	🍃							T		◑	●	Spring	5	214
Azalea 'Annabelle'	✳	🍃				🍂			Acid		◑	●	Spring/ Summer	5	91
Azalea 'Hollandia'	✳	🍃				🍂			Acid		◑	●	Spring/Summer	5	92
Azalea 'Orange Truffles'	✳	🍃				🍂			Acid		◑	●	Spring/ Summer	5	92
Cytisus scoparius 'Golden Sunlight'	✳	🍃							T	Sea	○	◊	Spring/ Summer	5	128
Chamaecyparis nootkatensis 'Compacta'	✳	🍃			🌲				T		◑	◗	Spring	4	109
Stachyurus praecox	✳	🍃							T		◑	◗	Spring	5	222
Forsythia 'Lynwood'	✳	🍃						⊔⊔⊔	T		◑	◗	Spring	4	143
Forsythia 'Beatrix Farrand'	✳	🍃							T		◑	◗	Spring	4	143
Corylopsis pauciflora	✳	🍃		�台					Acid		◑	◗	Spring	5	121
Cytisus × praecox	✳	🍃							T	Sea	○	◊	Spring	5	127
Cytisus × praecox 'Allgold'	✳	🍃							T	Sea	○	◊	Spring	5	127
Colutea arborescens	✳	🍃	🍒						T		◑	◗	Summer	5	118
Hypericum 'Hidcote'	✳	🍃			🌲				T		◑	◗	Summer/Autumn	5	160
Euonymus alatus	✳	🍃				🍂			Alkali		◑	◗	Summer	5	140
Jasminum humile 'Revolutum'	✳	🍃		�台	🌲		⊥		T		○	◗	Summer	8	164
Cytisus nigricans	✳	🍃							T	Sea	○	◗	Summer	5	127
Lomatia tinctoria	✳	🍃			🌲				T		◑	◗	Summer	7	173
Mahonia bealei	✳	🍃		�台	🌲				T		◑	◗	Winter	6	180
Mahonia 'Charity'	✳	🍃		�台	🌲				T		◑	◗	Winter	7	181
Mahonia japonica	✳	🍃		�台	🌲				T		◑	◗	Winter	7	181

Key (see also p 9 and p 11)	✳ Flower colour	🍃 Foliage colour	🍒 Berries/fruits/cones/seed heads colour
�台 Fragrant or aromatic	🌲 Evergreen	🍂 Good autumn colour	⊥ Climber or wall plant
⊔⊔⊔ Suitable for hedging	Soil Acid/alkali/tolerant	Sea Suitable for maritime or seaside conditions	○ Sun/shade requirements
◗ Moisture requirements	Season Season(s) of interest	Zone Climatic zone (see pages 59–62)	Page Page reference to Directory of Plants

SHRUBS AND TREES

Plant name	❋	leaf	berry	fan	▲	leaf	⊥	⊞	Soil	Sea	◐	◊	Season	Zone	Page
Lonicera × purpusii 'Winter Beauty'	●	●		●	●				T		◐	◊	Winter	5	176
Hamamelis mollis	●	●		●		●			Acid		◐	◊	Winter	5	151
Fuchsia 'Chillerton Beauty'	●	●	●	●					T	Sea	◐	◊	Summer/Autumn	5	144
Lonicera fragrantissima	●	●	●	●					T		◑	◊	Winter/Spring	6	174
Stranvaesia davidiana 'Palette'	●	●	●		●	●			T		◐	◊	Summer	6	223
Photinia glabra 'Variegata'	●	●			●				Alkali		◐	◊	Spring	8	191
Cornus alba 'Elegantissima'	●	●				●			T		◐	◆	Spring	2	119
Pieris japonica 'Variegata'	●	●		●	●				Acid		◐	◆	Spring	7	193
Osmanthus heterophyllus 'Variegatus'	●	●		●	●			⊞	T		○	◊	Autumn	8	185
Olearia × scilloniensis	●	●			●				T	Sea	○	◊	Summer	9	184
Leptospermum cunninghamii	●	●			●		⊥		Acid	Sea	○	◊	Summer	9	171
Leucothoe fontanesiana 'Rainbow'	●	●			●				Acid		Ⓣ	◊	Summer	6	171
Prunus × cistena	●	●	●					⊞	Alkali		◐	◊	Spring	3	200
Choisya ternata 'Sundance'	●	●		●	●				T	Sea	◐	◊	Summer/Autumn	7	111
Philadelphus coronarius 'Aureus'	●	●		●					Alkali		◐	◊	Summer	7	189
Cornus alba 'Spaethii'	●	●				●			T		◐	◆	Spring	2	119
Erica arborea 'Gold Tips'	●	●		●	●				Acid		○	◊	Spring	7	136
Elaeagnus × ebbingei 'Gilt Edge'	●	●		●	●				T		◑	◊	Autumn	5	134
Skimmia japonica 'Foremanii'	●	●	●	●	●				T	Sea	◐	◊	Spring	5	218
Prunus pumila 'Depressa'	●	●	●			●			Alkali		◐	◊	Spring	5	201
Rosa rugosa 'Blanc Double de Coubert'	●	●	●	●		●		⊞	T	Sea	○	◊	Summer	5	211
Nandina domestica	●	●	●		●	●			T		○	◊	Summer	8	183
Leycesteria formosa	●	●	●						T	Sea	◐	◊	Summer/Winter	7	172
Cotoneaster simonsii	●	●	●		●			⊞	T	Sea	◐	◊	Summer	5	124
Chaenomeles × speciosa 'Nivalis'	●	●	●				⊥		T		Ⓣ	◊	Spring	4	107
Osmanthus delavayi	●	●		●	●				T		◐	◊	Spring	7	185
Weigela 'Mont Blanc'	●	●							T		◐	◊	Spring/Summer/Autumn	5	234

SHRUBS AND TREES: 1.2 m – 2.5 m (4 ft – 8 ft)

Plant name	Flower	Foliage	Berries	Fragrant	Evergreen	Autumn	Climber	Hedging	Soil	Sea	Sun/shade	Moisture	Season	Zone	Page
Salix hastata 'Wehrhahnii'	✽	🌿							T		◐	●	Spring	4	213
Viburnum carlesii	✽	🌿	•:•	☀					T		◐	●	Spring	5	231
Viburnum × juddii	✽	🌿		☀		🍂			T		◐	●	Spring	5	232
Viburnum × carlcephalum	✽	🌿		☀		🍂			T		◐	●	Spring	5	231
Viburnum × burkwoodii	✽	🌿		☀	▲				T		◐	●	Spring	5	231
Rhododendron 'Unique'	✽	🌿			▲				Acid		◐	◐	Spring	5	205
Pieris japonica	✽	🌿		☀	▲				Acid		○	●	Spring	5	193
Pieris 'Brouwer's Beauty'	✽	🌿			▲		⊥		Acid		○	●	Spring	5	193
Pieris floribunda	✽	🌿			▲				Acid		◐	●	Spring	5	193
Azalea 'Raphael de Smet'	✽	🌿				🍂			Acid		◐	●	Spring	5	92
Spiraea × arguta	✽	🌿							T		○	◐	Spring	4	220
Prunus glandulosa 'Albiplena'	✽	🌿							Alkali		◐	◐	Spring	4	200
Spiraea thunbergii	✽	🌿							T		◐	◐	Spring	4	222
Skimmia japonica 'Fragrans'	✽	🌿		☀	▲				T	Sea	◐	◐	Spring	5	218
Spiraea prunifolia 'Plena'	✽	🌿				🍂			T		◐	◐	Spring	4	221
× Osmarea 'Burkwoodii'	✽	🌿		☀	▲			⊔⊔⊔	Alkali		◐	◐	Spring	6	185
Fothergilla major	✽	🌿		☀		🍂			Acid		◐	◐	Spring	5	143
Magnolia stellata	✽	🌿		☀					Acid		◐	◐	Spring	5	180
Enkianthus perulatus	✽	🌿				🍂			Acid		◐	◐	Spring	6	135
Erica arborea 'Alpina'	✽	🌿		☀	▲				Acid		○	◐	Spring	7	136
Cytisus × praecox 'Albus'	✽	🌿							T	Sea	○	◐	Spring	5	127
Hibiscus syriacus 'Hamabo' Hibiscus syriacus 'W.R. Smith'	✽	🌿							T		○	◐	Summer/Autumn	5	156

Key (see also p 9 and p 11)	✽	Flower colour	🌿	Foliage colour	•:•	Berries/fruits/cones/seed heads colour
☀	Fragrant or aromatic	▲	Evergreen	🍂	Good autumn colour	⊥	Climber or wall plant
⊔⊔⊔	Suitable for hedging	Soil	Acid/alkali/tolerant	Sea	Suitable for maritime or seaside conditions	○	Sun/shade requirements
◐	Moisture requirements	Season	Season(s) of interest	Zone	Climatic zone (see pages 59–62)	Page	Page reference to Directory of Plants

SHRUBS AND TREES

Plant name	Flower	Leaf	Berry	Fan	Tree	Autumn leaf	⊥	Hedge	Soil	Sea	○	◊	Season	Zone	Page
Clethra alnifolia	❋	leaf		fan		leaf			Acid	Sea	○	●	Summer/Autumn	3	117
Escallonia 'Donard White'	❋	leaf		fan	▲			hedge	T	Sea	○	◖	Summer/Autumn	3	139
Hydrangea arborescens 'Grandiflora'	❋	leaf							T		◑	●	Summer	5	157
Paeonia suffruticosa	❋	leaf							T		◑	●	Summer	6	187
Hydrangea quercifolia	❋	leaf				leaf			T		◑	●	Summer	7	159
Hydrangea macrophylla 'Veitchii'	❋	leaf							Alkali	Sea	◑	●	Summer	5	158
Cornus stolonifera 'Flaviramea'	❋	leaf				leaf			T		◑	●	Summer	2	120
Lyonia ligustrina	❋	leaf							Acid		◑	●	Summer	4	177
Deutzia × magnifica	❋	leaf							T		◑	◖	Summer	4	130
Deutzia vilmoriniae	❋	leaf							T		◑	◖	Summer	4	131
Spiraea × vanhouttei	❋	leaf							T		○	◖	Summer	4	220
Philadelphus × lemoinei	❋	leaf		fan					Alkali		◑	◖	Summer	5	189
Philadelphus 'Belle Etoile'	❋	leaf		fan					Alkali		◑	◖	Summer	5	189
Olearia × haastii	❋	leaf			▲			hedge	T	Sea	◑	◖	Summer	7	184
Stephanandra incisa	❋	leaf				leaf			T		◑	◖	Summer/Autumn	7	222
Stephanandra tanakae	❋	leaf				leaf			T		◑	◖	Summer/Autumn	5	222
Hebe salicifolia	❋	leaf			▲				Alkali	Sea	○	◖	Summer	7	153
Hebe brachysiphon	❋	leaf			▲			hedge	Alkali	Sea	◑	◖	Summer	5	151
Cistus × aguilari 'Maculatus'	❋	leaf			▲				T	Sea	○	◖	Summer	8	112
Lomatia myricoides	❋	leaf		fan	▲				T		◑	◖	Summer	7	173
Viburnum farreri	❋	leaf		fan					T		◑	●	Winter	6	232
Callicarpa bodinieri var. giraldii	❋	leaf	berry			leaf			T		◑	◖	Summer	6	98
Clematis macropetala	❋	leaf					⊥		Alkali		◑	◖	Spring/Summer	5	115
Rosmarinus officinalis 'Fastigiatus'	❋	leaf		fan	▲			hedge	T	Sea	○	◖	Spring/Summer	7	212
Rosmarinus officinalis	❋	leaf		fan	▲			hedge	T	Sea	○	◖	Spring/Summer	7	212
Ceanothus 'Southmead'	❋	leaf			▲		⊥		T		○	◖	Spring	7	104
Hydrangea villosa	❋	leaf							T		◑	●	Summer/Autumn	4	159

28

SHRUBS AND TREES: 1.2 m – 2.5 m (4 ft – 8 ft)

Plant name	✳	🍃	🍒	🔆	🌲	🍂	⊥	⊞	Soil	Sea	○	💧	Season	Zone	Page
Ceanothus 'A.T. Johnson'	✳	🍃			🌲		⊥		T		○	💧	Summer/Autumn	7	104
Ceanothus 'Burkwoodii'	✳	🍃			🌲		⊥		T		○	💧	Summer/Autumn	7	104
Hibiscus syriacus 'Blue Bird'	✳	🍃							T		○	💧	Summer/Autumn	5	156
Hydrangea aspera	✳	🍃							T		◑	💧	Summer	7	157
Hydrangea macrophylla 'Blue Wave'	✳	🍃							Acid	Sea	◑	💧	Summer	5	158
Ceanothus 'Gloire de Versailles'	✳	🍃		🔆			⊥		T		○	💧	Summer	9	104
Ceanothus 'Topaz'	✳	🍃					⊥		T		○	💧	Summer	7	104
Olearia stellulata 'Master Michael'	✳	🍃			🌲				T	Sea	○	💧	Summer	9	184
Hebe speciosa 'Veitchii'	✳	🍃			🌲				T	Sea	○	💧	Summer	8	153
Hebe 'Midsummer Beauty'	✳	🍃			🌲				Alkali	Sea	○	💧	Summer	7	152
Hebe × andersonii	✳	🍃			🌲				T	Sea	○	💧	Summer	7	151
Ceanothus 'Autumnal Blue'	✳	🍃			🌲		⊥		T		○	💧	Autumn	7	104
Griselinia littoralis 'Bantry Bay'		🍃			🌲			⊞	Alkali	Sea	○	💧		8	149
Chamaecyparis pisifera 'Squarrosa Sulphurea'		🍃			🌲				Acid		◑	💧		5	110
Buxus sempervirens 'Aureo-variegata'		🍃		🔆	🌲			⊞	T		Ⓣ	💧		5	98
Buxus sempervirens 'Elegantissima'		🍃		🔆	🌲			⊞	T		Ⓣ	💧		5	98
Lonicera nitida 'Baggesen's Gold'		🍃			🌲			⊞	T		○	💧		4	175
Thuja occidentalis 'Rheingold'		🍃			🌲				T		○	💧		4	227
Thuja orientalis 'Aurea Nana'		🍃	🍒		🌲				T		○	💧		5	228
Taxus baccata 'Semperaurea'		🍃			🌲				Alkali		◑	💧		6	226
Juniperus chinensis 'Kuriwao Gold'		🍃		🔆	🌲				T		◑	💧		5	165
Juniperus × media 'Old Gold'		🍃		🔆	🌲				Alkali		○	💧		5	166

Key (see also p 9 and p 11)	✳	Flower colour	🍃	Foliage colour	🍒	Berries/fruits/cones/seed heads colour
🔆	Fragrant or aromatic	🌲	Evergreen	🍂	Good autumn colour	⊥ Climber or wall plant
⊞	Suitable for hedging	Soil	Acid/alkali/tolerant	Sea	Suitable for maritime or seaside conditions	○ Sun/shade requirements
💧	Moisture requirements	Season	Season(s) of interest	Zone	Climatic zone (see pages 59–62)	Page Page reference to Directory of Plants

SHRUBS AND TREES: 1.2 m – 2.5 m (4 ft – 8 ft)

Plant name	✳	🍃	🍒	☼	🌲	🍂	⊥	⊔⊔⊔	Soil	Sea	◯	💧	Season	Zone	Page
Thuja plicata 'Rogersii'		🍃		☼	🌲				T		◯	◑		5	228
Juniperus × media 'Pfitzerana Aurea'		🍃		☼	🌲				Alkali		◯	◑		5	166
Abies lasiocarpa 'Compacta'		🍃	🍒		🌲				Acid		◐	●		5	75
Abies pinsapo 'Glauca'		🍃	🍒		🌲				T		◐	●		6	75
Juniperus virginiana 'Grey Owl'		🍃		☼	🌲				T		◐	◑		4	167
Pinus strobus 'Nana'		🍃	🍒		🌲				Acid		◯	●		3	196
Juniperus sabina 'Blue Danube'		🍃		☼	🌲				Alkali		◐	◑		5	167
Pinus mugo 'Gnom'		🍃	🍒		🌲				Alkali	Sea	◯	◑		2	194
Pinus pumila		🍃	🍒		🌲				Acid		◯	●		3	195
Salix caprea 'Pendula'		🍃							Alkali		◯	●	Spring	4	213
Picea glauca var. *albertiana* 'Conica'		🍃			🌲				Acid		◐	●		4	192
× Fatshedera lizei		🍃			🌲		⊥		T	Sea	◐	◌		6	142
Cephalotaxus harringtonia var. *drupacea*		🍃	🍒		🌲				Alkali		◐	◑		5	106
Tsuga canadensis 'Bennett'		🍃			🌲				Alkali		◐	◑		4	229
Juniperus chinensis 'Japonica'		🍃		☼	🌲				T		◐	◑		4	165
Chamaecyparis pisifera 'Filifera Nana'		🍃			🌲				Acid		◐	◑		5	109
Juniperus × media 'Hetzii'		🍃		☼	🌲				Alkali		◐	◑		4	166
Tsuga canadensis 'Pendula'		🍃			🌲				Alkali		◐	◑		5	229
Cedrus libani 'Nana'		🍃			🌲				T		◯	◑		6	105
Pinus sylvestris 'Beuvronensis'		🍃			🌲				T		◯	◑		3	196
Pinus nigra 'Pygmaea'		🍃			🌲	🍂			Alkali	Sea	◯	◑		4	195
Pinus mugo var. *pumilio*		🍃			🌲				Alkali	Sea	◯	◑		2	195
Pinus nigra 'Hornibrookiana'		🍃			🌲				Alkali	Sea	◯	◑		4	195
Chamaecyparis thyoides 'Ericoides'		🍃			🌲				Acid		◯	◑		5	110
Pinus densiflora 'Umbraculifera'		🍃			🌲				Acid		◯	◑		4	194
Chamaecyparis lawsoniana 'Tamariscifolia'		🍃			🌲				T		◐	◑		5	108
Lonicera nitida		🍃			🌲			⊔⊔⊔	T		Ⓣ	◑		4	175

Plant name	✳	🍃	🍓	☀	🌲	🍂	⊥	⎸⎹⎹⎹	Soil	Sea	◐	💧	Season	Zone	Page

SHRUBS AND TREES: 2.5 m – 6 m (8 ft – 20 ft)

Plant name	✳	🍃	🍓	☀	🌲	🍂	⊥	⎸⎹⎹⎹	Soil	Sea	◐	💧	Season	Zone	Page
Lonicera periclymenum 'Belgica'	✳	🍃	🍓	☀			⊥		T		◐	💧	Spring/Summer	5	176
Lonicera japonica var. *repens*	✳	🍃		☀	🌲		⊥		T		◐	💧	Summer/Autumn	5	175
Lonicera × *heckrottii*	✳	🍃		☀			⊥		T		◐	💧	Summer	5	174
Pittosporum tenuifolium 'Purpureum'	✳	🍃		☀	🌲			⎸⎹⎹⎹	Alkali		◐	💧	Spring	7	196
Pittosporum tenuifolium 'Garnettii'	✳	🍃		☀	🌲			⎸⎹⎹⎹	Alkali		◐	💧	Spring	7	196
Pittosporum tenuifolium 'Irene Paterson'	✳	🍃		☀	🌲			⎸⎹⎹⎹	Alkali		◐	💧	Spring	8	196
Pittosporum tenuifolium 'Abbotsbury Gold'	✳	🍃		☀	🌲			⎸⎹⎹⎹	Alkali		◐	💧	Spring	7	196
Magnolia 'Susan'	✳	🍃		☀					T		◐	💧	Spring	5	179
Leptospermum scoparium 'Burgundy Queen'	✳	🍃			🌲		⊥		Acid	Sea	○	💧	Summer	9	171
Leptospermum scoparium 'Nicholsii'	✳	🍃			🌲		⊥		Acid	Sea	○	💧	Summer	9	171
Leptospermum scoparium 'Red Damask'	✳	🍃			🌲		⊥		Acid	Sea	○	💧	Summer	9	171
Ribes speciosum	✳	🍃	🍓		🌲		⊥		T		○	💧	Spring/Summer	5	207
Rosa 'Altissimo'	✳	🍃		☀			⊥		T		○	💧	Summer	5	209
Magnolia × *soulangiana* 'Rustica Rubra'	✳	🍃							Acid		◐	💧	Spring/Summer	5	179
Magnolia 'Jane'	✳	🍃		☀					T		◐	💧	Spring/Summer	5	179
Syringa vulgaris 'Charles Joly'	✳	🍃		☀					Alkali		◐	💧	Spring/Summer	3	225
Syringa vulgaris 'Souvenir de Louis Späth'	✳	🍃		☀					Alkali		◐	💧	Spring/Summer	3	225
Magnolia liliiflora 'Nigra'	✳	🍃							Acid		◐	💧	Spring/Summer	5	179
Camellia japonica 'Adolphe Audusson'	✳	🍃			🌲				Acid		◐	💧	Spring	7	100
Camellia japonica 'Donckelarii'	✳	🍃			🌲				Acid		◐	💧	Spring	7	100
Camellia japonica 'Mathotiana'	✳	🍃			🌲				Acid		◐	💧	Spring	7	100

Key *(see also p 9 and p 11)*						
✳	Flower colour	🍃	Foliage colour	🍓	Berries/fruits/cones/seed heads colour
☀ Fragrant or aromatic		🌲 Evergreen		🍂 Good autumn colour		⊥ Climber or wall plant
⎸⎹⎹⎹ Suitable for hedging		**Soil** Acid/alkali/tolerant		**Sea** Suitable for maritime or seaside conditions		○ Sun/shade requirements
💧 Moisture requirements		**Season** Season(s) of interest		**Zone** Climatic zone *(see pages 59–62)*		**Page** Page reference to *Directory of Plants*

SHRUBS AND TREES: 2.5 m – 6 m (8 ft – 20 ft)

Plant name	✱	❦	●●	✺	▲	❧	⊥	ШШШ	Soil	Sea	○	◇	Season	Zone	Page
Crinodendron hookeranum	✱	❦			▲		⊥		Acid		◑	◆	Spring	8	125
Akebia quinata	✱	❦	●●	✺			⊥		T		Ⓣ	◈	Spring	4	81
Pittosporum tenuifolium	✱	❦		✺	▲			ШШШ	Alkali		◑	◈	Spring	7	196
Embothrium coccineum	✱	❦			▲				Acid		◑	◈	Spring	8	134
Rosa 'Sympathie' *Rosa* 'Crimson Showers'	✱	❦		✺			⊥		T		◑	◈	Summer/Autumn	5	208 209
Rosa 'Parkdirektor Riggers'	✱	❦					⊥		T		○	◈	Summer/Autumn	5	208
Corylus maxima 'Purpurea'	✱	❦	●●				⊥		T		○	◈	Spring/Winter	5	122
Eccremocarpus scaber	✱	❦			▲		⊥		T		○	◈	Summer/Autumn	9	133
Lapageria rosea	✱	❦			▲		⊥		Acid		◑	◈	Summer/Autumn	8	169
Rosa 'Climbing Ena Harkness'	✱	❦		✺			⊥		T		○	◈	Summer	5	208
Lonicera × *brownii* 'Fuchsioides'	✱	❦		✺			⊥		T		◑	◈	Summer	5	174
Clematis 'Ernest Markham'	✱	❦					⊥		Alkali		◑	◈	Summer	5	116
Calycanthus occidentalis	✱	❦		✺					T		○	◈	Summer	4	99
Buddleia davidii 'Royal Red'	✱	❦		✺					Alkali		○	◈	Summer	5	97
Desfontainea spinosa	✱	❦			▲				T		◑	◈	Summer	8	130
Berberidopsis corallina	✱	❦			▲		⊥		Acid		●	◈	Summer	4	93
Ribes sanguineum 'Pulborough Scarlet'	✱	❦	●●	✺					T		Ⓣ	◇	Spring	5	207
Magnolia × *soulangiana*	✱	❦							Acid		◑	◈	Spring	5	179
Jasminum polyanthum	✱	❦		✺			⊥		T		○	◈	Spring/Summer	9	164
Magnolia × *loebneri* 'Leonard Messel'	✱	❦		✺					T		◑	◈	Spring/Summer	5	179
Prunus cerasifera 'Pissardii'	✱	❦							T		◑	◈	Spring	3	200
Cotinus coggyria 'Royal Purple'	✱	❦				❧			T		○	◈	Summer	4	123
Lonicera tatarica	✱	❦	●●						T		Ⓣ	◈	Summer	4	176
Lonicera korolkowii	✱	❦	●●						T		Ⓣ	◈	Summer	5	175
Malus floribunda	✱	❦	●●						T		◑	◈	Spring	4	181
Rhododendron 'Pink Pearl'	✱	❦			▲				T		◑	◆	Spring/Summer	5	175
Clematis 'Nelly Moser'	✱	❦					⊥		T		◑	◈	Spring/Summer	5	116

SHRUBS AND TREES: 2.5 m – 6 m (8 ft – 20 ft)

Plant name	✳	🍃	🫐	🎇	🌲	🍂	⊥	🪮	Soil	Sea	◐	💧	Season	Zone	Page
Syringa × josiflexa 'Bellicent'	✳	🍃		🎇					Alkali		◐	💧	Spring/Summer	3	224
Camellia 'Leonard Messel'	✳	🍃			🌲				Acid		◐	💧	Spring	7	100
Camellia japonica 'Lady Clare'	✳	🍃			🌲				Acid		◐	💧	Spring	7	100
Cornus florida var. rubra	✳	🍃	🫐			🍂			T		◐	💧	Spring	4	120
Rhododendron rubiginosum	✳	🍃			🌲				Acid		◐	💧	Spring	5	206
Prunus 'Amanogawa'	✳	🍃		🎇					Alkali		○	💧	Spring	5	200
Prunus triloba	✳	🍃							Alkali	Sea	◐	💧	Spring	5	202
Tamarix tetrandra	✳	🍃						🪮	T	Sea	○	💧	Spring	5	225
Prunus persica 'Clara Meyer'	✳	🍃							Alkali		○	💧	Spring	3	201
Rosa 'Aloha' Rosa 'Compassion'	✳	🍃		🎇			⊥		T		○	💧	Summer/Autumn	5	209
Rosa 'New Dawn'	✳	🍃		🎇			⊥		T		○	💧	Summer/Autumn	5	209
Rosa 'Pink Perpétue'	✳	🍃		🎇			⊥		T		○	💧	Summer/Autumn	5	209
Rosa 'Zéphirine Drouhin'	✳	🍃		🎇			⊥		T		○	💧	Summer/Autumn	5	209
Clematis 'Barbara Dibley'	✳	🍃					⊥		Alkali		◐	💧	Summer	5	116
Jasminum × stephanense	✳	🍃		🎇			⊥		T		○	💧	Summer	5	164
Buddleia davidii 'Pink Pearl'	✳	🍃		🎇					Alkali		◐	💧	Summer	5	97
Cotinus coggygria	✳	🍃				🍂			T		○	💧	Summer	4	122
Cotinus obovatus	✳	🍃				🍂			T		○	💧	Summer	5	123
Tamarix pentandra	✳	🍃						🪮	T	Sea	○	💧	Summer	4	225
Abelia schumannii	✳	🍃							T		○	💧	Summer	9	74
Viburnum × bodnantense	✳	🍃		🎇					T		◐	💧	Winter	5	231
Sambucus nigra 'Pulverulenta'	✳	🍃	🫐	🎇					T		◐	💧	Summer	5	214

Key (see also p 9 and p 11)	✳	Flower colour	🍃	Foliage colour	🫐	Berries/fruits/cones/seed heads colour
🎇	Fragrant or aromatic	🌲	Evergreen	🍂	Good autumn colour	⊥	Climber or wall plant
🪮	Suitable for hedging	**Soil**	Acid/alkali/tolerant	**Sea**	Suitable for maritime or seaside conditions	○	Sun/shade requirements
💧	Moisture requirements	**Season**	Season(s) of interest	**Zone**	Climatic zone (see pages 59–62)	**Page**	Page reference to Directory of Plants

SHRUBS AND TREES

Plant name	Flower	Leaf	Berries	Fan	Tree	Autumn leaf	⊥	Comb	Soil	Sea	○	◊	Season	Zone	Page
Cytisus battandieri	✱	●		✱			⊥		T	Sea	○	◐	Summer	7	127
Hippophae rhamnoides	✱	●	●					⊞	T	Sea	◐	◊	Spring	3	156
Sambucus racemosa 'Plumosa Aurea'	✱	●	●						T		◐	◆	Spring	5	215
Coronilla emerus var. emeroides	✱	●		✱	▲				T		◐	◊	Summer	7	121
Cornus mas	✱	●	●			✦			T		◐	◆	Spring/Winter	4	120
Berberis × stenophylla	✱	●	●		▲			⊞	T		◐	◊	Spring	5	94
Berberis linearifolia 'Orange King'	✱	●	●		▲			⊞	T		◐	◊	Spring	6	94
Berberis darwinii	✱	●	●		▲			⊞	T		◐	◊	Spring	5	94
Lonicera involucrata	✱	●	●						T	Sea	Ⓣ	◊	Summer	5	174
Decaisnea fargesii	✱	●	●						T		◐	◊	Summer	5	129
Rhododendron wardii	✱	●			▲				Acid		◐	◆	Spring/Summer	5	206
Syringa vulgaris 'Primrose'	✱	●		✱					Alkali		◐	◊	Spring/Summer	3	225
Rosa banksiae 'Lutea'	✱	●		✱	▲		⊥		T		○	◊	Spring/Summer	5	210
Jasminum nudiflorum	✱	●					⊥		T		Ⓣ	◊	Spring/Winter	5	164
Corylus avellana 'Contorta'	✱	●							T		◐	◊	Spring/Winter	4	122
Corylus avellana 'Pendula'	✱	●	●						T		◐	◊	Spring/Winter	4	122
Salix matsudana 'Tortuosa'	✱	●							T		◐	◆	Spring	4	214
Salix sachalinensis 'Sekka'	✱	●							T		◐	◆	Spring	4	214
Laburnum anagyroides	✱	●		✱					T		○	◊	Spring	5	169
Betula pendula 'Youngii'	✱	●							Acid		◐	◊	Spring	2	96
Forsythia suspensa 'Nymans'	✱	●					⊥		T		◐	◊	Spring	4	143
Azara lanceolata	✱	●		✱	▲		⊥		T		◐	◊	Spring	7	93
Kerria japonica 'Pleniflora'	✱	●							T		Ⓣ	◊	Spring	4	168
Enkianthus campanulatus	✱	●				✦			Acid		◐	◊	Spring	4	135
Laurus nobilis	✱	●		✱	▲			⊞	Alkali		○	◊	Spring	5	170
Jasminum mesnyi	✱	●					⊥		T		◐	◊	Spring	8	163
Rosa 'Golden Showers'	✱	●		✱			⊥		T		Ⓣ	◊	Summer/Autumn	5	209

Plant name	✳	🍃	●	☼	▲	❧	⊥	▥	Soil	Sea	○	💧	Season	Zone	Page
Rosa 'Maigold'	✳	🍃		☼			⊥		T		Ⓣ	◑	Summer/Autumn	5	209
Rosa 'Climbing Lady Hillingdon'	✳	🍃		☼			⊥		T		◑	◑	Summer/Autumn	7	209
Clematis orientalis	✳	🍃	●	☼			⊥		Alkali		◑	◑	Summer/Autumn	5	115
Clematis tangutica	✳	🍃	●				⊥		Alkali		◑	◑	Summer/Autumn	5	116
Rosa 'Schoolgirl'	✳	🍃		☼			⊥		T		○	◑	Summer/Autumn	5	209
Fremontodendron californicum	✳	🍃			▲		⊥		Alkali		○	◑	Summer/Autumn	8	143
Genista aetnensis	✳	🍃							T		○	◑	Summer	6	146
Rosa 'Emily Gray'	✳	🍃		☼			⊥		Acid		○	◑	Summer	5	209
Aristolochia macrophylla	✳	🍃					⊥		T		◑	◑	Summer	4	86
Spartium junceum	✳	🍃		☼	▲				T	Sea	○	◑	Summer	7	220
Pittosporum tobira	✳	🍃		☼	▲		⊥		Alkali		○	◑	Summer	8	197
Chimonanthus praecox	✳	🍃		☼			⊥		Alkali		○	◑	Winter	5	110
Clematis cirrhosa var. balearica	✳	🍃			▲		⊥		Alkali		○	◑	Winter	7	114
Prunus lusitanica 'Variegata'	✳	🍃	●	☼	▲			▥	Alkali		◑	◑	Summer	6	201
Actinidia kolomikta	✳	🍃	●	☼					Acid		○	◑	Summer	4	80
Ligustrum lucidum 'Tricolor'	✳	🍃			▲				T		◑	◑	Summer	6	172
Myrtus communis 'Variegata'	✳	🍃	●	☼	▲		⊥		T	Sea	○	◑	Summer Autumn	9	183
Cornus alternifolia 'Argentea'	✳	🍃							T		◑	●	Spring	5	119
Pyrus salicifolia 'Pendula'	✳	🍃					⊥		T		○	◑	Spring	5	204
Pieris forrestii 'Wakehurst'	✳	🍃			▲				Acid		◑	●	Spring	5	193
Photinia × fraseri 'Red Robin'	✳	🍃			▲				Alkali		◑	◑	Spring	8	191
Aucuba japonica 'Variegata'	✳	🍃	●		▲			▥	Alkali	Sea	○	◑	Spring	7	91

Key (see also p 9 and p 11)	✳ Flower colour	🍃 Foliage colour	● Berries/fruits/cones/seed heads colour
☼ Fragrant or aromatic	▲ Evergreen	❧ Good autumn colour	⊥ Climber or wall plant
▥ Suitable for hedging	Soil Acid/alkali/tolerant	Sea Suitable for maritime or seaside conditions	○ Sun/shade requirements
💧 Moisture requirements	Season Season(s) of interest	Zone Climatic zone (see pages 59–62)	Page Page reference to Directory of Plants

SHRUBS AND TREES: 2.5 m – 6 m (8 ft – 20 ft)

Plant name	✳	leaf	berry	fan	tree	autumn	⊥	comb	Soil	Sea	Sun	Water	Season	Zone	Page
Ligustrum lucidum 'Excelsum Superbum'	✳	leaf			tree				T		◐	◊	Summer	6	172
Myrtus apiculata 'Glenleam Gold'	✳	leaf	berry	fan	tree				T		○	◊	Autumn	9	182
Euonymus japonicus 'Ovatus Aureus'	✳	leaf			tree			comb	T	Sea	○	◊	Summer	5	141
Elaeagnus × ebbingei 'Limelight'	✳	leaf		fan	tree				T		◐	◊	Autumn	5	134
Elaeagnus pungens 'Dicksonii'	✳	leaf		fan	tree				T		◐	◊	Autumn	5	134
Elaeagnus pungens 'Maculata'	✳	leaf		fan	tree				T		◐	◊	Autumn	5	134
Prunus laurocerasus 'Rotundifolia'	✳	leaf	berry		tree			comb	T		Ⓣ	◊	Spring	6	200
Prunus lusitanica	✳	leaf	berry	fan	tree			comb	Alkali		Ⓣ	◊	Summer	5	201
Rosa omeiensis var. pteracantha	✳	leaf	berry						T		○	◊	Spring/Summer	5	211
Viburnum opulus	✳	leaf	berry			autumn			T		◐	◆	Spring/Summer	3	232
Viburnum rhytidophyllum	✳	leaf	berry		tree				T		◐	◆	Spring/Autumn	7	232
Prunus padus 'Watereri'	✳	leaf	berry	fan					Alkali		○	◊	Spring	4	201
Euonymus europaeus 'Red Cascade'	✳	leaf	berry			autumn			Alkali		◐	◊	Spring/Autumn	5	140
Stranvaesia davidiana	✳	leaf	berry		tree	autumn			T		◐	◊	Summer	5	223
Pyracantha 'Orange Glow'	✳	leaf	berry		tree		⊥	comb	T		◐	◊	Summer/Winter	5	203
Pyracantha coccinea 'Lalandei'	✳	leaf	berry		tree		⊥	comb	T		◐	◊	Summer/Winter	5	203
Pyracantha atalantioides	✳	leaf	berry		tree		⊥	comb	T		◐	◊	Summer/Winter	5	203
Magnolia sieboldii	✳	leaf	berry	fan					Acid		◑	◊	Summer	5	179
Cotoneaster salicifolius	✳	leaf	berry		tree				T	Sea	◐	◊	Summer	6	124
Rosa filipes 'Kiftsgate'	✳	leaf	berry	fan	tree				T		○	◊	Summer	5	210
Lonicera maackii	✳	leaf	berry	fan					T		◐	◊	Summer	4	175
Rhus typhina	✳	leaf	berry			autumn			T		○	◊	Summer/Autumn	3	207
Malus × robusta 'Yellow Siberian'	✳	leaf	berry						T		◐	◊	Spring	4	181
Stranvaesia davidiana 'Fructuluteo'	✳	leaf	berry		tree	autumn			T		◐	◊	Summer	5	223
Cotoneaster 'Rothschildianus'	✳	leaf	berry		tree				T	Sea	◐	◊	Summer	6	124
Pyracantha rogersiana 'Flava'	✳	leaf	berry		tree				T		◐	◊	Summer/Winter	5	203
Cornus amomum	✳	leaf	berry		tree			comb			○	◆	Autumn/Winter	5	119

SHRUBS AND TREES: 2.5 m – 6 m (8 ft – 20 ft)

Plant name	Flower	Foliage	Berries	Fragrant	Evergreen	Autumn	Climber	Hedging	Soil	Sea	Sun	Moisture	Season	Zone	Page
Amelanchier lamarckii	✳	●	●			●			T		◐	◐	Spring	4	82
Clerodendrum trichotomum	✳	●	●	●					T		○	◐	Summer/Autumn	5	117
Cornus controversa	✳	●	●			●			T		◐	●	Summer	5	120
Ligustrum ovalifolium	✳	●	●	●	●			●	T		Ⓣ	◐	Summer	5	172
Myrtus apiculata	✳	●	●	●	●		⊥		T		○	◐	Autumn	9	182
Myrtus communis	✳	●	●	●	●		⊥		T		○	◐	Summer	8	183
Garrya elliptica	✳	●	●		●		⊥		T	Sea	◐	◐	Winter	5	146
Viburnum plicatum plicatum	✳	●							T		◐	●	Spring/Summer	4	232
Viburnum opulus 'Sterile'	✳	●				●			T		◐	●	Spring/Summer	3	232
Rhododendron 'Sappho'	✳	●			●				Acid		○	●	Spring/Summer	5	205
Magnolia × loebneri 'Merrill'	✳	●		●					T		◐	◐	Spring/Summer	5	179
Syringa vulgaris 'Madame Lemoine'	✳	●		●					Alkali		◐	●	Spring/Summer	3	225
Parrotiopsis jacquemontiana	✳	●				●			T		◐	◐	Spring/Summer	7	187
Magnolia × soulangiana 'Lennei'	✳	●					⊥		Acid		◐	◐	Spring/Summer	5	179
Clematis 'Duchess of Edinburgh'	✳	●		●			⊥		Alkali		◐	◐	Spring/Summer	5	116
Viburnum tinus	✳	●			●			●	T	Sea	◐	●	Winter/Spring	7	233
Camellia 'Cornish Snow'	✳	●			●				Acid		○	●	Spring	7	100
Camellia japonica 'Contessa Lavinia Maggi'	✳	●			●				Acid		◐	●	Spring	7	100
Camellia japonica 'Devonia'	✳	●			●				Acid		○	●	Spring	7	100
Camellia japonica 'Mathotiana Alba'	✳	●			●				Acid		○	●	Spring	7	100
Cornus alba	✳	●				●			T		◐	●	Summer/Winter	2	119
Cornus nuttallii	✳	●	●			●			Acid		◐	●	Spring/Autumn	6	120

Key (see also p 9 and p 11)	✳ Flower colour		● Foliage colour		● Berries/fruits/cones/seed heads colour
❋ Fragrant or aromatic	▲ Evergreen		● Good autumn colour		⊥ Climber or wall plant
⊞ Suitable for hedging	Soil Acid/alkali/tolerant		Sea Suitable for maritime or seaside conditions		○ Sun/shade requirements
◐ Moisture requirements	Season Season(s) of interest		Zone Climatic zone (see pages 59–62)		Page Page reference to Directory of Plants

SHRUBS AND TREES: 2.5 m – 6 m (8 ft – 20 ft)

Plant name	✳	🍃	🍒	🌿	🌲	🍂	⊥	ⅢⅢ	Soil	Sea	○	💧	Season	Zone	Page
Pieris 'Forest Flame'	✳	🍃			▲				Acid		◐	●	Spring	5	193
Rubus tridel	✳	🍃							T		◐	◗	Spring	5	212
Magnolia denudata	✳	🍃		🌿					Acid		◐	◗	Spring	5	178
Magnolia × highdownensis	✳	🍃		🌿					Alkali		◐	◗	Spring	5	178
Drimys winteri	✳	🍃		🌿	▲		⊥		T		◐	◗	Spring	8	133
Halesia carolina	✳	🍃	🍒						Acid		◐	◗	Spring	5	150
Clematis armandii	✳	🍃		🌿	▲		⊥		Alkali		○	◗	Spring	8	114
Exochorda × macrantha 'The Bride'	✳	🍃							Acid		○	◗	Spring	5	142
Pileostegia viburnoides	✳	🍃			▲		⊥		T		Ⓣ	●	Summer/Autumn	5	194
Clematis flammula	✳	🍃		🌿			⊥		Alkali		◐	◗	Summer/Autumn	5	114
Rosa 'Climbing Iceberg'	✳	🍃					⊥		T		○	◗	Summer/Autumn	5	209
Rosa 'White Cockade'	✳	🍃		🌿			⊥		T		○	◗	Summer/Autumn	5	209
Rosa 'Swan Lake'	✳	🍃					⊥		T		○	◗	Summer/Autumn	5	209
Escallonia 'Donard Seedling'	✳	🍃		🌿	▲			ⅢⅢ	T	Sea	○	◗	Summer/Autumn	5	139
Choisya ternata	✳	🍃		🌿	▲		⊥		T	Sea	◐	◗	Summer/Autumn	7	111
Eucryphia glutinosa	✳	🍃				🍂			Acid		◐	●	Summer	6	140
Eucryphia × nymansensis 'Nymansay'	✳	🍃			▲				Acid		◐	●	Summer	6	140
Hydrangea paniculata 'Grandiflora'	✳	🍃							T		◐	●	Summer	5	159
Chionanthus virginicus	✳	🍃		🌿			⊥		T		○	◗	Summer	4	111
Cornus kousa	✳	🍃	🍒						T		◐	◗	Summer	5	120
Deutzia scabra 'Macrocephala'	✳	🍃							T		◐	◗	Summer	4	131
Sorbaria aitchisonii	✳	🍃							T		◐	◗	Summer	5	220
Euonymus japonicus	✳	🍃			▲			ⅢⅢ	T	Sea	Ⓣ	◗	Summer	5	141
Oxydendrum arboreum	✳	🍃				🍂			Acid		Ⓣ	◗	Summer	5	185
Itea ilicifolia	✳	🍃		🌿	▲				Acid		◐	◗	Summer	5	163
Olearia ilicifolia	✳	🍃		🌿	▲			ⅢⅢ	T	Sea	◐	◗	Summer	8	184
Trachelospermum asiaticum	✳	🍃		🌿	▲		⊥		Acid		○	◗	Summer	7	229

Plant name	✳	🍃	●	Fan	▲	Leaf	⊥	Hedge	Soil	Sea	○	💧	Season	Zone	Page
Trachelospermum jasminoides	✳	🍃		Fan	▲		⊥		Acid		○	💧	Summer	7	229
Hoheria glabrata	✳	🍃		Fan			⊥		T		◐	💧	Summer	6	156
Hoheria sexstylosa	✳	🍃			▲		⊥		T		◐	💧	Summer	8	157
Philadelphus 'Virginal'	✳	🍃		Fan					Alkali		◐	💧	Summer	5	190
Olearia macrodonta	✳	🍃			▲			Hedge	T	Sea	◐	💧	Summer	7	184
Stuartia malacodendron	✳	🍃				Leaf			Acid		◐	💧	Summer	6	223
Clematis florida 'Sieboldii'	✳	🍃					⊥		Alkali		○	💧	Summer	5	114
Carpenteria californica	✳	🍃		Fan	▲		⊥		T		○	💧	Summer	9	103
Buddleia davidii 'White Bouquet'	✳	🍃		Fan					Alkali		○	💧	Summer	5	97
Clethra barbinervis	✳	🍃		Fan		Leaf			Acid	Sea	○	●	Summer	5	117
Leptospermum scoparium 'Album Flore Pleno'	✳	🍃			▲		⊥		Acid	Sea	○	●	Summer	9	171
Cordyline australis	✳	🍃		Fan	▲				T	Sea	○	●	Summer	8	118
Fatsia japonica	✳	🍃			▲				T		Ⓣ	💧	Autumn	7	142
Elaeagnus × ebbingei	✳	🍃	●	Fan	▲			Hedge	T	Sea	◐	💧	Autumn	5	134
Clematis cirrhosa	✳	🍃	●		▲		⊥		Alkali		○	●	Winter/Spring	7	114
Buddleia 'Lochinch'	✳	🍃		Fan					T		○	💧	Summer	5	98
Rhododendron 'Purple Splendour'	✳	🍃			▲				Acid		◐	●	Spring/Summer	5	205
Syringa vulgaris 'Katherine Havemeyer'	✳	🍃		Fan					Alkali		◐	💧	Spring/Summer	3	225
Abutilon vitifolium	✳	🍃					⊥		T		○	💧	Spring/Summer	8	76
Wisteria floribunda	✳	🍃		Fan			⊥		T		○	💧	Spring/Summer	4	235
Wisteria floribunda 'Macrobotrys'	✳	🍃		Fan			⊥		T		○	💧	Spring/Summer	4	235
Clematis 'Mrs Cholmondeley'	✳	🍃					⊥		Alkali		◐	💧	Spring/Summer	5	116

Key (see also p 9 and p 11)	✳	Flower colour		🍃	Foliage colour		●	Berries/fruits/cones/seed heads colour
Fan	Fragrant or aromatic	▲	Evergreen	Leaf	Good autumn colour	⊥		Climber or wall plant
Hedge	Suitable for hedging	Soil	Acid/alkali/tolerant	Sea	Suitable for maritime or seaside conditions	○		Sun/shade requirements
💧	Moisture requirements	Season	Season(s) of interest	Zone	Climatic zone (see pages 59–62)	Page		Page reference to Directory of Plants

SHRUBS AND TREES: 2.5 m – 6 m (8 ft – 20 ft)

Plant name	✳	🍃	🫐	🪭	🌲	🍂	⊥	⫿	Soil	Sea	○	💧	Season	Zone	Page
Clematis 'Vyvyan Pennell'	✳	🍃					⊥		Alkali		◑	💧	Spring/Summer	5	116
Rhododendron augustinii	✳	🍃			🌲				Acid		◑	◆	Spring	5	205
Ceanothus 'Delight'	✳	🍃			🌲		⊥		T		○	💧	Spring/Summer	7	104
Ceanothus impressus	✳	🍃			🌲		⊥		T		○	💧	Spring	7	104
Solanum crispum 'Glasnevin'	✳	🍃			🌲		⊥		Alkali		◑	💧	Summer/Autumn	8	219
Clematis × jackmanii	✳	🍃					⊥		Alkali		◑	💧	Summer/Autumn	5	115
Clematis 'Jackmanii Superba'	✳	🍃					⊥		Alkali		◑	💧	Summer/Autumn	5	116
Clematis 'The President'	✳	🍃					⊥		Alkali		◑	💧	Summer/Autumn	5	116
Clematis viticella 'Abundance'	✳	🍃					⊥		Alkali		◑	💧	Summer/Autumn	5	116
Clematis 'William Kennett'	✳	🍃					⊥		Alkali		◑	💧	Summer	5	116
Lippia citriodora	✳	🍃		🪭			⊥		T		○	💧	Summer	8	173
Buddleia alternifolia	✳	🍃		🪭					T		◑	💧	Summer	5	97
Buddleia davidii 'Black Knight'	✳	🍃		🪭					T		◑	💧	Summer	5	97
Buddleia davidii 'Empire Blue'	✳	🍃		🪭					T		◑	💧	Summer	5	97
Buddleia davidii 'Ile de France'	✳	🍃		🪭					T		◑	💧	Summer	5	97
Disanthus cercidifolius	✳	🍃				🍂			Acid		◑	◆	Autumn	7	132
Chamaecyparis laws. 'Ellwood's White'		🍃			🌲				T		◑	💧		6	108
Chamaecyparis lawsoniana 'Albovariegata'		🍃			🌲			⫿	T		◑	💧		6	108
Hedera canariensis 'Gloire de Marengo'		🍃			🌲		⊥		T		◑	💧		5	154
Ilex aquifolium 'Argenteo-marginata'		🍃	🫐		🌲			⫿	T	Sea	◑	💧	Spring/Winter	5	161
Ilex aquifolium 'Silver Queen'		🍃			🌲			⫿	T	Sea	◑	💧		5	161
Cryptomeria japonica 'Elegans'		🍃			🌲	🍂			Acid		◑	💧	Spring	5	125
Hedera helix 'Chicago'		🍃			🌲		⊥		T		◑	💧		5	154
Acer palmatum 'Atropurpureum'		🍃							T		◑	💧	Summer	5	77
Acer palmatum 'Dissectum Atropurpureum'		🍃							Acid		◑	💧	Summer	5	77
Vitis vinifera 'Purpurea'		🍃	🫐			🍂	⊥		T		◑	💧		6	234
Ligustrum ovalifolium 'Aureum'		🍃	🫐	🪭	🌲			⫿	T		◑	💧	Summer	5	173

SHRUBS AND TREES: 2.5 m – 6 m (8 ft – 20 ft)

Plant name	✳	🌿	🍒	☀	🌲	🍂	⊥	▥	Soil	Sea	○	💧	Season	Zone	Page
Ilex × altaclarensis 'Golden King'		✓	✓		▲			▥	T	Sea	◑	●	Winter	6	160
Thuja plicata 'Aureovariegata'		✓	✓	☀	▲			▥	T		○	●		5	228
Calocedrus decurrens 'Aureovariegata'		✓			▲				T		○	●		5	99
Taxus baccata 'Fastigiata Aurea'		✓	✓		▲				Alkali		◑	○		6	226
Chamaecyparis laws. 'Ellwood's Gold'		✓			▲				T		◑	●		6	108
Juniperus chinensis 'Aurea'		✓		☀	▲				T		○	●		5	165
Juniperus chinensis 'Kaizuka Aurea'		✓		☀	▲				T		○	●		4	165
× Cupressocyparis leylandii 'Castlewellan'		✓			▲			▥	T	Sea	◑	●		5	126
Chamaecyparis pisifera 'Filifera Aurea'		✓			▲				Acid		◑	●		5	109
Chamaecyparis pisifera 'Plumosa Aurea'		✓			▲				Acid		○	●		5	109
Juniperus × media 'Plumosa Aurea'		✓		☀	▲				Alkali		◑	●		5	166
Cedrus atlantica 'Aurea'		✓			▲				T		○	●		7	105
Cedrus deodara 'Aurea'		✓			▲				T		○	●		6	105
Chamaecyparis nootkatensis 'Lutea'		✓			▲				T		○	●		4	109
Cupressus macrocarpa 'Goldcrest'		✓		☀	▲				T		○	●		7	126
Pinus contorta		✓	✓		▲			▥	Acid	Sea	○	●		7	194
Thuja orientalis 'Conspicua'		✓	✓	☀	▲				T		○	●		5	228
Thuja occidentalis 'Lutea Nana'		✓		☀	▲				T		○	●		5	227
Chamaecyparis lawsoniana 'Lanei'		✓			▲				T		◑	●		6	108
Chamaecyparis lawsoniana 'Spek'		✓			▲				T		○	●		6	108
Juniperus communis 'Hibernica'		✓		☀	▲				Alkali		○	●		4	166
Juniperus virginiana 'Burkii'		✓		☀	▲				Alkali		◑	●		4	167

Key (see also p 9 and p 11)	✳	Flower colour	🌿	Foliage colour	🍒	Berries/fruits/cones/seed heads colour
☀	Fragrant or aromatic	▲	Evergreen	🍂	Good autumn colour	⊥	Climber or wall plant
▥	Suitable for hedging	Soil	Acid/alkali/tolerant	Sea	Suitable for maritime or seaside conditions	○	Sun/shade requirements
💧	Moisture requirements	Season	Season(s) of interest	Zone	Climatic zone (see pages 59–62)	Page	Page reference to Directory of Plants

SHRUBS AND TREES: 2.5 m – 6 m (8 ft – 20 ft)

Plant name	✳	🍃	🍒	�·	🌲	🍂	⊥	⫴	Soil	Sea	◐	💧	Season	Zone	Page
Juniperus virginiana 'Skyrocket'		🍃		�·	🌲				Alkali		◐	💧		5	167
Juniperus squamata 'Meyeri'		🍃		�·	🌲				Alkali		◐	💧		5	167
Juniperus virginiana 'Blue Heaven'		🍃		�·	🌲				Alkali		◐	💧		4	167
Juniperus chinensis 'Pyramidalis'		🍃		�·	🌲				T		◐	💧		5	165
Picea pungens 'Hoopsii'		🍃			🌲				Acid		◐	💧		2	192
Chamaecyparis laws. 'Chilworth Silver'		🍃			🌲				T		◐	💧		6	108
Picea abies 'Acrocona'		🍃	🍒		🌲				T		◐	💧		4	192
Pseudotsuga menziesii 'Fletcheri'		🍃	🍒	�·	🌲				Acid		◯	💧		5	202
Taxus baccata 'Fastigiata'		🍃	🍒		🌲				Alkali		◐	💧		6	225
Vitis 'Brandt'		🍃	🍒			🍂	⊥		T		◐	💧		6	234
Abies koreana		🍃	🍒		🌲				Acid		◐	💧		5	75
Ilex aquifolium		🍃	🍒		🌲			⫴	T	Sea	◐	💧	Winter	5	161
Ilex aquifolium 'Bacciflava'		🍃	🍒		🌲			⫴	T	Sea	◐	💧	Autumn/Winter	5	161
Ilex aquifolium 'Pyramidalis'		🍃	🍒		🌲			⫴	T	Sea	◐	💧	Winter	5	161
Ilex aquifolium 'J.C. van Tol'		🍃	🍒		🌲			⫴	T	Sea	◐	💧	Winter	5	161
Thuja occidentalis 'Holmstrup'		🍃		�·	🌲				T		◐	💧		4	227
Thuja occidentalis 'Smaragd'		🍃		�·	🌲			⫴	T		◐	💧		4	227
Acer griseum		🍃				🍂			T		◐	💧	Autumn/Winter	5	77
Acer japonicum		🍃				🍂			Acid		◐	💧	Spring/Autumn	5	77
Acer palmatum 'Dissectum Viridis'		🍃				🍂			Acid		◐	💧	Summer/Autumn	5	77
Acer palmatum 'Heptalobum Osakazuki'		🍃				🍂			Acid		◐	💧	Summer/Autumn	5	77
Nyssa sinensis		🍃				🍂			Acid		◯	💧		6	183
Arundinaria japonica		🍃			🌲				T		◯	💧		5	87
Griselinia littoralis		🍃							Alkali	Sea	Ⓣ	💧		6	149
Chamaecyparis lawsoniana 'Ellwoodii'		🍃							T		◐	💧		5	108
Chamaecyparis laws. 'Ellwood's Pillar'		🍃			🌲				T		◐	💧		5	108
Juniperus chinensis 'Kaizuka'		🍃		�·	🌲				T		◐	💧		4	165

SHRUBS AND TREES: 2.5 m – 6 m (8 ft – 20 ft)

Plant name	Flower	Foliage	Berries	Fragrant	Evergreen	Autumn	Climber	Hedging	Soil	Sea	Sun	Moisture	Season	Zone	Page
Chamaecyparis thyoides 'Andelyensis'		Foliage			Evergreen				Acid		◐	◆		5	110
Juniperus × media 'Blaauw'		Foliage		Fragrant	Evergreen				Alkali		◐	◊		4	166
Calocedrus decurrens		Foliage		Fragrant	Evergreen				T		○	◊		5	99
Pinus sylvestris 'Watereri'		Foliage			Evergreen				T		○	◊		3	196
Pinus aristata		Foliage			Evergreen				Acid		○	◊		5	194

SHRUBS AND TREES: over 6 m (20 ft)

Plant name	Flower	Foliage	Berries	Fragrant	Evergreen	Autumn	Climber	Hedging	Soil	Sea	Sun	Moisture	Season	Zone	Page
Lonicera sempervirens	Flower	Foliage			Evergreen		Climber		T		○	◊	Summer	5	176
Crataegus oxyacantha 'Coccinea Plena'	Flower	Foliage			Evergreen				T	Sea	◐	◊	Spring	4	125
Campsis radicans	Flower	Foliage					Climber		T		○	◊	Summer/Autumn	8	103
Campsis × tagliabuana 'Madame Galen'	Flower	Foliage					Climber		T		○	◊	Summer/Autumn	8	103
Clematis montana 'Tetrarose'	Flower	Foliage					Climber		Alkali		◐	◊	Spring	5	115
Clematis montana var. rubens	Flower	Foliage					Climber		Alkali		◐	◊	Spring	5	115
Prunus sargentii	Flower	Foliage							Alkali		○	◊	Spring	5	201
Prunus 'Accolade'	Flower	Foliage							Alkali		○	◊	Spring	5	199
Rosa 'Albertine'	Flower	Foliage		Fragrant			Climber		T		Ⓣ	◊	Summer	5	209
Solanum jasminoides 'Album'	Flower	Foliage			Evergreen		Climber		Alkali		◐	◊	Summer/Autumn	8	219
Acer platanoides 'Drummondii'	Flower	Foliage							Alkali		◐	◆	Spring	5	78
Acer platanoides 'Crimson King'	Flower	Foliage							Alkali		◐	◊	Spring	5	78
Salix alba 'Chermesina'	Flower	Foliage							T		◐	◆	Spring	2	213
Salix × chrysocoma	Flower	Foliage							T		◐	◆	Spring	2	213
Rhododendron falconeri	Flower	Foliage		Fragrant	Evergreen				Acid		◐	◆	Spring	5	205

Key (see also p 9 and p 11)	✹ Flower colour	⬭ Foliage colour	🍒 Berries/fruits/cones/seed heads colour
☀ Fragrant or aromatic	▲ Evergreen	🍁 Good autumn colour	⊥ Climber or wall plant
⊞ Suitable for hedging	**Soil** Acid/alkali/tolerant	**Sea** Suitable for maritime or seaside conditions	○ Sun/shade requirements
◊ Moisture requirements	**Season** Season(s) of interest	**Zone** Climatic zone (see pages 59–62)	**Page** Page reference to Directory of Plants

SHRUBS AND TREES: over 6 m (20 ft)

Plant name	✳	🍂	⚫⚫	☀	▲	🍁	⊥	⊞	Soil	Sea	○	◌	Season	Zone	Page
Laburnum × watereri 'Vossii'	✳	🍂		☀					T		○	half	Spring	5	169
Betula pendula	✳	🍂							T		half	◌	Spring	2	97
Acacia dealbata	✳	🍂		☀	▲				Acid		Ⓣ	◌	Spring	9	76
Lonicera japonica 'Halliana'	✳	🍂		☀	▲		⊥		T		half	◌	Summer/Autumn	5	175
Rosa 'Mermaid'	✳	🍂			▲		⊥		T		half	◌	Summer/Autumn	5	209
Quercus ilex	✳	🍂	⚫⚫		▲			⊞	T	Sea	○	◌	Summer	7	204
Lonicera × americana	✳	🍂		☀			⊥		T		half	◌	Summer	5	174
Passiflora caerulea	✳	🍂	⚫⚫		▲		⊥		T		half	◌	Summer/Autumn	8	188
Sorbus aria 'Lutescens'	✳	🍂	⚫⚫						Alkali	Sea	half	◌	Spring/Summer	2	220
Cornus controversa 'Variegata'	✳	🍂	⚫⚫						T		half	●	Summer	5	120
Lonicera japonica 'Aureoreticulata'	✳	🍂		☀	▲		⊥		T		○	◌	Summer/Autumn	7	174
Malus 'John Downie'	✳	🍂	⚫⚫	☀					T		half	◌	Spring	4	181
Sorbus aucuparia	✳	🍂	⚫⚫			🍁			Acid		half	◌	Spring/Autumn	2	220
Sorbus hupehensis	✳	🍂	⚫⚫			🍁			T		half	◌	Summer/Autumn	4	220
Rhododendron sinogrande	✳	🍂			▲				Acid		half	●	Spring	6	206
Clematis montana	✳	🍂					⊥		Alkali		half	◌	Spring	5	115
Prunus × yedoensis	✳	🍂		☀					Alkali		○	◌	Spring	5	202
Polygonum baldschuanicum	✳	🍂					⊥		T		half	◌	Summer/Autumn	5	197
Jasminum officinale	✳	🍂		☀			⊥		T		○	◌	Summer/Autumn	6	164
Eucalyptus niphophila	✳	🍂		☀	▲				Acid		○	●	Summer	6	139
Hydrangea petiolaris	✳	🍂					⊥		T		Ⓣ	●	Summer	4	159
Magnolia grandiflora	✳	🍂		☀	▲		⊥		Acid		half	◌	Summer	7	178
Rosa 'Albéric Barbier'	✳	🍂		☀	▲		⊥		T		○	◌	Summer	5	209
Prunus subhirtella 'Autumnalis'	✳	🍂							Alkali		○	◌	Autumn/Winter	3	201
Wisteria sinensis	✳	🍂		☀			⊥		T		○	◌	Spring/Summer	5	235
Paulownia tomentosa	✳	🍂		☀					T		○	◌	Spring	6	188
Parthenocissus henryana		🍂	⚫⚫			🍁	⊥		T		half	◌		6	187

SHRUBS AND TREES: over 6 m (20 ft)

Plant name	❋	🍃	🍒	🎇	🌲	🍂	⊥	⑊	Soil	Sea	◑	💧	Season	Zone	Page
Hedera helix 'Glacier'		🍃			🌲		⊥		T		◑	💧		△5	154
Acer negundo 'Variegatum'		🍃							T		◑	💧	Spring/Summer	△5	77
Chamaecyparis laws. 'Columnaris Aurea'		🍃			🌲				T		◑	💧		△6	108
Chamaecyparis lawsoniana 'Lutea'		🍃			🌲				T		◑	💧		△6	108
Chamaecyparis lawsoniana 'Maas'		🍃			🌲				T		◑	💧		△5	108
Chamaecyparis lawsoniana 'Stewartii'		🍃			🌲				T		◑	💧		△6	108
Chamaecyparis laws. 'Winston Churchill'		🍃			🌲				T		◑	💧		△6	108
Robinia pseudoacacia 'Frisia'		🍃		🎇					T		○	💧	Summer	△3	207
Gleditsia triacanthos 'Sunburst'		🍃	🍒						T		Ⓣ	💧		△3	149
Chamaecyparis obtusa 'Crippsii'		🍃			🌲				T		◑	💧		△5	109
Chamaecyparis lawsoniana 'Erecta Aurea'		🍃			🌲				T		◑	💧		△6	108
Chamaecyparis lawsoniana 'Westermannii'		🍃			🌲				T		◑	💧		△5	108
Hedera colchica 'Dentata Variegata'		🍃			🌲		⊥		T		◑	💧		△5	154
Hedera colchica 'Paddy's Pride'		🍃			🌲		⊥		T		◑	💧		△5	154
Hedera helix 'Goldheart'		🍃			🌲		⊥		T		Ⓣ	💧		△5	154
Chamaecyparis lawsoniana 'Allumii'		🍃			🌲				T		◑	💧		△5	108
Chamaecyparis lawsoniana 'Blue Nantais'		🍃			🌲				T		◑	💧		△5	108
Chamaecyparis laws. 'Columnaris Glauca'		🍃			🌲				T		◑	💧		△6	108
Chamaecyparis lawsoniana 'Pembury Blue'		🍃			🌲				T		◑	💧		△6	108
Abies procera 'Glauca'		🍃	🍒		🌲				Acid		◑	💧		△2	75
Picea pungens var. *glauca*		🍃			🌲				Acid		◑	💧		△2	192
Picea pungens 'Koster'		🍃			🌲				Acid		◑	💧		△2	192

Key	(see also p 9 and p 11)	❋	Flower colour		🍃	Foliage colour		🍒	Berries/fruits/cones/seed heads colour
🎇	Fragrant or aromatic	🌲	Evergreen		🍂	Good autumn colour		⊥	Climber or wall plant
⑊	Suitable for hedging	**Soil**	Acid/alkali/tolerant		**Sea**	Suitable for maritime or seaside conditions		○	Sun/shade requirements
💧	Moisture requirements	**Season**	Season(s) of interest		**Zone**	Climatic zone (*see pages 59–62*)		**Page**	Page reference to *Directory of Plants*

SHRUBS AND TREES: over 6 m (20 ft)

Plant name	❋	🍃	berry	fan	tree	leaf	⊥	comb	Soil	Sea	○	◊	Season	Zone	Page
Pinus parviflora		🍃	●		▲				Acid		○	◆		5	195
Cupressus glabra 'Conica'		🍃		☀	▲				T		◑	◗		7	126
Cedrus atlantica var. glauca		🍃	●		▲				T	Sea	○	◊		6	105
Cedrus atlantica 'Glauca Pendula'		🍃	●		▲				T	Sea	○	◊		6	105
Abies lasiocarpa 'Arizonica'		🍃	●		▲				Acid		◑	◆		5	75
Pseudotsuga menziesii		🍃	●	☀	▲			comb	Acid		○	◆		5	202
Taxus baccata		🍃	●		▲			comb	Alkali		Ⓣ	◊		6	225
Pinus sylvestris		🍃	●		▲				T		○	◊		3	196
Pinus pinea		🍃	●		▲				T	Sea	○	◊		8	195
Pinus nigra		🍃	●		▲				Alkali	Sea	○	◊		4	195
Taxodium distichum		🍃	●			leaf			T		◑	◆		4	225
Pinus leucodermis		🍃	●		▲				Alkali		○	◊		5	194
Parthenocissus quinquefolia		🍃	●			leaf	⊥		T		Ⓣ	◗	Autumn	5	187
Parthenocissus tricuspidata 'Veitchii'		🍃	●			leaf	⊥		T		Ⓣ	◗	Autumn	5	187
Vitis coignetiae		🍃	●			leaf	⊥		T		◑	◆	Autumn	5	234
Picea abies		🍃			▲				Acid		◑	◆		4	192
Thuja plicata		🍃		☀	▲			comb	T		◑	◆		5	228
Chamaecyparis lawsoniana 'Fletcheri'		🍃			▲				T		◑	◊		5	108
Chamaecyparis lawsoniana 'Green Pillar'		🍃			▲				T		◑	◗	Spring	5	108
Chamaecyparis lawsoniana 'Pottenii'		🍃			▲				T		◑	◗	Spring	6	108
Chamaecyparis lawsoniana 'Wisselii'		🍃			▲				T		◑	◊		5	108
Chamaecyparis nootkatensis 'Pendula'		🍃	●		▲				T		◑	◊		4	109
Metasequoia glyptostroboides		🍃	●			leaf			T		○	◆	Spring/Autumn	5	182
Larix decidua		🍃	●			leaf			T		○	◆	Spring/Autumn	2	169
Buxus sempervirens		🍃		☀	▲			comb	T		Ⓣ	◗		5	98
Celastrus orbiculatus		🍃	●			leaf	⊥		T		◑	◗	Autumn	3	105
Sequoiadendron giganteum		🍃			▲				T		○	◆		6	218

SHRUBS AND TREES: over 6 m (20 ft)

Plant name	✳	🍃	●	☼	🌲	🍂	⊥	⊞	Soil	Sea	◐	💧	Season	Zone	Page
Quercus coccinea		🍃	●			🍂			T		○	◆	Autumn	4	204
Nyssa sylvatica		🍃				🍂			Acid		○	◆	Autumn	6	183
Populus nigra 'Italica'		🍃							T	Sea	○	◗		2	197
Chamaecyparis lawsoniana 'Erecta Viridis'		🍃			🌲				T		◐	◗		6	108
× Cupressocyparis leylandii		🍃			🌲			⊞	T	Sea	◐	◗		5	126
Cupressus macrocarpa		🍃	●	☼	🌲			⊞	T	Sea	◐	◗		6	126
Tsuga canadensis		🍃	●		🌲				Alkali		◐	◗		4	229
Chamaecyparis lawsoniana		🍃			🌲			⊞	T		◐	◗		5	107
Araucaria araucana		🍃	●		🌲				T		○	◗		6	85
Cedrus deodara		🍃	●		🌲				T		○	◗		6	105
Cedrus libani		🍃	●		🌲				T		○	◗		6	105
Cupressus sempervirens 'Stricta'		🍃		☼	🌲				T		○	◊		8	126
Pinus cembra		🍃			🌲				Acid		○	◗		4	194
Ginkgo biloba		🍃				🍂			T		○	◗	Autumn	4	149

SHRUBS AND TREES

Key *(see also p 9 and p 11)*	✳	Flower colour	🍃	Foliage colour	●	Berries/fruits/cones/seed heads colour
☼ Fragrant or aromatic	🌲	Evergreen	🍂	Good autumn colour	⊥	Climber or wall plant
⊞ Suitable for hedging	**Soil**	Acid/alkali/tolerant	**Sea**	Suitable for maritime or seaside conditions	○	Sun/shade requirements
💧 Moisture requirements	**Season**	Season(s) of interest	**Zone**	Climatic zone *(see pages 59–62)*	**Page**	Page reference to *Directory of Plants*

HERBACEOUS AND ROCK PLANTS

Plant name	✳	leaf	berry	fan	▲	oak leaf	⊥	R	Soil	Sea	○	◊	Season	Zone	Page
Antennaria dioica var. rubra	✳	leaf			▲			R	Acid		○	◊	Spring/Summer	7	84
Bergenia 'Ballawley'	✳	leaf			▲	oak			Alkali		◑	◆	Spring	4	96
Epimedium × rubrum	✳	leaf			▲	oak		T			●	◊	Spring	7	135
Aubrieta deltoidea	✳	leaf			▲			R	Alkali		○	◐	Spring	4	90
Primula × pruhoniciana 'Wanda'	✳	leaf						R	Acid		◑	◆	Winter/Spring	4	199
Sedum spurium 'Schorbusser Blut'	✳	leaf			▲			R T		Sea	○	◊	Summer/Autumn	3	217
Sedum cauticola	✳	leaf						R T		Sea	○	◊	Summer/Autumn	3	216
Echinacea purpurea	✳	leaf							T		◑	◊	Summer/Autumn	4	133
Polygonum affine 'Darjeeling Red'	✳	leaf				oak			T		◑	◊	Summer/Autumn	4	197
Potentilla atrosanguinea 'Gibson's Scarlet'	✳	leaf							T		○	◊	Summer	4	198
Dianthus deltoides 'Brilliant'	✳	leaf						R	T		◑	◊	Summer	5	·131·
Aster novi-belgii 'Jenny'	✳	leaf							T		◑	◆	Autumn	4	89
Sedum spectabile	✳	leaf			▲				Alkali	Sea	○	◊	Summer/Autumn	3	217
Potentilla nitida 'Rubra'	✳	leaf							T		○	◊	Summer	4	199
Dianthus alpinus	✳	leaf			▲			R	Alkali	Sea	○	◊	Spring/Summer	4	131
Dianthus × allwoodii	✳	leaf			▲				Alkali	Sea	○	◊	Summer/Autumn	5	132
Dianthus Old fashioned pinks	✳	leaf							T	Sea	○	◊	Summer/Autumn	5	132
Bergenia × schmidtii	✳	leaf			▲				Alkali		◑	◆	Spring/Summer	4	96
Androsace sarmentosa var. chumbyi	✳	leaf						R	Alkali		○	◊	Spring/Summer	7	83
Geranium endressii	✳	leaf							T		◑	◊	Spring/Summer	4	148
Armeria maritima	✳	leaf			▲			R	T	Sea	○	◊	Spring/Summer	6	86
Arabis aubrietioides	✳	leaf			▲			R	T		◑	◊	Spring/Summer	4	85
Phlox amoena	✳	leaf						R	T		○	◊	Spring/Summer	5	190
Incarvillea delavayi	✳	leaf							T		○	◊	Spring/Summer	5	161
Saxifraga umbrosa var. primuloides	✳	leaf			▲			R	T		◑	◊	Spring/Summer	5	216
Helleborus orientalis	✳	leaf			▲				T		◑	◆	Winter/Spring	5	156
Bergenia cordifolia	✳	leaf			▲	oak			Alkali		◑	◆	Spring	2	96

HERBACEOUS AND ROCK PLANTS: up to 60 cm (2 ft)

Plant name	✳	🍃	🍒	🔅	🌲	🍂	⊥	R	Soil	Sea	○	💧	Season	Zone	Page
Aethionema 'Warley Rose'	✳	🍃						R	T		○	💧	Spring	5	80
Aubrieta deltoidea	✳	🍃			🌲			R	Alkali		○	💧	Spring	4	90
Saxifraga moschata 'Atropurpurea'	✳	🍃			🌲			R	T		◑	💧	Spring	5	216
Anemone × hybrida 'Bressingham Glow'	✳	🍃							T		◑	💧	Summer/Autumn	5	83
Geranium 'Ballerina'	✳	🍃						R	T		◑	💧	Summer/Autumn	5	147
Geranium sanguineum 'Lancastriense'	✳	🍃							T		◑	💧	Summer/Autumn	4	148
Astrantia major	✳	🍃							T		◑	💧	Summer	4	90
Gypsophila repens 'Fratensis'	✳	🍃						R	Alkali	Sea	○	💧	Summer	4	150
Gypsophila repens 'Rosea'	✳	🍃						R	Alkali	Sea	○	💧	Summer	5	150
Sempervivum montanum	✳	🍃			🌲			R	T	Sea	○	💧	Summer	5	217
Erigeron mucronatus	✳	🍃						R	T		○	💧	Summer	5	138
Geranium dalmaticum	✳	🍃				🍂		R	T		◑	💧	Summer	4	148
Thymus serpyllum	✳	🍃		🔅	🌲			R	T		○	💧	Summer	5	228
Sempervivum arachnoideum	✳	🍃			🌲			R	T	Sea	○	💧	Summer	3	217
Crepis incana	✳	🍃						R	T		○	💧	Summer	5	125
Aster novi-belgii 'Little Pink Baby'	✳	🍃							T		◑	💧	Autumn	4	89
Alyssum montanum	✳	🍃		🔅	🌲			R	Alkali		○	💧	Spring/Summer	4	81
Alyssum saxatile	✳	🍃			🌲			R	Alkali		○	💧	Spring/Summer	4	82
Raoulia australis	✳	🍃			🌲			R	T		○	💧	Spring	7	204
Sedum spathulifolium 'Cappa Blanca'	✳	🍃			🌲			R	T	Sea	○	💧	Summer/Autumn	3	217
Anthemis sancti-johannis	✳	🍃		🔅					Alkali		○	💧	Summer	6	84
Achillea taygetea 'Moonshine'	✳	🍃							T		○	💧	Summer	5	79

Key (see also p 9 and p 11)	✳	Flower colour		🍃	Foliage colour		🍒	Berries/fruits/cones/seed heads colour
🔅	Fragrant or aromatic	🌲	Evergreen	🍂	Good autumn colour	⊥		Climber or wall plant
R	Suitable for rock gardens	Soil	Acid/alkali/tolerant	Sea	Suitable for maritime or seaside conditions	○		Sun/shade requirements
💧	Moisture requirements	Season	Season(s) of interest	Zone	Climatic zone (see pages 59–62)	Page		Page reference to Directory of Plants

49

HERBACEOUS AND ROCK PLANTS: up to 60 cm (2 ft)

Plant name	✱	🍃	●●	fan	▲	🍂	⊥	R	Soil	Sea	○	◇	Season	Zone	Page
Sedum spathulifolium 'Purpureum'	✱	🍃			▲			R	T	Sea	○	◇	Summer/Autumn	3	217
Paeonia mlokosewitschii	✱	🍃	●●			🍂			T		◑	◈	Spring/Autumn	5	186
Geum chiloense 'Lady Stratheden'	✱	🍃							T		◑	◈	Spring/Summer	6	148
Doronicum caucasicum	✱	🍃							T		◑	◆	Spring	5	132
Trollius europaeus 'Superbus'	✱	🍃							T		◑	◆	Spring/Summer	3	229
Tellima grandiflora	✱	🍃			▲				T		◑	◈	Spring/Summer	4	227
Caltha palustris 'Flore Plena'	✱	🍃							Acid		◑	◆	Spring	4	99
Adonis vernalis	✱	🍃							T		◑	◆	Spring	7	80
Iris pumila	✱	🍃						R	Alkali		◑	◆	Spring	4	162
Helleborus corsicus	✱	🍃			▲				T		◑	◆	Spring	6	155
Euphorbia epithymoides	✱	🍃			▲				T		◑	◈	Spring	4	141
Saxifraga 'Elizabethae'	✱	🍃			▲				T		◑	◈	Spring	5	216
Coreopsis grandiflora	✱	🍃							Alkali		○	◆	Summer/Autumn	3	118
Coreopsis verticillata	✱	🍃							Alkali		○	◈	Summer/Autumn	3	118
Inula hookeri	✱	🍃							T		○	◈	Summer/Autumn	5	161
Alchemilla mollis	✱	🍃							T		◑	◆	Summer	3	81
Aster linosyris	✱	🍃							T		◑	◆	Summer	5	89
Oenothera missouriensis	✱	🍃							T		○	◈	Summer	4	183
Rudbeckia fulgida 'Deamii'	✱	🍃							T		◑	◈	Summer	3	212
Helianthemum nummularium	✱	🍃			▲				Alkali		○	◈	Summer	5	155
Achillea tomentosa	✱	🍃							T		○	◇	Summer/Autumn	5	79
Cerastium biebersteinii	✱	🍃			▲				T		○	◇	Spring/Summer	4	106
Androsace villosa var. *arachnoidea*	✱	🍃							Alkali		○	◇	Spring/Summer	6	83
Arabis ferdinandi-coburgii 'Variegata'	✱	🍃			▲				T		○	◈	Spring/Summer	4	85
Actaea alba	✱	🍃	●●					R	T		◑	◈	Spring/Summer	5	80
Anaphalis margaritacea	✱	🍃			▲				Alkali		◑	◈	Summer	5	82
Dryas octopetala	✱	🍃			▲			R	Alkali		○	◈	Spring/Summer	5	133

HERBACEOUS AND ROCK PLANTS: up to 60 cm (2 ft)

Plant name	✳	🍃	🫐	🔆	🌲	🍂	⊥	R	Soil	Sea	◐	💧	Season	Zone	Page
Arenaria balearica	✳	🍃			🌲				T		●	◐	Spring/Summer	5	86
Arenaria montana	✳	🍃			🌲				T		Ⓣ	◐	Spring/Summer	5	86
Arabis albida	✳	🍃			🌲				T		◑	◐	Spring/Summer	4	85
Arabis albida 'Flore Pleno'	✳	🍃			🌲				T		◑	◐	Spring/Summer	4	85
Silene alpestris	✳	🍃			🌲				T		◑	◐	Spring/Summer	5	218
Helleborus niger	✳	🍃			🌲				T		●	●	Spring/Winter	4	156
Iris pumila	✳	🍃							Alkali		◑	●	Spring	4	162
Epimedium youngianum 'Niveum'	✳	🍃			🌲	🍂			T		◑	◐	Spring	7	135
Anacyclus depressus	✳	🍃							T		○	◇	Summer	5	82
Leontopodium alpinum	✳	🍃							T		○	◇	Summer	3	171
Aster novi-belgii 'Snowsprite'	✳	🍃							T		◑	●	Autumn	4	89
Saxifraga fortunei	✳	🍃			🌲				T		◑	●	Autumn	5	216
Aubrieta deltoidea 'Variegata'	✳	🍃			🌲				Alkali		○	◐	Spring/	4	91
Hosta undulata 'Medio-variegata'	✳	🍃							T		◑	●	Summer	4	157
Hosta fortunei 'Albopicta'	✳	🍃							T		◑	●	Summer	4	157
Ajuga reptans 'Multicolor'	✳	🍃			🌲				T		◑	●	Spring/Summer	6	81
Ajuga reptans 'Burgundy Glow'	✳	🍃			🌲				T		●	●	Spring/Summer	6	81
Stachys lanata	✳	🍃			🌲				T		◑	◐	Summer	4	222
Festuca cinerea	✳	🍃			🌲				T		○	◐	Summer	4	142
Hosta sieboldiana	✳	🍃							T		●	●	Summer	4	157
Nepeta × faassenii	✳	🍃							T		○	◐	Spring–Autumn	4	183
Veronica incana	✳	🍃							T		◑	◐	Summer	5	230

Key *(see also p 9 and p 11)*	✳	Flower colour	🍃	Foliage colour	🫐	Berries/fruits/cones/seed heads colour
🔆 Fragrant or aromatic	🌲	Evergreen		🍂	Good autumn colour	⊥ Climber or wall plant
R Suitable for rock gardens	**Soil**	Acid/alkali/tolerant	**Sea**	Suitable for maritime or seaside conditions	○	Sun/shade requirements
💧 Moisture requirements	**Season**	Season(s) of interest	**Zone**	Climatic zone *(see pages 59–62)*	**Page**	Page reference to *Directory of Plants*

HERBACEOUS AND ROCK PLANTS: up to 60 cm (2 ft)

Plant name	❋	🍃	🍒	🎆	🌲	🍂	⊥	R	Soil	Sea	○	💧	Season	Zone	Page
Aquilegia alpina	❋	🍃							R	T		◑	●	Spring/Summer	4	84
Centaurea montana	❋	🍃								T		◑	◐	Spring/Summer	3	106
Ajuga pyramidalis	❋	🍃			▲					T		◑	●	Spring/Summer	6	80
Polemonium caeruleum	❋	🍃								T		◑	◐	Spring/Summer	4	197
Phlox douglasii	❋	🍃							R			◑	◐	Spring/Summer	5	191
Helleborus foetidus	❋	🍃			▲					T		●	●	Spring/Winter	4	155
Iris unguicularis	❋	🍃		🎆	▲					Alkali		○	○	Winter/Spring	5	163
Primula denticulata	❋	🍃							R	T		◑	●	Spring	3	199
Iris pumila	❋	🍃							R	Alkali		◑	●	Spring	4	162
Gentiana acaulis	❋	🍃							R	Alkali		◑	◐	Spring	5	147
Aubrieta deltoidea	❋	🍃			▲				R	Alkali		○	◐	Spring	4	90
Catananche caerulea 'Major'	❋	🍃								T		○	○	Summer/Autumn	6	103
Clematis integrifolia 'Hendersonii'	❋	🍃								Alkali		○	◐	Summer/Autumn	5	114
Campanula poscharskyana	❋	🍃							R	T		○	◐	Summer/Autumn	4	102
Stokesia laevis	❋	🍃								T		◑	○	Summer/Autumn	5	222
Scabiosa caucasica	❋	🍃								Alkali		○	◐	Summer/Autumn	4	216
Iris laevigata	❋	🍃								T		◑	●	Summer	5	162
Eryngium maritimum	❋	🍃								Alkali	Sea	○	○	Summer/Autumn	6	138
Aster alpinus	❋	🍃							R	T		○	◐	Summer	5	88
Erigeron × speciosum 'Dignity'	❋	🍃								T		○	◐	Summer	5	138
Linum narbonense	❋	🍃								T		○	◐	Summer	6	173
Astilbe chinensis var. pumila	❋	🍃								T		◑	◐	Summer	4	90
Campanula carpatica	❋	🍃							R	T		◑	◐	Summer	5	101
Campanula cochlearifolia Campanula garganica	❋	🍃							R	T		◑	◐	Summer	4	101
Campanula glomerata 'Superba'	❋	🍃								T		◑	◐	Summer	5	102
Campanula lactiflora 'Pouffe'	❋	🍃								T		◑	◐	Summer	6	102
Erigeron macranthus	❋	🍃								T		◑	◐	Summer	5	138

HERBACEOUS AND ROCK PLANTS: up to 60 cm (2 ft)

Plant name	✳	🍃	🍒	☀	🌲	🍂	⊥	R	Soil	Sea	○	💧	Season	Zone	Page
Aster amellus	✳	🍃									◐	◑	Summer / Autumn	6	88
Veronica spicata	✳	🍃									◐	◑	Summer	4	230
Erinus alpinus 'Dr Hanelle'	✳	🍃			🌲			R			○	◑	Summer	6	138
Lithospermum diffusum 'Heavenly Blue'	✳	🍃			🌲			R	Acid		○	●	Summer	7	173
Aster novi-belgii 'Audrey'	✳	🍃									◐	●	Autumn	4	89
Gentiana × macaulayi	✳	🍃						R	Acid		◐	◑	Autumn	5	147
Acaena microphylla		🍃	🍒					R			○	◑	Autumn	5	76

HERBACEOUS PLANTS: 60 cm – 1.2 m (2 ft – 4 ft)

Plant name	✳	🍃	🍒	☀	🌲	🍂	⊥	R	Soil	Sea	○	💧	Season	Zone	Page
Gaillardia aristata	✳	🍃						T			◐	◑	Summer / Autumn	5	146
Euphorbia griffithii	✳	🍃						T			◐	◑	Spring / Summer	3	141
Papaver orientale	✳	🍃						T			○	◑	Spring / Summer	7	187
Liatris pycnostachya	✳	🍃						T			○	●	Summer / Autumn	5	172
Lythrum salicaria 'Firecandle'	✳	🍃						T			◐	●	Summer / Autumn	3	178
Monarda didyma	✳	🍃		☀				T			◐	●	Summer / Autumn	4	182
Kniphofia caulescens	✳	🍃						T		Sea	○	◑	Summer / Autumn	7	168
Kniphofia galpinii	✳	🍃						T		Sea	○	◑	Summer / Autumn	7	169
Astilbe × arendsii 'Fanal'	✳	🍃						T			◐	●	Summer	4	90
Astilbe × arendsii 'Granat'	✳	🍃						T			◐	●	Summer	4	90
Lychnis chalcedonica	✳	🍃						T			◐	●	Summer	4	177
Hemerocallis hybrids	✳	🍃						T			◐	●	Summer	4	156
Phlox paniculata	✳	🍃		☀				T			◐	●	Summer	4	191
Aquilegia 'McKana Hybrid'	✳	🍃						T			◐	◑	Summer	4	84

Key (see also p 9 and p 11)

Symbol	Meaning	Symbol	Meaning	Symbol	Meaning
✳	Flower colour	🍃	Foliage colour	🍒	Berries/fruits/cones/seed heads colour
☀	Fragrant or aromatic	🌲	Evergreen	🍂	Good autumn colour	⊥	Climber or wall plant
R	Suitable for rock gardens	Soil	Acid/alkali/tolerant	Sea	Suitable for maritime or seaside conditions	⊥	Climber or wall plant
💧	Moisture requirements	Season	Season(s) of interest	Zone	Climatic zone (see pages 59–62)	○	Sun/shade requirements
				Page	Page reference to Directory of Plants		

HERBACEOUS PLANTS: 60 cm – 1.2 m (2 ft – 4 ft)

Plant name	✱	leaf	berries	fan	▲	leaf (solid)	⊥	R	Soil	Sea	○	drop	Season	Zone	Page
Paeonia lactiflora	✱	leaf		fan					T		◑	half drop	Summer	3	186
Lupinus 'Russell Hybrids'	✱	leaf							Acid		◑	half drop	Summer	5	177
Iris, tall bearded	✱	leaf							Alkali		○	half drop	Summer	4	163
Aster novi-belgii 'Crimson Brocade'	✱	leaf							T		◑	full drop	Autumn	4	89
Achillea millefolium 'Cerise Queen'	✱	leaf							T		○	half drop	Summer	5	78
Dicentra spectabilis	✱	leaf							T		◑	half drop	Spring/Summer	3	132
Centranthus ruber	✱	leaf	berries						Alkali		○	half drop	Summer/Autumn	6	106
Chrysanthemum rubellum 'Clara Curtis'	✱	leaf		fan					Alkali		○	half drop	Summer/Autumn	7	112
Anemone × hybrida 'Queen Charlotte'	✱	leaf							T		◑	half drop	Summer/Autumn	5	84
Astilbe × arendsii 'Bressingham Pink'	✱	leaf							T		◑	full drop	Summer	4	90
Hemerocallis hybrids	✱	leaf							T		◑	full drop	Summer	4	156
Phlox paniculata	✱	leaf		fan					T		◑	full drop	Summer	4	191
Filipendula hexapetala	✱	leaf							T		◑	full drop	Summer	4	142
Campanula lactiflora 'Loddon Anna'	✱	leaf							T		◑	half drop	Summer	5	102
Aquilegia 'McKana Hybrid'	✱	leaf							T		◑	half drop	Summer	4	84
Sidalcea malvaeflora	✱	leaf							T		◑	half drop	Summer	4	218
Physostegia virginiana 'Vivid'	✱	leaf							T		◑	half drop	Summer	6	191
Paeonia lactiflora	✱	leaf		fan					T		◑	half drop	Summer	3	186
Lupinus 'Russell Hybrids'	✱	leaf							Acid		◑	half drop	Summer	5	177
Asclepias incarnata	✱	leaf							Acid		○	half drop	Summer	8	88
Delphinium 'Belladonna Hybrids'	✱	leaf							T		○	half drop	Summer/Autumn	5	130
Iris, tall-bearded	✱	leaf							Alkali		○	half drop	Summer	4	163
Aster novi-belgii 'Fellowship'	✱	leaf							T		◑	full drop	Autumn	4	89
Iris foetidissima	✱	leaf	berries						T		◑	half drop	Summer	5	162
Euphorbia wulfenii	✱	leaf			▲				T		◑	half drop	Spring/Summer	6	142
Doronicum plantagineum	✱	leaf							T		◑	full drop	Spring/Summer	5	133
Helenium autumnale 'Wyndley'	✱	leaf							T		◑	half drop	Summer/Autumn	5	154

HERBACEOUS PLANTS: 60 cm – 1.2 m (2 ft – 4 ft)

Plant name	✳	🍃	🍒	🎆	🔺	🍂	⊥	R	Soil	Sea	○	💧	Season	Zone	Page
Solidago virgaurea	✳	🍃							T		◑	💧	Summer/Autumn	3	219
Hemerocallis hybrids	✳	🍃							T		◑	💧	Summer	4	156
Heliopsis scabra	✳	🍃							T		○	💧	Summer	5	155
Aquilegia 'McKana Hybrid'	✳	🍃							T		◑	💧	Summer	4	84
Alstroemeria aurantiaca 'Dover Orange'	✳	🍃							T		◑	💧	Summer	9	81
Lupinus 'Russell Hybrids'	✳	🍃							Acid		◑	💧	Summer	5	177
Achillea filipendulina 'Coronation Gold'	✳	🍃							T		○	💧	Summer	5	78
Iris, tall-bearded	✳	🍃							Alkali		○	💧	Summer	4	163
Acanthus spinosus	✳	🍃							T		◑	💧	Summer	7	76
Acanthus mollis var. latifolius	✳	🍃							T		◑	💧	Summer	6	76
Artemisia 'Silver Queen'	✳	🍃							T		◑	💧	Summer	5	87
Delphinium Belladonna Hybrid'	✳	🍃							T		○	💧	Summer/Autumn	5	130
Anemone × hybrida 'Alba'	✳	🍃							T		◑	💧	Summer/Autumn	5	83
Astilbe × arendsii 'Deutschland'	✳	🍃							T		◑	💧	Summer	4	90
Phlox paniculata	✳	🍃		🎆					T		◑	💧	Summer	4	191
Gypsophila paniculata	✳	🍃							Alkali	Sea	○	💧	Summer	4	150
Campanula lactiflora 'Alba'	✳	🍃							T		Ⓣ	💧	Summer	5	102
Aquilegia 'McKana Hybrid'	✳	🍃							T		◑	💧	Summer	4	84
Paeonia lactiflora	✳	🍃		🎆					T		◑	💧	Summer	3	186
Lupinus 'Russell Hybrids'	✳	🍃							Acid		◑	💧	Summer	5	177
Achillea ptarmica 'The Pearl'	✳	🍃							T		○	💧	Summer	3	78
Chrysanthemum maximum 'Wirral Supreme'	✳	🍃							Alkali		○	💧	Summer	5	111

Key *(see also p 9 and p 11)*	✳	Flower colour	🍃	Foliage colour	🍒	Berries/fruits/cones/seed heads colour
🎆 Fragrant or aromatic	🔺	Evergreen	🍂	Good autumn colour	⊥	Climber or wall plant
R Suitable for rock gardens	Soil	Acid/alkali/tolerant	Sea	Suitable for maritime or seaside conditions	○	Sun/shade requirements
💧 Moisture requirements	Season	Season(s) of interest	Zone	Climatic zone *(see pages 59–62)*	Page	Page reference to *Directory of Plants*

HERBACEOUS AND ROCK PLANTS

Plant name	❋	🍃	🍒	🎆	🌲	🍂	⊥	R	Soil	Sea	◯	💧	Season	Zone	Page
Iris, tall-bearded	❋	🍃							Alkali		◯	●	Summer	4	163
Aster novi-belgii 'Blandie'	❋	🍃							T		◑	●	Autumn	4	89
Cimicifuga foetida 'White Pearl'	❋	🍃							T		◑	●	Autumn	4	112
Aster ericoides	❋	🍃							T		◑	◒	Autumn	6	89
Thalictrum aquilegifolium	❋	🍃							T		◑	●	Spring/Summer	5	227
Iris pallida 'Variegata'	❋	🍃		🎆					Alkali		◑	◒	Spring/Summer	5	162
Meconopsis betonicifolia	❋	🍃							Acid		◑	●	Spring	5	181
Clematis heracleifolia	❋	🍃							Alkali		◯	●	Summer/Autumn	5	114
Aster × frikartii	❋	🍃							Alkali		◯	●	Summer/Autumn	6	89
Aconitum × arendsii	❋	🍃							T		◑	●	Summer/Autumn	3	79
Aconitum fischeri	❋	🍃							T		◑	●	Summer/Autumn	3	79
Geranium pratense 'Johnson's Blue'	❋	🍃							T		◑	◒	Summer/Autumn	4	148
Agapanthus 'Headbourne Hybrid'	❋	🍃							T		◯	●	Summer/Autumn	8	80
Delphinium 'Belladonna Hybrids'	❋	🍃							T		◯	◒	Summer/Autumn	5	130
Echinops ritro	❋	🍃							Alkali		◯	◒	Summer/Autumn	5	133
Phlox paniculata	❋	🍃		🎆					T		◑	●	Summer	4	191
Iris kaempferi	❋	🍃							Acid		◑	●	Summer	5	162
Iris sibirica	❋	🍃							Acid		◑	●	Summer	4	162
Hosta fortunei	❋	🍃							T		◑	●	Summer	4	157
Aconitum napellus 'Bressingham Spire'	❋	🍃							T		◑	●	Summer	3	79
Eryngium alpinum	❋	🍃							T	Sea	◯	◌	Summer	6	138
Anchusa azurea 'Loddon Royalist'	❋	🍃							T		◯	◒	Summer	5	83
Aquilegia 'McKana Hybrid'	❋	🍃							T		◑	◒	Summer	4	84
Campanula persicifolia	❋	🍃			🌲				T		◑	◒	Summer	4	102
Lupinus 'Russell Hybrids'	❋	🍃							Acid		◑	◒	Summer	5	177
Iris, tall-bearded	❋	🍃							Alkali		◯	◒	Summer	4	163
Aster novi-belgii 'Ada Ballard'	❋	🍃							T		◑	●	Autumn	4	89

HERBACEOUS PLANTS: 60 cm – 1.2 m (2 ft – 4 ft)

Plant name	✳	🍃	🫐	🎇	🌲	🍂	⊥	R	Soil	Sea	○	💧	Season	Zone	Page
Aster novi-belgii 'Chequers'	✳	🍃							T		◑	●	Autumn	△4	89
Aster novi-belgii 'Marie Ballard'	✳	🍃							T		◑	●	Autumn	△4	89

HERBACEOUS PLANTS: 1.2 m – 2.5 m (4 ft – 8 ft)

Plant name	✳	🍃	🫐	🎇	🌲	🍂	⊥	R	Soil	Sea	○	💧	Season	Zone	Page
Rheum palmatum	✳	🍃							T		○	●	Summer	△3	204
Aster novae-angliae 'September Ruby'	✳	🍃							T		◑	●	Autumn	△5	89
Eremurus elwesii	✳	🍃		🎇					Alkali		○	◗	Spring	△6	135
Delphinium 'Pacific Hybrids'	✳	🍃							T		○	◗	Summer/Autumn	△5	130
Aster novae-angliae 'Harrington's Pink'	✳	🍃							T		◑	●	Autumn	△5	89
Helianthus decapetalus	✳	🍃							T		○	◗	Summer/Autumn	△5	155
Anthemis tinctoria 'Grallagh Gold'	✳	🍃							T		○	◗	Summer	△6	84
Delphinium 'Pacific Hybrid'	✳	🍃							T		○	◗	Summer/Autumn	△5	130
Artemisia lactiflora	✳	🍃		🎇					Acid		◑	◗	Summer/Autumn	△4	87
Crambe cordifolia	✳	🍃							Alkali		○	◗	Summer	△7	125
Aruncus dioicus	✳	🍃							T		●	◗	Summer	△3	87
Cortaderia selloana	✳	🍃			🌲				T		○	◗	Autumn	△7	121
Thalictrum dipterocarpum	✳	🍃							T		◑	●	Summer	△5	227
Delphinium 'Pacific Hybrids'	✳	🍃							T		○	◗	Summer/Autumn	△5	130

Key *(see also p 9 and p 11)*	✳	Flower colour		🍃	Foliage colour		🫐	Berries/fruits/cones/seed heads colour
🎇	Fragrant or aromatic		🌲	Evergreen		🍂	Good autumn colour		⊥	Climber or wall plant
R	Suitable for rock gardens	**Soil**	Acid/alkali/tolerant	**Sea**	Suitable for maritime or seaside conditions		○	Sun/shade requirements
💧	Moisture requirements	**Season**	Season(s) of interest	**Zone**	Climatic zone *(see pages 59–62)*	**Page**	Page reference to *Directory of Plants*

Guidelines for Successful Growing

This book lists over 1,100 garden plants which are suitable for planting in most districts. It is impossible to be totally accurate in describing all the qualities of a plant as these vary according to the circumstances.

Climate

In the matter of hardiness, no one can be absolutely sure where a borderline should come, as winters can be unpredictable in their severity. A winter with severe frosts can prove to be less damaging than a slightly warmer one in which there is excessive near-freezing rain. A persistent freezing wind can lower the ambient·air temperature by several degrees through wind chill. A reasonable fall of snow can serve to protect completely some small plants, and the lower parts of larger ones, from the direct adverse effects of frosts and wind.

Probably the worst type of winter is one in which there is excessive dampness. This is particularly harmful to evergreens which have to maintain transpiration at all times. So while a climate might, in theory, suit a shrub in a matter of average winter temperature, it might not be ideal for average winter precipitation.

The rock plants, for instance, come from the high mountain regions of the world. There they have the winter protection of snow. In lowland gardens of Northern Europe and climatically similar areas of North America, the winters can be comparatively mild and wet at the time when alpine plants should be experiencing a cold, dry period of rest. While it is not possible to provide snow, the required dryness can be provided to some degree by planting on the raised areas of the rock garden, and by incorporating grit into the compost and on the surface around the plants.

Wall protection is often advocated for garden plants which originate in climates warmer than those in which they are to be planted as this gives them some protection against damage from biting north or east winds, and to some extent from frosts.

The climatic conditions of the district in which the garden is situated must be a prime consideration when deciding what to plant, but even within the garden itself there will be some areas that will be warmer than others. While some may be exposed to the directions from which the coldest winds will come, others will be protected by shrubs, hedges or walls.

Zones

The Plant Hardiness Zone System used in this book is based on the system devised by *The United States Department of Agriculture* for use in southern Canada and the United States (excluding Alaska and the Hawaiian Islands).

An attempt has been made here to increase the scope of the system to include Australia, New Zealand, South Africa and Western Europe, including the United Kingdom and Eire.

As will be seen from the zone map of the USA, the USDA system divides North America into 10 climatic zones separated by average **minimum** winter temperatures, in stages of 10°F from −50°F and below at Zone 1, up to +40°F at Zone 10.

For the purpose of this book, a rough translation to Celsius has been made and both the Fahrenheit and the Celsius figures are shown in the key to the maps.

Every plant included in the charts has been given a zone number indicating

Early summer in an English garden, with lilacs or syringas (Clare College, Cambridge).

ZONE 1 Below −45°C
(−50°F)
ZONE 2 −45°C to −39°C
(−50°F to −40°F)
ZONE 3 −39°C to −35°C
(−40°F to −30°F)
ZONE 4 −35°C to −29°C
(−30°F to −20°F)
ZONE 5 −29°C to −23°C
(−20°F to −10°F)
ZONE 6 −23°C to −18°C
(−10°F to 0°F)
ZONE 7 −18°C to −12°C
(0°F to 10°F)
ZONE 8 −12°C to −6°C
(10°F to 20°F)
ZONE 9 −6°C to −1°C
(20°F to 30°F)
ZONE 10 −1°C to 4°C
(30°F to 40°F)

that it should withstand the **average
minimum winter temperature of
that zone** and **also those zones with
higher numbers** and therefore higher
minimum temperatures. For more de-
tailed range of zones refer to the entry in
the Plant Directory. It must, however, be
realised that other factors, such as precipitation patterns and high maximum
summer temperatures, may well make
life insupportable for plants with low
zone numbers.

No claim is made as to precise
accuracy.

It is indeed difficult to contemplate a
climatic zone system that can be 100%
accurate, simply because the variations
in annual temperatures and precipitation can be so considerable from one year
to another. Working as one must from a
basis of averages means that, in all prob-
ability, there will be few if any seasons in
any area that fully correspond to the
averages in any climatic consideration.

Within each zone there are bound to
be local variations in climate due to a
variety of circumstances. Low-lying
areas can be frost pockets, while only a
few metres higher up a hillside the growing season may be a good two weeks
longer than in a garden near the top.

In temperate areas of low summer
rainfall, while the climate may be suitable in every other way, unless there is
sufficient mains or stored water for the
garden, survival of plants may be uncer-
tain unless chosen with care.

By observing what grows in other
people's gardens, or in municipal parks
nearby, it is possible to make a reasonable
assessment of the planting possibilities for
your own garden.

Every plant has a transpiration rate

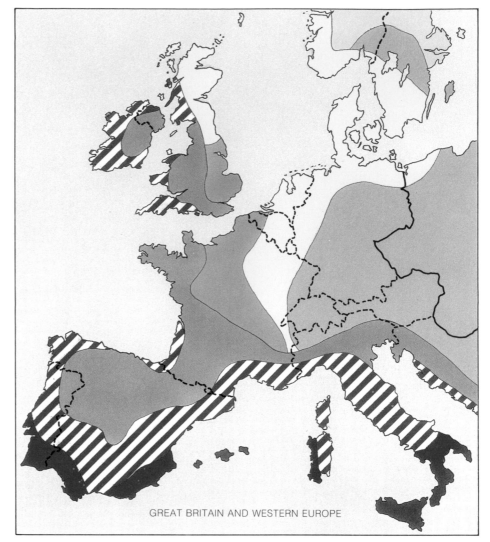

GREAT BRITAIN AND WESTERN EUROPE

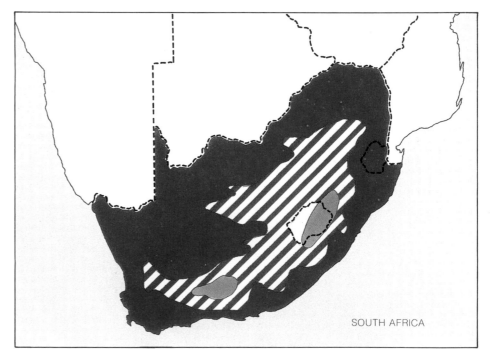

SOUTH AFRICA

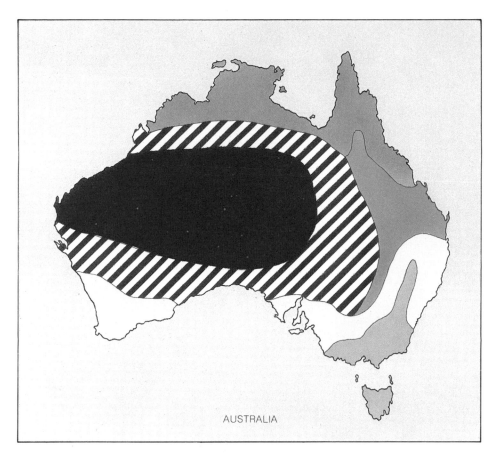

AUSTRALIA

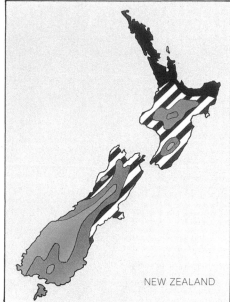

NEW ZEALAND

(the amount of water loss through the leaves) suited to the climate of its natural habitat. Thus, plants indigenous to areas of high humidity are unsuited to areas of excessive dryness, even though temperatures may be suitable, because their roots would be unable to supply sufficient water to satisfy an increased rate of transpiration.

Equally, plants found in very dry areas and having a slower rate of transpiration are prone to rotting in wetter climates even though temperatures may be comparable.

Statistics showing levels of annual rainfall are of little use. It is the distribution of the total throughout the year that is of most significance. Two regions, while having roughly the same levels of annual precipitation, and even similar winter and summer temperatures, will not both be able to satisfy the requirements of a given plant if the total rainfall of one region is concentrated within a few months while the other has a more even distribution throughout the year.

In South Africa, for instance, there is a very marked difference in the levels of annual precipitation between the east and the west coasts. The east coast is swept by the warm Agulhas current which flows from north to south. This not only keeps the eastern coastal margin warm and frost free, but also ensures adequate levels of rainfall throughout the year well into the interior.

The current which flows up the west coast roughly from Cape Town north-

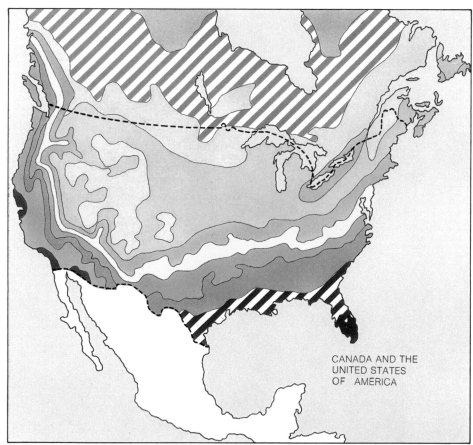

CANADA AND THE
UNITED STATES
OF AMERICA

wards, known as the Benguela current, is considerably cooler, chilling the lower air which, interacting with hotter upper layers, establishes exceptionally stable conditions in which rainfall is rare.

In the Durban region on the east coast over 1,000 mm of rain falls over the year. At Port Nolloth on the west coast less than 60 mm falls, almost all of it in the winter. Temperatures here are in fact cooler throughout the year than those of Durban.

Soil

For those with a new garden or a well-established one my advice is to take the trouble to know your garden. Do not rush off to the nearest garden centre to purchase that special shrub you've always cherished. First ascertain whether your new garden is suitable for it. We all have our favourites and with care, forethought and preparation it is quite possible that we may be able to accommodate them.

There are a great number of garden plants to suit almost any situation, but it is vitally important to understand the characteristics of the situation before selecting the plants.

Soil types vary and you must get to know yours before designing the garden or selecting your plants. A really enthusiastic gardener may even look at the soil before buying the house.

The soil test kits obtainable at garden centres can be useful if used correctly and with necessary care.

The most important difference in soil types is between acid (lime-free) and alkaline (chalky or limy) – for this dictates many of the plants that can satisfactorily be grown.

For simplicity, soils are normally divided into three basic types: acid, neutral or normal and alkaline or chalk. The acid soils are usually peaty or black and sandy, though some clay soils may be acid.

Neutral soils have a reasonable level of humus and all necessary nutrients. They are generally quite workable in all but the most adverse weather conditions. They are also readily adaptable to the soil requirements of most hardy garden plants, merely by incorporating a mixture of well-rotted manure or garden compost suitable for their needs into the hole when planting.

Highly alkaline soils, in extreme cases can pose the greatest problems for, not only do you have to be selective in choice of plants, but also the soil may be difficult to penetrate with a spade or fork where a thin layer of chalky clay sits only 10 cm (4 in) or so thick on the underlying solid white chalk.

However, not all are as bad as that, and any soil can be termed alkaline, if its pH is over 7.00 (see page 64).

Aspect

Once the type of soil is known and understood, there are several other factors it is advisable to examine, such as, which areas lie wet in winter or are excessively dry in summer, are shaded by trees or houses and never actually see the sun, are exposed to winter winds, or are at the end of narrow passage-ways which will be extremely draughty.

Look out the windows, especially those most used, to see if any neighbouring houses overlook you, or if there are any unsightly views you may wish to screen.

Planning your garden

The best way to make a start is to draw up a plan or bird's eye view of the plot on squared paper using reasonably accurate paced-out measurements. Mark in steps and paths you wish to retain and walls, and the position of windows and doors of the dwelling.

It is better to design the layout of the garden as a single entity from the outset, even if you complete the construction of it over a period of years.

Then comes the fascinating job of filling in the details. Try to involve all the family. Future recriminations will be avoided and, if the garden is of sufficient size, most tastes and requirements can be catered for. Remember very young children, and even children as yet unborn, for it would not be advisable to incorporate a pond nor those shrubs with vicious spines or prickly leaves, or plants with poisonous berries or fruits. If you must have them, plant them where inquisitive toddlers are unable or unlikely to go. The Yucca with its needle-sharp tips to the rigid sword-like leaves could so easily damage eyes if a child should run or fall into it.

In a sitting-out area there are several considerations. Sunny, private positions are usually desired, which are sheltered from the wind and have a pleasant view. If you like to have meals outside, site it near the house.

What is the purpose of your lawn? Is it to be a play area or to become the perfect greensward?

For some smaller gardens paving would be more suitable than a lawn. Where lack of time or age are considerations to be taken into account an area of paving with borders round and gaps left at intervals for planting can be very attractive and trouble-free once laid.

Plants should be chosen according to soil and aspect. For instance, in a shady part of a garden with cool moist soil it is possible to grow a wide range of flowering and foliage plants such as ivies, hostas and ferns.

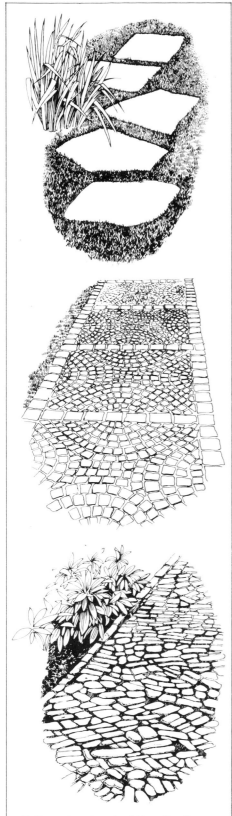

Paths and paving should be attractive as well as utility features. Stepping stones set in a lawn create an informal effect, as do old paviours and random stone.

Be certain that you have chosen the paving you want, be it natural stone, crazy-paving or manufactured slabs, and that it is well laid. Once it is down it is costly to lift and replace.

Paving will also be needed for a patio area, although it will be used in association with a lawn and planted borders. If possible, it should be laid so that it's surface is fractionally lower than that of the lawn, to allow the mower to run over it, minimizing the need for hand-trimming the lawn edge.

Manures, compost and fertilizers

There is a certain amount of confusion as to the difference between fertilizers and manures.

Manures

Manures are *organic* and bulky. They include farmyard manure, stable manure, garden compost, sewage sludge and seaweed. These are all excellent means of supplying organic matter to the soil. If farmyard manure is fresh, and the straw has hardly started to decompose, it will be at its highest state of nutritional value, but it can prove fatal to plants if it is incorporated near their roots. It might also contain a fair amount of weed seeds.

The nitrogen level in organic manures is fairly rapidly diminished once it is spread, so, if it is to be dug in, it should be left in heaps and not spread over the ground until the work of digging can be done.

Well-rotted, or fully decomposed manures are of most use for they are practically odourless, and easy to handle and improve the structure of the soil, even though they have lost much of their nutritional value during the rotting process. However, this loss can be made up with concentrated artificial or organic fertilizers. Chicken manure from deep litter houses is the most concentrated, and care is needed not to over-use it as this again can damage plant roots.

Garden compost

Most garden owners have access to some of the following: fallen leaves, lawn mowings, soft clippings and vegetable refuse from the kitchen, all of which can be composted to make a valuable source of organic matter for the garden with

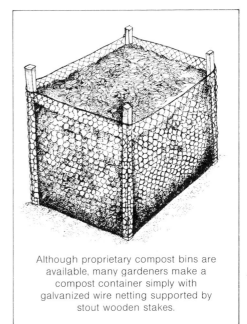

Although proprietary compost bins are available, many gardeners make a compost container simply with galvanized wire netting supported by stout wooden stakes.

very little effort and expense.

Larger and coarser refuse, such as woody prunings from shrubs and long herbaceous stems, if of sufficient quantity to be worth the expense, can be broken down with electric shredders that reduce them to a state suitable for incorporation into the compost heap. Hard twigs and long herbaceous stems must never be used in the compost heap unless chopped up finely as they will keep it too open, and prevent the breaking down process from taking place. At the other extreme, short lawn mowings will pack down too densely if used on their own. Air will be excluded, and the heap will not heat up sufficiently.

Consider the site of the compost heap. It is best to select a position that is accessible but hidden from view. Generally, an area of approximately 1–1.5 sq m (10–15 sq ft) seems about right. Too small and it will not heat up properly. Too large and air may not reach the centre, so again it will not heat properly. The width should be 90 cm (3 ft), though the length can be more.

Compost heaps are made on the surface, though any turf must always be removed first. They can be completely open-sided, or fenced-in with bricks, boards or corrugated iron, so long as holes are provided for the passage of air. Two heaps are even better, for one can then be rotting down while the other is being built up. Proprietary compost bins can also be obtained.

The first layer of refuse, preferably of mixed materials, should be spread over the area, and firmed down to a thickness of 15 cm (6 in) or so, before covering the surface with a compost accelerator which will contain both nitrogen and lime. Then spread another 15 cm (6 in) layer of refuse topped with a sprinkling of accelerator, and so on up to a height of about 1.2 m (4 ft). Each layer should be well watered. As an alternative to a proprietary accelerator, one can alternate a dressing of sulphate of ammonia with a dressing of garden lime (calcium carbonate). When the heap is completed, leave it undisturbed until ready for use.

Fertilizers

The subject of fertilizers can be extremely complicated, but the amateur gardener has no need to know more than a few basic rules.

So long as there is no obvious imbalance in a garden soil, the general purpose or balanced compound fertilizers will do a good job if used correctly. Some of these are organic based, while others are inorganic (artificial). The latter are cheaper, but return no organic matter to the soil, and, while it is always good advice to incorporate some form of bulk humus when applying any fertilizer, it is essential when the fertilizers are inorganic.

If in doubt about the fertility of your soil, soil test kits can tell you the levels of nitrogen (N), phosphates (P) and potash (K), and also the pH – the acidity/alkalinity level. Use them with care following the instructions on the pack or they will be a waste of money, and totally misleading. If you apply fertilizer according to the results arrived at by use of a soil test kit, then you will use a mixture of straight fertilizers and not a ready-made compound fertilizer.

Nitrogen (N) is essential for growth and foliage colour. Any deficiency will show in stunted growth and yellowing of the leaves which will also be small. The most usually recommended source for amateurs is sulphate of ammonia.

Phosphorus (P) is needed for the encouragement of good root formation, and it also helps in the ripening of seed and fruit. Bonemeal is an organic source of supply, but only in acid soils. Superphosphate is the generally accepted source, and is suitable on all soil types.

Potash (K) stimulates healthy grown, and also encourages good flowering and fruiting. Wood or plant ash is a source of potassium, usually in the form of K_2O. Other elements include magnesium, iron, and phosphorus, and sometimes a little manganese. The form of potash most easily purchased by amateur gardeners is sulphate of potash.

Lime is not, strictly speaking, a plant food, but is essential to their well-being. Only when lime is present can plant foods in the soil be made available. Lime is lost from cultivated soils in various ways. Fertilizers or manures use up lime in the processes that make the food values available to plants. Rainfall 'leaches' out more and, in any case, lime tends to sink in the ground, eventually to below the area in which it is needed.

The soil test kits for lime will indicate the amount of lime necessary to achieve a pH level suitable for the plants or crops to be grown. Most soils benefit in terms of improved drainage, and general workability from applications of lime.

pH This is a measure of acidity and alkalinity. Soils with a pH of 7.0 are referred to as neutral soils. Those with a pH level of less than 7 are referred to as acid soils and, above that figure, as alkaline soils. pH4 is very acid, but pH5 is ideal for many plants, such as rhododendrons and camellias, which are calcifuges and cannot tolerate any lime in the soil.

Planting

The vast majority of plants, be they trees, shrubs or herbaceous perennials, are purchased container grown. Some types that form exceptions are the cheaper hedging plants which are not worth the expense of potting.

Container-grown plants

The benefits of the container-growing 'revolution' are considerable to both the purchaser and the vendor, for it allows plants to be sold and planted at any time of the year. So long as they are watered as necessary, they may be left unplanted for a reasonable time without worry. It has become possible to see a shrub or even a tree in full flower at the garden centre on a morning in spring or summer and to have it planted in your own garden the same afternoon.

There is an important difference to be found between 'container grown' and 'containerized' plants. The former are plants that have lived in pots since their early days, being potted on to selling size without root disturbance, while the latter are bare-rooted plants that are potted later in life.

Sometimes such plants are offered for sale before they have sufficiently re-established their roots. It should be possible to pick up a container-grown plant by the stem, using necessary care, of course. If the container and soil drop off, don't buy the plant.

Before planting a container-grown plant always prepare the planting hole properly. This should mean double-digging a hole of generous size, i.e. digging two spits (spade blades) deep, turning over the lower spit on its own level. If time does not permit, then the

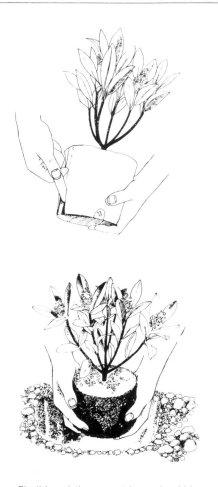

Flexible polythene containers should be slit and carefully peeled away before inserting plants in well-prepared planting holes which have been double-dug.

lower spit should at least be forked over to loosen it up. Then incorporate well-rotted manure or garden compost; fresh manures and composts which have not properly rotted should never be used. Position the plant in the hole and replace the soil, firming well as you go, so that the new soil level coincides with the soil level in the container.

Bare-rooted plants

The planting of bare-rooted shrubs and trees is best done in the autumn while the soil is still warm. If this is not possible, then there is no great harm done by planting at any time between autumn and early spring, as long as the soil is workable. If planting becomes impossible, and a bare-rooted shrub or tree is delivered, then its roots should be moistened and wrapped well in damp sacking or cloth, and the plant stored in a garage or shed until the ground becomes workable. This treatment will also apply if the ground becomes waterlogged after a prolonged period of heavy rains. Never wrap the roots in plastic as this does not 'breath' and roots can rot.

When a break in the weather permits, planting should be carried out as follows. Firstly, dig a hole larger than the area of root spread so that the roots can be spread out. The soil from the hole should be mixed well with peat and fertilizer, and, after forking over the bottom of the hole, some of the mixture should be placed in the centre to form a shallow mound so the roots sit naturally. Do not prepare the hole before the plant is available for planting, as both the hole and the soil removed from it may become too wet or too frozen for successful planting. There are many usable fertilizers available. My preference is for organic rather than chemical, and with a reasonably high potash element to encourage flowers and fruits.

Any damaged or over-long roots should be trimmed back with sharp secateurs. If, in the case of deciduous ornamental or fruit trees, there is a markedly greater spread of branches than of roots, cut back the branches to equal the root size. The cuts should be cleanly done with sharp secateurs immediately above a bud or pair of buds.

When planting a standard or a half-standard tree, hammer in a stake before the hole is filled in to avoid damaging the roots of the plant. When the stake is

firmly in place, the tree can be attached with a tree tie, or, if the stem requires straightening or is of a weak or floppy nature, two tree ties might be needed, one at the top and the other about half way up. Nylon stockings make very effective tree ties. Once the tree is attached to the stake the mixture of soil, peat and fertilizer should be returned to the hole working it well round the roots. When the hole is filled, tread the soil down firmly. Firm planting is essential to the tree's future success, but should not be done when the ground is sticky or waterlogged when you should not be planting anyway.

Shrubs or trees with a close-knit mass of fibrous roots should be gently moved up and down several times once sufficient fine soil has been returned to the hole to cover the roots. This settles the soil down well among the fibrous roots. If a stake is needed, it should be hammered into position before the roots are covered, and the plant tied to it at the end of the planting operation.

General guidelines

After a period of exceptionally frosty weather go round and firm any plants lifted by the frost, especially the more shallow-rooted subjects.

Plant to the previous planting depth using the soil mark on the stem as your guide. Many ornamental trees, some shrubs and nearly all fruit trees, are propagated by grafting or budding onto a chosen rootstock, which will determine the growth habit of the plant. The planting depth should leave the union of stock and scion between 10–15 cm (4–6 in) above ground level. If they are planted above the union, or mulching raises the soil level above it, then either rooting of the scion will take place (which will defeat the object of the graft), or buried stems of lower branches may rot and the ultimate result will be the death of the plant.

One exception, where deep planting is desirable, is with clematis where it can prevent the loss of the plant through clematis wilt. This fungus disease can attack and kill all the above ground parts of a clematis with remarkable speed, but does not attack the roots or any of the stem below ground. Deeper planting makes it possible for the clematis to produce new growth from the buried lower stem.

Some heathers are tolerant of deepish

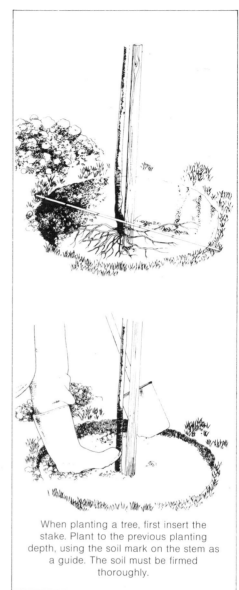

When planting a tree, first insert the stake. Plant to the previous planting depth, using the soil mark on the stem as a guide. The soil must be firmed thoroughly.

planting where it results in the production of roots. The new plants that result can later be lifted, separated and planted elsewhere.

Pruning

It is essential to use sharp cutting instruments for all pruning, cutting-back, trimming or clipping.

Tools and their use

It pays to buy the best quality tools you can afford. Cheap ones will almost certainly have cutting blades of inferior material. Considerable damage can be done by blunt cutting edges, and the work becomes much harder. All tools should be kept clean, well-oiled and rust-free so as to be ready to do the best job when required.

Never over-strain a tool by trying to make it do more than the tasks for which it is designed. This particularly applies to secateurs. It is tempting to save a journey back to the shed to collect a saw or the loppers in order to cut one thick branch when the secateurs have managed all others. So the secateurs are opened wide, and all the strength of both hands applied to wrench back and forth until the branch falls away with a bruised and jagged cut. These secateurs will probably never again be capable of a true, clean cut. Going up a scale, loppers can suffer the same way if used too roughly.

Pruning cuts

Where possible when using pruning saws or loppers, the outward end of the branch to be cut should be supported to avoid tearing of the bark at the cutting point just before the cut is completed.

All cuts should be cleaned up with a sharp pruning knife, and, where the branches cut are of suitable diameter, they should be painted over with a proprietary sealing compound, which will help to keep out damp and frost, and protect against harmful organisms.

Where possible, all cuts should be made at an angle to the horizontal, so as to form a water-shed so no water remains on bare wood to start up any rot.

Pruning cuts on shrubs and trees should always be just above a bud and sloping away from it, or, in the case where there is a pair of buds opposite each other, then the cut should slope sideways to avoid water shedding off into the buds. Cuts should never be made too close to the buds (the bud will be damaged), nor too far above as the resulting stump will almost certainly die back.

When to prune, what to prune

Many people are frightened of pruning their shrubs or trees, because they are afraid of damaging or even killing them. The fact is that pruning is essential for many plants in the garden. It keeps them within a certain area and it can help in the production of flowers and decorative foliage. In the case of the red- or yellow-stemmed dogwoods and some coloured-stemmed willows, hard pruning or cutting back of about one third of the stems every year keeps the wood young and at its most colourful.

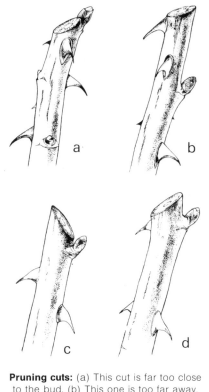

Pruning cuts: (a) This cut is far too close to the bud. (b) This one is too far away. (c) A cut should not slope to a bud. (d) A correct pruning cut.

The difference between pruning and cutting back is that whereas pruning is a surgical operation done with the intention of benefiting the plant, cutting-back is carried out to achieve a size or a shape that suits the gardener. Weak, dead or damaged stems should be pruned out, as should any over-abundance of twiggery. If this is done the chances of fungal and insect problems are likely to be considerably reduced, not only by the reduction of branches on which these problems can occur, but by increasing the circulation of air around those that remain.

The strict theory of pruning is fairly complicated, as it affects the length of a plant's life, season of flowering and whether, in fact, the plant will flower at all. For instance, pruning of spring- or early summer-flowering plants should be carried out immediately after flowering. If left to the autumn much, if not all, of the initiating flower buds will be destroyed. These may not be visible to the eye, but are nevertheless forming within the plant.

However, some plants definitely need pruning or cutting back. The butterfly bush (*Buddleia davidii*) is a good example

as it puts on so much growth each season, which is unattractive if left standing in the winter months. The long flowering stems of the previous summer may be cut back to just above a pair of buds near the base of the plant at any time during late autumn, winter or spring. The earlier the better if the unsightly branches are not to cause a blemish on the beauty of your winter garden, but any time during the dormant season will do. A later flowering season than normal can be manipulated simply by leaving the pruning until late spring, well after the plant has started into strong growth. This may be useful if the buddleia is required to blend with, say, Michaelmas daisies round its base.

Winter pruning may be done on any shrub that flowers on new growth in summer or autumn just so long as it is sufficiently hardy. With caryopteris, fuchsias and other plants where hardiness is in doubt, pruning is best left until the spring, judging each season as it comes. The old flower heads and branches give a measure of protection to new growth.

Other shrubs that are best tackled in the winter when the leaves are off and you can see what you are doing, are deutzias, philadelphus, weigelas, early-flowering spiraeas and the beauty bush (*Kolkwitzia amabilis*).

Wall shrubs

Choosing a shrub to train against a wall requires a fair amount of thought. Don't rush into purchasing any plant that takes your fancy. It is important to know something of the potential growth of the plant and, if hard pruning is going to be required to keep it within a restricted area, what damage is going to be done to its flowering potential. Pyracanthas, for instance, often surprise people by the amount of growth they can produce each season, and, if the longest flowering life span is to be achieved, there must be enough space to avoid the need for drastic cutting at least for some years.

An evergreen ceanothus also makes an excellent wall shrub. There are two important facts to remember regarding pruning. Never cut beyond the base of the previous season's growth as ceanothus, as well as a number of other plants, do not readily break from older wood. Always prune immediately after flowering, for if it is left until the autumn thousands of next season's potential flowers will be destroyed. There are no

berries to consider so there is no reason to delay the task.

Neglected plants

If you are faced with overgrown and tangled shrubs in a negelected garden there are two alternatives. Dig out the offending tangle and start again with new plants, or prune right back to the main stems, removing all but the best young shoots which emanate from a reasonably low level. This somewhat drastic treatment does not suit all shrubs. An overgrown Spanish broom (*Spartium junceum*) for instance could succumb to grey mould (*Botrytis*). It would be much simpler and better to replace with a young plant.

Hedges

The pruning of hedges is normally referred to as clipping or trimming with shears or an electric hedge trimmer.

While these are excellent tools for use on many, or perhaps even most, hedging plants, they are not the ideal tool for pruning larger leaved hedging plants, such as laurel or holly. These are better

pruned with sharp secateurs, as shears tend to damage a lot of leaves making the hedge unsightly.

There are rules that should be applied to the clipping of even the simplest of hedges. Some, such as beech and hornbeam, should not be cut at all for the first two years after planting, while most

Large-leaved hedging plants are best pruned with secateurs as shears tend to damage a lot of leaves.

Contrast in foliage colours from shrubs and conifers. (Garden designed by Kathleen Chattaway.)

other deciduous hedges are best cut back hard to about 30 cm (1 ft) in their first spring. Privets and *Lonicera nitida*, require the same treatment.

The Leyland cypress, × *Cupressocyparis leylandii*, or the golden 'Castlewellan', are among the best conifers for hedging. Growing at a rate of approximately 75 cm ($2\frac{1}{2}$ ft) per year they form an excellent thick, sound absorbing screen when stopped at not less than 1.8 m (6 ft).

Clipping should be done twice a year in spring and late summer. For the thickest and most beautiful screen, the ends of *all* branches should be tipped during the year after planting. This must include those growing lengthways as well as those growing out from the line of the hedge, and will have the effect of thickening the growth. It should be repeated until the individual plants have knitted together, after which the hedge is trimmed twice a year along its sides and top in the usual manner.

Hedges should be trained from an early age so that they are narrower at the top than at the base. The reverse must never be allowed to occur, or browning off of the bottom growth may be the result.

All hedges should be shaped so as to be rather narrower across at the top than at their base. The reverse must never be allowed to occur, or browning off of the bottom growths will probably result.

Topiary is a specialized form of hedging where specific shapes are the end result. Peacocks, globes, spirals, or even more ambitious projects can be brought to rewarding fruition by careful and patient clipping. The best subjects for this treatment are box and yew.

Propagation

There is a great deal of satisfaction to be had from raising your own plants, for it is both calming and an exciting challenge. You can also save yourself some money. Although not all plants are easy to propagate, most can be increased quite simply and quickly.

There are two main methods of increasing plants. The first is from seeds or, in the case of ferns, spores. The second is by vegetative means of which there are several methods.

Seed

This is, in theory, possible for all plants, but the resultant seedlings are not identically true to the form of either parent; each one has its own genetic character. This difference is minimal, and of no concern in the species, but is not acceptable for the perpetuation of cultivars or hybrids.

For the successful germination of seed and the raising of seedlings, there are three essential basic requirements – warmth, air and moisture. Failure to provide any one of these can result in failure, as can too much moisture or too high a temperature.

Care should be taken in the selection of seed compost. John Innes composts are still popular and reputable brands bearing the John Innes symbol of approval may be used with great success. There are also many peat-based or soil-less composts which are also very good. These universal or seed and potting composts are suitable for most purposes, pricking-out and potting-on, as well as seed sowing, whereas with the John Innes there are four separate strengths for different uses, including sowing seed. The main disadvantage with the peat-based compost is that if allowed to get too dry it becomes difficult to re-wet.

Seed of plants from cold or temperate climates can be sown outdoors in prepared seedbeds. Some hardcoated seed require a period of freezing to break their dormancy, and such conditions are provided by sowing outdoors in autumn. Soaking for two or three days in warm water will help to soften hard seed covers. Seeds of plants from warmer climates must be sown in warmth. The seed compost should be about 15–20°C (60–68°F) and this is best provided by thermostatically controlled electric soil-heating cables set at about 27°C (80°F).

Seeds should always be sown in previously moistened compost. Sow thinly, as overcrowding will result in spindly weak seedlings. As a general rule, seeds should be covered to approximately twice their own depth with moist compost, although the finest seed is best left uncovered.

Seed sown in trays of seed compost should be stood on a bench or in a propagator if heat is required. Cover the trays with a sheet of glass and some sheets of newspaper, or something similar until germination. The glass avoids moisture loss, and the paper keeps seed in the dark and slows down evaporation. The paper must be removed at the first sign of

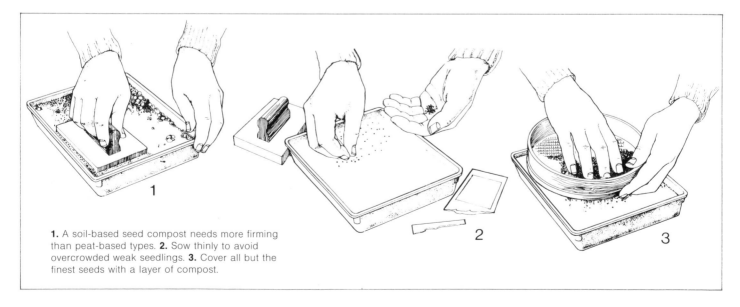

1. A soil-based seed compost needs more firming than peat-based types. **2.** Sow thinly to avoid overcrowded weak seedlings. **3.** Cover all but the finest seeds with a layer of compost.

germination. The glass should be slightly raised at one side on germination and taken off completely after a few days. When the seedlings are large enough to handle they can be pricked out into small individual pots.

Vegetative propagation

The most commonly used method of vegetative propagation is by means of cuttings. This entails the removal from the plant of sections of stems or roots, or in some cases leaves or buds. Eventually they will grow into a new plant identical in all respects to their parent.

Cuttings

Certain conditions apply to all kinds of cuttings. For successful rooting, there must be sufficient moisture, warmth, light and air. The rooting medium must, therefore, be moisture-retentive, and yet well enough drained to ensure the free passage of air. It must also be free of pests and diseases. John Innes seed compost is suitable. Other good rooting mediums consist of equal parts by volume of coarse (not builders') sand and peat, or peat and vermiculite.

If taken at the right time, cuttings will usually root fairly readily, but, for extra security, rooting hormones may be used. They are readily obtainable as a liquid dip, or as a powder from garden centres, and must be used in accordance with the manufacturers' instructions.

For the majority of hardy garden plants, cuttings of semi-ripe growth taken during summer can be induced to root in an unheated greenhouse or cold frame. Hardwood cuttings taken in the autumn need only a sheltered site in the open, but leaf or bud cuttings, and cuttings taken in the winter months from actively growing plants, require in addition the assistance of some artificially provided heat. A temperature of 13–18°c (55–64°F) is generally sufficient, though some subjects may require more. This can be provided in a frame or greenhouse by soil-warming cables or, for a few cuttings, by a small electric propagator. Whichever the case, a high humidity should be maintained using glass or plastic covers. This is necessary in order to provide the close moist conditions that will reduce transpiration (water loss through the leaves). It is also beneficial to spray the cuttings with tepid water occasionally.

Softwood cuttings These are taken from immature shoot tips, and on outdoor plants are best removed in early to mid-summer. Short, non-flowering sideshoots about 5–10 cm (2–4 in) long are best. They must be rooted under warm conditions in a frame or propagator. When the selected shoots have been severed from the plant, they should be cut cleanly with a sharp knife or razor blade just below a node. These, termed nodal cuttings, are generally considered to root most easily, but in some cases, such as clematis, it is preferable to cut between the nodes, that is inter-nodally.

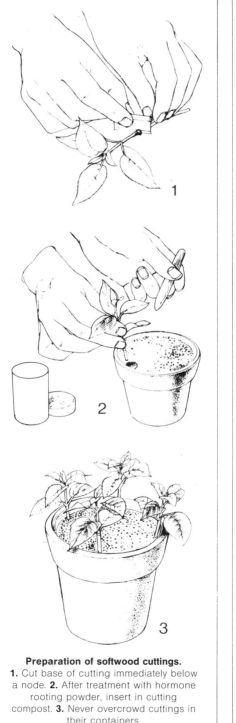

Preparation of softwood cuttings.
1. Cut base of cutting immediately below a node. **2.** After treatment with hormone rooting powder, insert in cutting compost. **3.** Never overcrowd cuttings in their containers.

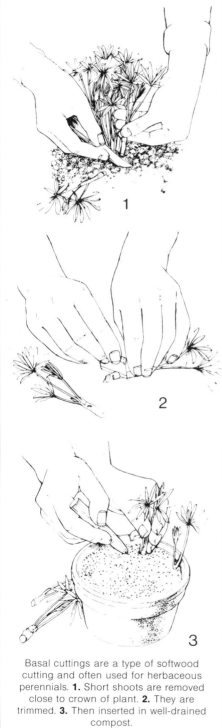

Basal cuttings are a type of softwood cutting and often used for herbaceous perennials. **1.** Short shoots are removed close to crown of plant. **2.** They are trimmed. **3.** Then inserted in well-drained compost.

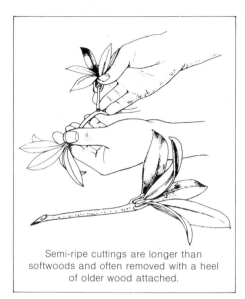

Semi-ripe cuttings are longer than softwoods and often removed with a heel of older wood attached.

Semi-ripe cuttings These are taken from midsummer to early autumn and require no heat. But, while some might root successfully in the open, most need the protection of a cold frame or cloche. This is the method best suited for increasing deciduous and evergreen shrubs, and for many conifers.

Semi-ripe cuttings take longer to root than softwood ones, so, since they will use up more of their own food reserves, they should be about 10–15 cm (4–6 in) long. Leaves should be removed from the lower half which is to be inserted in the rooting medium, but left on the top half.

Hardwood cuttings These afford the easiest method of propagation for shrubs

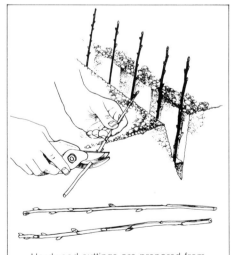

Hardwood cuttings are prepared from well-ripened current-year's wood and inserted in an outdoor bed, in a sand-lined slit trench. Firm them well in.

and trees. They are taken from mid-autumn through winter, and inserted in a sheltered bed outdoors. Rooting takes even more time than semi-ripe cuttings, and the cuttings should be 20–38 cm (8–15 in). In many cases they root more successfully if taken with a heel of older wood (a strip of the main stem that remains when a side shoot is pulled away). If the tip is soft and unripened it should be removed just above a bud using a sharp knife.

Propagation of conifers
Cuttings are the most commonly used method of propagating conifers, as cultivars do not come true from seed. Cuttings of most species are not difficult to strike, but it is difficult to get good results from cultivars of *Cedrus*, *Cupressus*, *Pinus* and *Pseudotsuga*. These must be increased either by seed or by grafting.

Hardwood cuttings The simplest method is to take these in late autumn. The length will vary from 10–25 cm (4–10 in) according to species. Cuttings should be of firm wood of the current season's growth, taken with a 'heel'.

Most conifers pose a problem to propagation by reason of their high resin content inhibiting rooting. For this reason, it is better to take cuttings from young established plants rather than old trees. Some of the resin that appears at the base of the cutting may be removed by immersing for a few minutes in luke-warm water, about 38°C (100°F).

Remove the lower leaves as you would for any evergreen plant and use a rooting hormone, either powder or liquid. The cuttings should then be inserted into a clay pot or seed tray containing equal parts by volume of peat and sharp sand, and well firmed in. Place in a light situation, but not in direct sunlight, in a cold frame or outside covered with a sheet of glass to reduce transpiration.

Some cuttings may have rooted by the following spring, while others may take as long as two years.

Semi-ripe cuttings These are taken in summer. Shoot tips of the current year's growth are taken 5–15 cm (2–6 in) long. Cut from just beneath a bud and remove the bottom leaves. After dipping in rooting hormone, liquid or powder, they should be inserted into a cutting medium consisting of a peat and sharp sand mix,

roughly equal parts by volume, or a peat and vermiculite mix.

Place cuttings in a greenhouse or cold frame and if possible supply some bottom heat by means of electric soil-warming cables laid in sand or use an electrically heated propagator. A temperature of 18°C (65°F) is sufficient, and this may well be equalled or exceeded by nature in a reasonable summer.

Conifer cuttings tend to dry out very quickly. Therefore cover the cuttings with the lid of the propagator, sheets of glass, clear polythene, or ideally, if intended production merits the expense, use a mist propagator. The latter will certainly lead to greater percentage success, and considerably quicker rooting.

Rooting should take place before winter sets in. As soon as a root system has formed pot up separately, protect from frost for the winter months, and then either plant out into a nursery bed or pot on into containers and place outside in late spring, to grow on to planting size.

Root cuttings
This method is used for propagating many herbaceous plants and some shrubs that have fleshy roots. They are taken during the dormant period in autumn or winter. If only a small quantity are needed they can, with care, be taken from

Thin root cuttings are best laid on the surface of compost in a seed tray, and then covered with a thin layer of compost. Insert thick cuttings vertically.

the plant *in situ*, but generally they are taken from lifted plants. While the thickness of root will vary from one plant type to another, cuttings of woody plants, and of thick fleshy-rooted shrubs should be about $\frac{1}{2}$–1 cm ($\frac{1}{4}$–$\frac{1}{2}$ in) in thickness, and 5–15 cm (2–6 in) in length. They are prepared by making a horizontal cut at the top and a diagonal one at the bottom. They are then inserted, sloping cut downwards, either in open ground or in pots or trays in a compost made up of equal parts by volume of peat, coarse sand and loam.

Some herbaceous perennials, for example border phlox, with thinner roots may also be increased readily by root cuttings. In these cases, cuttings about 8–10 cm (3–4 in) are taken and laid horizontally in trays of rooting medium and covered by 1 cm ($\frac{1}{2}$ in) of sand.

Layering

This is a method whereby a stem, while remaining attached to a plant, is encouraged to produce roots. It has several advantages, not least of which is that it more-or-less looks after itself until rooted, being supplied with nutrients and water from the parent plant. Also, as a layered shoot is usually considerably larger than a cutting, a larger plant is achieved in a shorter time. However, these advantages only really apply where very few new plants are required, as the actual time needed for individual preparation is much greater than for cuttings.

This is the best and simplest method for all rhododendron cultivars, including the azaleas. Dig out a shallow hole and fill it with a mixture of peat, sand and leafmould. Choose a young, low-growing branch. It should be fastened to a short stake with raffia or twine and pegged down where it passes through the trench. If the stem is split lengthwise where it is buried, rooting will be hastened. Never allow the rooting area to become too dry.

Stooling

This is another method of branch rooting similar to layering. The shrub to be increased is cut down to just above ground level, and covered with humusrich soil, so only the tips show. The shoots eventually produce roots, and later they can be separated from the parent and planted in their new situation. It is a popular method of increasing heathers, pinks and border carnations.

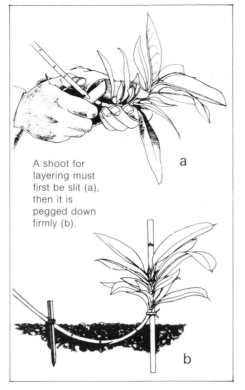

A shoot for layering must first be slit (a), then it is pegged down firmly (b).

Division

This is a much used method for increasing herbaceous perennials. It entails lifting a clump of plants with care and separating out individual or small groups of growing points, each with a root or two attached. Division can be carried out anytime between late autumn and the onset of spring. The lifted clumps can either be teased apart by hand or cut into small pieces with a knife or spade. The old central portion should be discarded and the outer parts planted out in their growing positions.

Grafting

This last method is one not normally of interest to the amateur gardener. A portion of the plant to be increased is grafted on to a suitable rootstock, and this method is used by commercial nurserymen in a variety of ways, from the **budding** of roses to the grafting of fruit and ornamental trees. It is a complex subject and beyond the scope of this book.

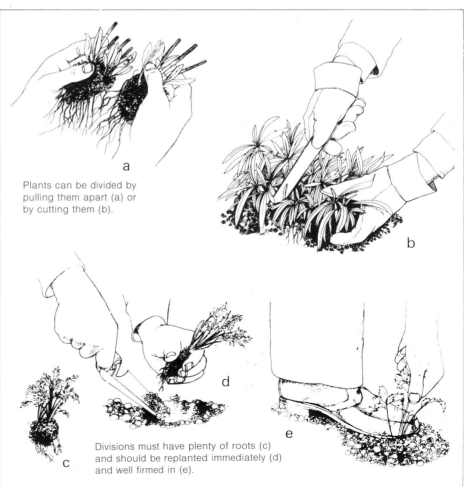

Plants can be divided by pulling them apart (a) or by cutting them (b).

Divisions must have plenty of roots (c) and should be replanted immediately (d) and well firmed in (e).

Directory of Plants

In this section the plants are listed under their full botanical names. Then follows the name of the family to which the plant belongs. If the plant has one, the common or colloquial name follows. The zone numbers come next, together with an indication of the type of plant (in other words, shrub; herbaceous perennial, conifer, etc.).

It is important that both sections of the book are used together. Consult either the plant selection charts first, or this plant directory, but always use the two together to enable you to choose quickly exactly the right plant for a specific situation or a set of requirements.

Those who are not familiar with many garden plants will find the illustrations invaluable as an aid to plant selection. Most, but not all, of the hundreds of plants described here are illustrated.

The descriptions of the plants are necessarily brief due to the very large number of plants included in this book, but nevertheless they give all the information that is needed.

Heights of plants are given in every instance, in both metric and imperial. There are descriptions of flowers, and in every instance flowering time is stated. As appropriate there are descriptions of berries, cones and fruits.

Foliage details for every plant include colour and shape, and whether it is evergreen (holds its leaves all the year round) or deciduous (loses them in the autumn). Autumn leaf colour is described where appropriate.

The best position for each plant is recommended – for instance, sun, shade, shelter and so on. Included are soil requirements, and you will see that many plants tolerate a wide range of soils.

The habit of the plant follows. This refers mainly to the shape of the plant.

The method (or methods) of propagation is given for each plant, together with the best time of the year. Pruning details, too, are given, if applicable. Remember that more detail on soils, propagation, pruning, planting and so on can be found in the 'Guidelines for Successful Growing'.

Further useful tips and hints are given under most entries, such as suggested uses of plants, and suggestions for plant associations. Plus any further noteworthy characteristics or habits.

A traditional herbaceous border in mid-summer, featuring delphiniums.

Abelia floribunda
Caprifoliaceae
ZONES 9–10   SHRUB
Height: 1.8–2.5 m (6–8 ft), **Flowers:** bright carmine-red, late spring – mid-summer, **Foliage:** mid-green, evergreen, **Position:** wall shelter even in mild areas, **Soil:** suits most soil, **Habit:** rounded, bushy, **Propagation:** cuttings in mid-summer from current season's growth.
□A very bright and attractive, free-flowering shrub if you have a cosy enough position against a south-facing wall. Cut out very old stems after flowering.

Abelia × grandiflora
Caprifoliaceae
ZONES 7–10   SHRUB
Height: 1.8–2.5 m (6–8 ft), **Flowers:** pinkish white, slightly scented, mid-summer – mid-autumn, **Foliage:** bright green, semi-evergreen, **Position:** sunny, protect from cold winds, **Soil:** suits most soils, **Habit:** rounded, bushy, **Propagation:** cuttings in mid-summer from current season's wood.
□Looks well in association with golden foliage shrubs and, for flower contrast, with *Ceratostigma willmottianum* or *Caryopteris × clandonensis*. Cut out very old stems after flowering.

Right: *Abelia floribunda*

Abelia × grandiflora 'Francis Mason'
Caprifoliaceae
ZONES 7–10   SHRUB
Height: 1.8–2.5 m (6–8 ft), **Flowers:** pinkish white, slightly scented, mid-summer – mid-autumn, **Foliage:** variegated with light golden green, semi-evergreen, **Position:** sunny, protect from cold winds, **Soil:** most soils, **Habit:** rounded, bushy, **Propagation:** cuttings in mid-summer from the current season's wood.
□Well partnered by red-purple-leaved shrubs or foliage of *Berberis darwinii*. Cut out old stems after flowering.

Abelia schumannii
Caprifoliaceae
ZONES 8–10   SHRUB
Height: 3 m (10 ft), **Flowers:** pink, early summer – early autumn, **Foliage:** dark green, deciduous, **Position:** sunny, sheltered from cold winds, **Soil:** most soils, **Habit:** bushy, **Propagation:** cuttings in mid-summer from previous season's wood.
□Somewhat delicate and tips may be damaged by frosts, but the shrub is not generally killed. Cut out very old stems in late winter.

Abeliophyllum distichum
Oleaceae
ZONES 7–10   SHRUB
Height: 1 m (3 ft), **Flowers:** white, tinted with pink, fragrant, late winter – early spring, **Foliage:** green, deciduous, **Position:** sunny, better with wall protection in cold districts, **Soil:** any reasonable, well drained soil, **Habit:** elegant growth, erect shoots, slow grower, **Propagation:** cuttings or layering.
□Prune back fairly hard after flowering. Looks good planted with garrya.

Top left: *Abies balsamea* 'Hudsonia'
Top right: *Abies pinsapo* 'Glauca'
Below: *Abies lasiocarpa* 'Compacta'

Abies balsamea 'Hudsonia'
Pinaceae Silver Fir
ZONES 3–9   CONIFER
Height: 30 cm (1 ft), **Spread:** 45 cm (1½ ft) after 10 years. Eventually attains 90 cm (3 ft) in height, **Flowers:** and cones: of no particular decorative merit, **Foliage:** shiny green with two greyish-white bands underneath, evergreen, **Position:** sun or partial shade avoiding exposed situations, **Soil:** a slightly acid soil preferred, moist, but well-drained, **Habit:** a flattish topped, spreading bush, **Propagation:** by grafting in spring.
□ Useful for rock or heather garden.

Abies koreana
Pinaceae Silver fir, Korean fir
ZONES 5–9   CONIFER
Height: 1.8 m (6 ft) after 10 years, eventually attains 15 m (50 ft), **Cones:** bright purple/blue, produced at an early age, **Foliage:** shiny green above, whitish below, evergreen, **Position:** sun or partial shade, **Soil:** a deep, slightly acid soil preferred, moist but well-drained, **Habit:** conical, **Propagation:** seed sown in spring.
□ Makes a good lawn specimen in large gardens.

Abies lasiocarpa 'Arizonica'
Pinaceae Cork fir
ZONES 5–9   CONIFER
Height: 4 m (13 ft) after 10 years, eventual height 15 m (50 ft), **Flowers:** purple or violet-blue, spring, not significant, followed by purple cones, **Foliage:** silver-grey, evergreen, **Position:** sun or partial shade, **Soil:** a deep, moist but well-drained, slightly acid soil preferred, **Habit:** conical, **Propagation:** by seed sown in spring.
□ Maintain a single dominant leading shoot. Lawn specimen for large garden.

Abies lasiocarpa 'Compacta'
Pinaceae Silver fox
ZONES 5–9   CONIFER
Height: 60 cm (2 ft) after 10 years, eventually attains 2.4 m (8 ft), **Cones:** purple when young, cylindrical, **Foliage:** blue-grey, very attractive in spring and early summer, evergreen, **Position:** sun or partial shade, **Soil:** a well-drained but moist slightly acid soil preferred, **Habit:** dense compact and irregularly conical, **Propagation:** by grafting in spring.
□ Useful conifer for heather gardens.

Abies pinsapo 'Glauca'
Pinaceae Spanish fir
ZONES 6–9   CONIFER
Height: 1.8–2.5 m (6–8 ft) after 10 years. Eventually attains 24 m (80 ft), **Cones:** cylindrical, **Foliage:** distictive blue-grey, radially arranged, evergreen, **Position:** sun or partial shade, **Soil:** a deep, moist but well-drained, slightly acid soil preferred, but also lime tolerant, **Habit:** pyramidal, **Propagation:** by grafting in spring.
□ Ensure a single dominant leading shoot. Often used as a lawn specimen in large gardens.

Abies procera 'Glauca'
(**syn.** *A. nobilis*)
Pinaceae Noble fir
ZONES 6–9   CONIFER
Height: 2.5–3 m (8–10 ft) after 10 years. Eventually attains 24 m (80 ft), **Cones:** brown, upright and cylindrical, large, **Foliage:** blue-grey, evergreen, **Position:** sun or partial shade, **Soil:** a deep, moist but well-drained, slightly acid soil preferred, **Habit:** slender and conical, **Propagation:** best raised by grafting in spring.
□ This Abies is ultimately rather too large for most gardens.

Abutilon vitifolium
Malvaceae
ZONES 8–9   SHRUB
Height: 2.5 m (8–12 ft), **Flowers:** pinkish mauve, early summer – early autumn, **Foliage:** mid-green covered with short white hairs, semi-evergreen, **Position:** sunny, with wall protection, **Soil:** any reasonably well-drained soil, **Habit:** bushy in mild climates, elsewhere less branched, **Propagation:** seed sown in spring.
□ Somewhat delicate and will only reach full height in warm, sheltered positions. In other areas may be short lived.

Acacia dealbata
Leguminosae   Silver wattle, mimosa
ZONES 9–10   TREE
Height: 4.5–7.5 m (15–25 ft), **Flowers:** yellow, fragrant, borne in long sprays, mid – late spring, **Foliage:** greyish, feathery or fernlike, evergreen, **Position:** sunny and sheltered, suitable for warmer districts only, **Soil:** preferably slightly acid, **Habit:** quick-growing, spreading tree, **Propagation:** seeds sown in mid-spring in seed compost at 16°C (61°F).
□ If plant becomes too tall, cut it back when flowering is over.

Acaena microphylla
Rosaceae   New Zealand burr
ZONES 5–10   ROCK PLANT
Height: 2–5 cm (1–2 in), **Flowers:** insignificant, but followed by attractive crimson burrs or seed heads, **Foliage:** bronze-green, ferny, deciduous, **Position:** full sun, **Soil:** well-drained, **Habit:** ground cover spreading to 60 cm (2 ft), excellent for planting in paving, **Propagation:** seeds sown early autumn – early spring, or by dividing and replanting early autumn – early spring.

Acanthus mollis var. latifolius
Acanthaceae   Bear's breeches
ZONES 6–10   HERBACEOUS PERENNIAL
Height: 1 m (3 ft), **Flowers:** white and purple on 45 cm (18 in) long stems, summer, **Foliage:** mid green, glossy, large and spectacular, deciduous, **Position:** sun or partial shade, **Soil:** well-drained, **Habit:** striking perennial, upright flower spikes and ornamental foliage, a good companion for purple-foliage shrubs or shrub roses, **Propagation:** root cuttings in winter; seeds sown in light compost in spring; or by division in spring or autumn.

Acanthus spinosus
Acanthaceae   Bear's breeches
ZONES 7–10   HERBACEOUS PERENNIAL
Height: 90–120 cm (3–4 ft), **Flowers:** white and purple, carried on 45 cm (18 in) spikes, summer, **Foliage:** spiny, deeply cut, dark green, deciduous, **Position:** sun or partial shade, **Soil:** any reasonably well-drained soil, **Habit:** striking perennial with upright flower spikes and ornamental foliage, excellent companion for shrubs, **Propagation:** root cuttings in winter; seeds sown in light compost in spring; or by division in spring or autumn.

Left: Handsome spikes of *Acanthus spinosus*

76

Acer griseum

Aceraceae Paperbark maple

ZONES 5–9   TREE

Height: about 6 m (20 ft), **Flowers:** insignificant, **Foliage:** green, trifoliate, brilliant scarlet and crimson colour in autumn, deciduous, **Position:** sun or partial shade, sheltered, **Soil:** well-drained but moisture-retentive, **Habit:** upright branched tree, narrowish domed head, **Propagation:** seeds sown in mid-autumn in a garden frame, or, where possible, by layering in autumn.

☐ Very attractive russet-coloured peeling bark gives interest throughout the year, especially in winter. Underplant with winter-flowering heathers.

Acer japonicum

Aceraceae Downy Japanese maple

ZONES 5–9   TREE

Height: 4.5–6 m (15–20 ft), **Flowers:** insignificant, **Foliage:** pale green, lobed, colour brilliant crimson in autumn, deciduous, **Position:** sun or dappled shade, sheltered, **Soil:** cool, moist, well drained, neutral or slightly acid, **Habit:** slow growing tree, bushy habit, **Propagation:** seed sown in mid-autumn in a garden frame.

☐ An excellent companion plant is pampas grass (cortaderia).

Acer negundo 'Variegatum'

Aceraceae Variegated box elder

ZONES 5–8   TREE

Height: about 6 m (20 ft), **Flowers:** insignificant, **Foliage:** white and green variegated pinnate leaves, deciduous, **Position:** sun or partial shade, **Soil:** well-drained but moisture-retentive, **Habit:** spreading, rounded head, **Propagation:** grafting.

☐ Popular specimen tree, ideal for town gardens.

Acer palmatum 'Atropurpureum'

Aceraceae Japanese maple

ZONES 5–9   SHRUB

Height: 6 m (20 ft), **Flowers:** yellow, insignificant, early summer, **Foliage:** reddish bronze, deciduous, **Position:** sun or dappled shade, protect from wind, **Soil:** humus rich, reasonably lime tolerant, **Habit:** upright rounded , ultimately tree-like, growth is slow, **Propagation:** layering or grafting.

☐ This beautiful shrub will grow in partial shade, but its colour will be enhanced in full sun provided shelter against wind is given. Try an underplanting of hostas for contrast in foliage shape and colour.

Acer palmatum 'Dissectum Atropurpureum'

Aceraceae Japanese maple

ZONES 5–9   SHRUB

Height: 3 m (10 ft), **Flowers:** yellow, insignificant, early summer, **Foliage:** reddish bronze, finely cut, deciduous, **Position:** sun or partial shade, protect from wind, **Soil:** humus-rich, neutral or slightly acid, **Habit:** low spreading bush, **Propagation:** layering or grafting.

☐ Associates well with evergreen azaleas and golden callunas. *Choisya ternata* 'Sundance' will make a lovely partner.

Acer palmatum 'Dissectum Viridis'

Aceraceae Japanese maple

ZONES 5–9   SHRUB

Height: 3 m (10 ft), **Flowers:** yellow, not significant, early summer, **Foliage:** bright green turning yellow and orange in autumn, deciduous, **Position:** sun or partial shade, protect from wind, **Soil:** humus-rich, neutral or slightly acid, **Habit:**

Top left: *Acer griseum* **Top right:** *Acer palmatum* 'Dissectum Atropurpureum' **Above:** *Acer japonicum*

low spreading bush, **Propagation:** layering or grafting.

☐ Good companion for evergreen azaleas.

Acer palmatum 'Heptalobum Osakazuki'

Aceraceae Japanese maple

ZONES 5–9   SHRUB

Height: 6 m (20 ft), **Flowers:** yellow, insignificant, early summer, **Foliage:** medium green, magnificent autumn colour, deciduous, **Position:** sun or partial shade, protect from wind, **Soil:** humus-rich, neutral or slightly acid, **Habit:** upright rounded, shrub or small tree, **Propagation:** layering.

☐ The leaves of the Heptalobum group of Japanese maples are larger than those of the species and usually seven-lobed.

☐ Try pampas grass (cortaderia) as a companion for this maple.

Acer platanoides 'Crimson King'
Aceraceae Purple-leafed Norway maple
ZONES 5–9 TREE
Height: 9–12 m (30–40 ft), **Flowers:** yellow, small but attractive, spring, **Foliage:** intense purple – crimson, deciduous, **Position:** sun or partial shade, tolerant of atmospheric pollution, **Soil:** moist, tolerates chalk soils, **Habit:** broad headed, **Propagation:** grafting or layering.
☐ Looks well with golden-foliage shrubs or *Robinia pseudoacacia* 'Frisia' as a partner.

Acer platanoides 'Drummondii'
Aceraceae Variegated form of Norway maple
ZONES 5–9 TREE
Height: 9–12 m (30–40 ft), **Flowers:** yellow, inconspicuous, spring, **Foliage:** green with a neat white edge, true maple-leaf shape, deciduous, **Position:** sun or partial shade; tolerant of atmospheric pollution, **Soil:** moist, tolerates chalk soils, **Habit:** broad headed tree, **Propagation:** by grafting or layering.
☐ Useful for lighting up a dark backdrop.

Right: Useful for lighting up a dark backdrop, *Acer platanoides* 'Drummondii'

Achillea filipendulina 'Coronation Gold'
Compositae Yarrow
ZONES 5–10 HERBACEOUS PERENNIAL
Height: 90–120 cm (3–4 ft), **Flowers:** yellow in flat heads, summer, **Foliage:** medium green, deciduous, **Position:** full sun, **Soil:** any soil which is well-drained, **Habit:** hardy and upright perennial, flowers dry well for indoor decoration, **Propagation:** by dividing and replanting in autumn or spring.
☐ Good companion for delphiniums.

Achillea millefolium 'Cerise Queen'
Compositae Milfoil
ZONES 5–10 HERBACEOUS PERENNIAL
Height: 60–75 cm (2–2½ ft), **Flowers:** bright red, early – mid-summer, **Foliage:** dark green, deciduous, **Position:** full sun, **Soil:** suits most well-drained soils, **Habit:** hardy and upright perennial, **Propagation:** by dividing and replanting in autumn or spring.
☐ Looks good with silver-foliage perennials.

Achillea ptarmica 'The Pearl'
Compositae Sneezewort
ZONES 3–10 HERBACEOUS PERENNIAL
Height: 60–75 cm (2–2½ ft), **Flowers:** white, double, in loose clusters, mid-summer – early autumn, **Foliage:** long, medium green notched, deciduous, **Position:** sun, **Soil:** any soil which is well-drained, **Habit:** perennial with upright stems, informal flowers, **Propagation:** by division and replanting in autumn or spring.
☐ Good companion for strong-coloured perennials.

Achillea taygetea 'Moonshine'
Compositae Yarrow
ZONES 5–10   HERBACEOUS PERENNIAL
Height: 60 cm (2 ft), **Flowers:** light yellow, carried in flat heads, early summer – early autumn, **Foliage:** attractively cut, silvery, deciduous, **Position:** full sun, **Soil:** any soil which is well-drained, **Habit:** stiff-stemmed, upright perennial, **Propagation:** by division and replanting in autumn or spring.
☐ Useful cut flower. Delphiniums make good companions.

Achillea tomentosa
Compositae 'Alpine yarrow'
ZONES 5–9   ROCK PLANT
Height: 15 cm (6 in), **Flowers:** yellow, in flat heads, mid-summer – early autumn, **Foliage:** greyish, finely divided, deciduous, **Position:** full sun, **Soil:** poor, well-drained, **Habit:** forms a prostrate mat spreading to 30 cm (1 ft); **Propagation:** divide clumps in spring.
☐ Grown on rock garden, in paving or at edge of border.

Aconitum × arendsii
Ranunculaceae Monkshood
ZONES 3–9   HERBACEOUS PERENNIAL
Height: 1.2 m (4 ft), **Flowers:** brilliant blue, hooded, in loose spikes, late summer – mid-autumn, **Foliage:** mid green, deeply cut, deciduous, **Position:** partial shade, ideal for planting under trees, **Soil:** humus-rich, moisture-retentive, **Habit:** strong growing perennial, sturdy and upright, needs no support, **Propagation:** divide clumps in autumn or spring.
☐ Every part of this plant is poisonous.

Aconitum fischeri
Ranunculaceae Monkshood
ZONES 3–9   HERBACEOUS PERENNIAL
Height: 1 m (3 ft), **Flowers:** deep-blue, hooded, in racemes, late summer – early autumn, **Foliage:** deep green, shiny, deep cut, deciduous, **Position:** partial shade, ideal for planting under trees, **Soil:** humus-rich, moisture-retentive, **Habit:** strong-growing perennial, sturdy and upright, needs no support, **Propagation:** divide clumps in autumn or spring.
☐ Every part of this plant is poisonous.

Aconitum napellus 'Bressingham Spire'
Ranunculaceae Monkshood
ZONES 3–9   HERBACEOUS PERENNIAL
Height: 1 m (3 ft), **Flowers:** deep-blue, in bold spikes, mid – late summer, **Foliage:** deep green, ferny, deciduous, **Position:** partial shade, ideal for planting under trees, **Soil:** any humus-rich, moisture-retentive soil, **Habit:** strong-growing perennial, sturdy and upright, needs no support, **Propagation:** divide clumps in autumn or spring.
☐ Every part of this plant is poisonous.

Left: *Aconitum napellus* 'Bressingham Spire'

Actaea alba
(**syn. *A. pachypoda***)
Ranunculaceae Baneberry
ZONES 5–9   ROCK PLANT
Height: 45 cm (18 in), **Flowers:** white, in loose spikes, late spring – early summer, followed by white berries on red stalks, **Foliage:** golden green, deciduous, **Position:** partial or full shade, **Soil:** humus-rich, **Habit:** bushy, needs no support, **Propagation:** by seeds sown in spring; or by division in autumn or spring.
☐ Very attractive foliage plant for the rock garden. Good for cutting.

Actinidia kolomikta
Actinidiaceae Kolomikta vine
ZONES 4–10   CLIMBER
Height: 2.5–4 m (8–13 ft), **Flowers:** white, rounded, slightly fragrant, yellow fruits (on female plants), **Foliage:** deep green, marked with white and pink at tip end, deciduous, **Position:** south-facing wall, full sun, **Soil:** well-drained, humus-rich and lime-free, **Habit:** hardy twining climber, **Propagation:** by seed sown in garden frame in autumn; or by cuttings of half-ripe shoots in sand and peat mix in a garden frame in summer.
☐ Thin out old stems in late winter.

Adonis vernalis
Ranunculaceae
ZONES 7–9   ROCK PLANT
Height: 15–30 cm (6–12 in), **Flowers:** yellow, mid – late spring, **Foliage:** green ferny, deciduous, **Position:** sun or partial shade, **Soil:** well-drained, moisture-retentive, plenty of humus, **Habit:** rounded and bushy perennial, disappears below ground by mid-summer, **Propagation:** sow seed in early – late summer in seed compost in a garden frame, or by division in early – mid-autumn.
☐ Looks attractive when planted with purple aubrieta.

Aethionema 'Warley Rose'
Cruciferae
ZONES 5–9   ROCK PLANT
Height: 10–15 cm (4–6 in), **Flowers:** deep pink, in fat spikes, mid – late spring, **Foliage:** long, thin, greyish, **Position:** sunny, **Soil:** well-drained, **Habit:** forms a dense carpet, **Propagation:** by cuttings of non-flowering growths taken in early – mid-summer.
☐ Good for ground cover. Also grow on rock garden or in paving.

Agapanthus 'Headbourne Hybrids'
Liliaceae African lily
ZONES 8–10   HERBACEOUS PERENNIAL
Height: 60–75 cm (2–2½ ft), **Flowers:** blue, in roughly spherical umbels, mid-summer – early autumn, **Foliage:** green, strap-like, generally deciduous outdoors, **Position:** full sun and shelter, not suitable for cold districts, **Soil:** rich, well-drained, moisture-retentive, **Habit:** perennial with upright flower stems, thick, brittle roots, **Propagation:** dividing in mid-spring.
☐ Agapanthus are excellent perennials for growing with shrubs. They are also suitable for ornamental containers.

Ajuga pyramidalis
Labiatae Bugle
ZONES 6–10   HERBACEOUS PERENNIAL
Height: 25 cm (10 in), **Flowers:** blue, in short spikes, mid-spring – early summer, **Foliage:** green, generally evergreen, **Position:** sun or partial shade, **Soil:** any moist soil in reasonable condition, **Habit:** perennial, excellent low-growing ground cover, **Propagation:** divide clumps in autumn or spring.
☐ A good companion plant is *Lysimachia nummularia* 'Aurea' with golden foliage.

Ajuga reptans 'Burgundy Glow'
Labiatae Bugle
Zones 6–10   Rock plant
Height: 10 cm (4 in), **Flowers:** pale blue, in short spikes, late spring – early summer, **Foliage:** shades of red, generally evergreen, **Position:** sun or partial shade, **Soil:** any moist soil in reasonable condition, **Habit:** prostrate and spreading, **Propagation:** divide clumps in autumn or spring.
☐ Good ground cover for a shrub border.

Ajuga reptans 'Multicolor'
  (**syn. 'Rainbow'**)
Labiatae Bugle
Zones 6–10   Rock plant
Height: 10 cm (4 in), **Flowers:** blue, late spring – early summer, **Foliage:** pink, yellow and bronzy leaves, evergreen, **Position:** sun or partial shade, **Soil:** moist soil in reasonable condition, **Habit:** prostrate and spreading; **Propagation:** divide clumps in autumn or spring.
☐ Good ground cover for a shrub border.

Akebia quinata
Lardizabalaceae
Zones 4–10   Climber
Height: about 6 m (20 ft), **Flowers:** scented, reddish purple, mid-spring, flowers followed by 8 cm (3 in) long purplish fruits, **Foliage:** mid green, comprising five oblong leaflets, semi-evergreen, **Position:** sun or shade, **Soil:** suits most soils, **Habit:** vigorous, hardy, twining, **Propagation:** by layering or by cuttings.
☐ Useful climber for growing through old trees or large shrubs.

Alchemilla mollis
Rosaceae Lady's mantle
Zones 3–9   Herbaceous perennial
Height: 30–45 cm (1–1½ ft), **Flowers:** greeny yellow, early – late summer, **Foliage:** pale green, palmate, **Position:** sun or partial shade, **Soil:** moisture-retentive yet well-drained, **Habit:** spreading self-seeding ground cover perennial, **Propagation:** by seeds which readily germinate, producing masses of self-sown seedlings.
☐ Good for flower arrangements. Excellent for cottage gardens and for ground cover in shrub borders.

Alstroemeria aurantiaca 'Dover Orange'
Alstroemeriaceae Peruvian lily
Zones 9–10   Herbaceous perennial
Height: 1 m (3 ft), **Flowers:** reddish-orange, lily-like, early summer – early autumn, **Foliage:** green, grassy, deciduous, **Position:** sun or partial shade, **Soil:** humus-rich, well-drained, **Habit:** somewhat invasive perennial, excellent cut flower, **Propagation:** by careful division of clumps in early or mid-spring; try not to disturb the roots too much.
☐ Good companions are silver-foliage perennials like artemisias.

Alyssum montanum
Cruciferae Madwort
Zones 4–9   Rock plant
Height: 8–10 cm (3–4 in), **Flowers:** yellow, fragrant, late spring – early summer, **Foliage:** greyish-green, evergreen, **Position:** plenty of sun needed, **Soil:** well-drained, preferably alkaline, **Habit:** low growing, spreading to 30 cm (1 ft), **Propagation:** by seeds sown in early spring and stood in a garden frame; or by cuttings in early summer.
☐ Cut back after flowering to keep compact. A good companion for aubrieta.

Alyssum saxatile

Cruciferae Gold dust

ZONES 4–9 ROCK PLANT

Height: 23–30 cm (9–12 in), **Flowers:** bright yellow, prolifically mid-spring – early summer, **Foliage:** greyish – good background for the flowers, evergreen, **Position:** best in full sun, **Soil:** well-drained, preferably alkaline, **Habit:** compact, free flowering perennial, spreading to 45 cm (1½ ft), **Propagation:** by seeds sown in early spring and stood in a garden frame; or by cuttings in early summer inserted in mix of peat and sand in a garden frame.

☐ Cut back after flowering to keep bushy and promote long life. Associates well with aubrieta and arabis.

Right: Yellow *Alyssum saxatile* and purple *Aubrieta deltoidia* growing over a drystone wall

Amelanchier lamarckii

Rosaceae Snowy mespilus, June berry

ZONES 4–9 SHRUB

Height: 5 m (16 ft), **Flowers:** white in pendulous clusters; mid-spring, **Foliage:** opening bronze, turning green with glorious autumn tints, deciduous, **Position:** sun or partial shade, **Soil:** fertile, moisture-retentive, **Habit:** slender upright, suckering, **Propagation:** seeds, layering or by separating rooted suckers.

☐ Outstanding at all seasons. Even the winter twigs are attractive, while the flowers in spring and autumn foliage colours are truly magnificent. Black edible fruits are produced.

Anacyclus depressus

Compositae Mount Atlas daisy

ZONES 5–9 ROCK PLANT

Height: 5 cm (2 in), **Flowers:** pure white, yellow centred daisies, reddish in bud, early – late summer, **Foliage:** greyish-green, ferny, **Position:** full sun essential, **Soil:** light, gritty and well drained, **Habit:** forms a colourful prostrate carpet spreading to about 30 cm (1 ft), **Propagation:** by seeds sown under glass in autumn; or by cuttings of non-flowering growth under glass in spring.

☐ Suitable for rock garden, scree bed or for gaps in paving.

Anaphalis margaritacea

Compositae Pearl everlasting

ZONES 5–9 HERBACEOUS PERENNIAL

Height: 30–45 cm (1–1½ ft), **Flowers:** white in flat heads, late summer, **Foliage:** greyish-green, evergreen, **Position:** sun or partial shade, **Soil:** well drained, **Habit:** erect clump-forming perennial, good cut flower, **Propagation:** cuttings placed in a garden frame in spring, or by division in autumn or spring.

☐ Flowers can be dried, and hold their colour and texture. Excellent for grouping with brightly coloured perennials.

Anchusa azurea 'Loddon Royalist' (Syn. *A. italica*)

Boraginaceae Alkanet, bugloss

ZONES 5–10   HERBACEOUS PERENNIAL

Height: 1 m (3 ft), **Flowers:** vivid blue, in large panicles, early – late summer, **Foliage:** medium-green, lanceolate, covered in prickly hairs, deciduous, **Position:** full sun, **Soil:** suits most well-drained soils, **Habit:** clump forming perennial, straggly, branching flower stems, needs support, **Propagation:** division in spring, or by root cuttings in winter.

☐ Dead-head faded flower stems. Plant with oriental poppies or achilleas.

Andromeda polifolia 'Compacta'

Ericaceae Bog rosemary

ZONES 3–9   SHRUB

Height: 30 m (1 ft), **Flowers:** pink, pitcher shaped; late spring – mid-summer, **Foliage:** grey-green, evergreen; autumn tints, **Position:** sun or partial shade, **Soil:** humus-rich, moist, acid, **Habit:** ground covering, **Propagation:** by seed, cuttings, division, or layering in spring.

☐ Associates well with callunas and ericas and *Gaultheria procumbens* among other dwarf Ericaceous shrubs.

Androsace sarmentosa var. *chumbyi*

Primulaceae Rock jasmine

ZONES 7–10   ROCK PLANT

Height: 10 cm (4 in), **Flowers:** pink, mid-spring – early summer, **Foliage:** green, neat rosettes, **Position:** full sun and shelter, **Soil:** well-drained, gritty, ideally alkaline, **Habit:** low and spreading to about 60 cm (2 ft), **Propagation:** by cuttings of rosettes or basal shoots in a garden frame during early summer.

☐ For the rock or scree garden; also ideal for paving and dry-stone walls.

Androsace villosa var. *arachnoidea*

Primulaceae Rock jasmine

ZONES 6–10   ROCK PLANT

Height: 5–8 cm (2–3 in), **Flowers:** white, primrose-like; late spring – early summer, **Foliage:** grey-green, very hairy, **Position:** full sun and shelter, **Soil:** well-drained, gritty, ideally alkaline, **Habit:** very compact perennial, spreading to 30 cm (1 ft), **Propagation:** by cuttings of rosettes or basal shoots in a garden frame during early summer.

☐ For the rock or scree garden; also ideal for paving or dry-stone walls.

Anemone × hybrida 'Alba' (syn. *A. japonica* 'Alba')

Ranunculaceae Windflower

ZONES 5–9   HERBACEOUS PERENNIAL

Height: 75–90 cm (2½–3 ft), **Flowers:** white, single, late summer – mid autumn, **Foliage:** mid green; deciduous, **Position:** sunny or semi-shaded spot, **Soil:** any type, well-drained, **Habit:** free-flowering perennial when it is fully established, **Propagation:** by root cuttings taken late autumn – mid-winter in sand and peat mix in a garden frame; or by dividing.

☐ Cut stems down to ground level after flowering. A useful cut flower and associates well with autumn-colouring shrubs.

Anemone × hybrida 'Bressingham Glow' (syn. *A. japonica*)

Ranunculaceae Windflower

ZONES 5–9   HERBACEOUS PERENNIAL

Height: 45–60 cm (1½–2 ft), **Flowers:** pink, semi-double, late summer – mid-autumn, **Foliage:** mid-green, deciduous, **Position:** sunny or semi-shaded spot, **Soil:** any type, well-drained, **Habit:** free-flowering perennial when it is fully established, **Propagation:** root cuttings late autumn – mid-winter; or by dividing.

☐ A useful cut flower and associates well with autumn-colouring shrubs.

Anemone × hybrida 'Queen Charlotte' (syn. *A. japonica*)

Ranunculaceae Windflower
ZONES 5–9   HERBACEOUS PERENNIAL
Height: 75 cm–1 m (2½–3 ft), **Flowers:** pink, single, **Foliage:** mid green, deciduous, **Position:** sunny or semi-shaded spot, **Soil:** any type, well-drained, **Habit:** free-flowering perennial when it is fully established, **Propagation:** by root cuttings taken late autumn – mid-winter; or by dividing.
☐ Useful cut flower and associates well with autumn-colouring shrubs.

Antennaria dioica var. *rubra*

Compositae
ZONES 7–10   ROCK PLANT
Height: 10 cm (4 in), **Flowers:** deep pinky-red in clusters, late spring – early summer, **Foliage:** greyish-green, evergreen, **Position:** full sun, **Soil:** normal, well-drained with added grit, preferably acid, **Habit:** slow-spreading mat, **Propagation:** by division in spring.
☐ For rock garden, scree bed or gaps in paving.

Anthemis sancti-johannis

Compositae
ZONES 6–10   HERBACEOUS PERENNIAL
Height: 45 cm (1½ ft), **Flowers:** brilliant orange daisies, early – late summer, **Foliage:** hairy and greyish, fragrant, deciduous, **Position:** full sun, **Soil:** well-drained, **Habit:** clumpy and compact, **Propagation:** by seeds sown in late winter in gentle heat, or in mid-spring outdoors; or by cuttings taken in summer and inserted in sand and peat mix in a garden frame; division in autumn or early spring.
☐ A good companion for grey-foliage perennials.

Anthemis tinctoria 'Grallagh Gold'

Compositae   Ox-eye chamomile
ZONES 6–10   HERBACEOUS PERENNIAL
Height: 75 cm (2½ ft), **Flowers:** deep yellow, early – late summer, **Foliage:** medium green, attractively lobed, deciduous, **Position:** full sun, **Soil:** well-drained, **Habit:** tall and erect, **Propagation:** by division in autumn or spring; or by cuttings in summer inserted in sand and peat mix in a garden frame.

Aquilegia alpina

Ranunculaceae   Columbine
ZONES 4–9   ROCK PLANT
Height: 30 cm (1 ft), **Flowers:** dark blue, spurred, late spring – early summer, **Foliage:** greyish-green, ferny, deciduous, **Position:** sun or partial shade, **Soil:** moist, well drained with added leafmould, **Habit:** graceful, but short lived, **Propagathon:** by seeds sown when ripe mid – late summer, or by division mid-autumn – early spring.
☐ Dead-head after flowering. Excellent for the rock garden or scree bed.

Aquilegia 'McKana Hybrids'

Ranunculaceae   Columbine
ZONES 4–9   HERBACEOUS PERENNIALS
Height: 60–90 cm (2–3 ft), **Flowers:** red, pink, white with yellow or white corolla; or yellow, or blue with white corolla; summer, **Foliage:** light green, prettily fern-like, compound, deciduous, **Position:** sun or partial shade, **Soil:** any well-drained humus-rich soil, **Habit:** elegant, short-lived, **Propagation:** by division of clumps in autumn or spring.
☐ When flowering is over, cut down the stems. Lovely cut flowers. Ideal for cottage gardens and for growing with border irises.

Arabis albida
(syn. *A. caucasica***)**
Cruciferae Wall or rock cress
ZONES 4–9 ROCK PLANT
Height: 23 cm (9 in), **Flowers:** white, single, late winter – early summer, **Foliage:** greyish-green, farinose, evergreen, **Position:** sun or partial shade, **Soil:** suits most well-drained soils, **Habit:** carpeting, can spread extensively if not cut back annually, **Propagation:** by dividing clumps in autumn; by cuttings in a garden frame in mid-summer; or by seed sown under glass in spring or summer.
☐ Cut back stems after flowering. Grow on steep bank as ground cover, or in a dry-stone wall. Good companion plants include the spring flowering aubrieta and yellow alyssum.

Arabis albida 'Flore Pleno'
Cruciferae Wall or rock cress
ZONES 4–9 ROCK PLANT
Height: 15 cm (6 in), **Flowers:** white, double, late winter – early summer, **Foliage:** greyish-green, farinose, evergreen, **Position:** sun or partial shade, **Soil:** suits most well-drained soils, **Habit:** more compact than the species, **Propagation:** by dividing clumps in autumn; or cuttings in a garden frame in mid-summer.
☐ Trim back stems after flowering.

Above: The wall or rock cress, *Arabis albida*, is ideal for drystone walls and for growing on steep banks

Arabis aubrietioides
Cruciferae Wall or rock cress
ZONES 4–9 ROCK PLANT
Height: 15 cm (6 in), **Flowers:** rose-pink, single; spring – early summer, **Foliage:** greyish-green, evergreen, **Position:** sun or partial shade, **Soil:** any well-drained soil, **Habit:** compact, **Propagation:** by dividing clumps in autumn; or by cuttings in a garden frame in mid-summer.
☐ Trim back stems after flowering. Useful for rock garden, paving and dry-stone walls.

Arabis ferdinandi-coburgii
'Variegata'
Cruciferae Wall or rock cress
ZONES 4–9 ROCK PLANT
Height: 10 cm (4 in), **Flowers:** white, single, spring – early summer, **Foliage:** green with attractive white edges, evergreen, **Position:** sunny, **Soil:** any well-drained soil, **Habit:** very neat and compact, spreading to 30 cm (1 ft), **Propagation:** by dividing clumps in autumn; or by cuttings in a garden frame in mid-summer.

Araucaria araucana
(syn. *A. imbricata***)**
Araucariaceae Monkey puzzle
ZONES 6–10 CONIFER
Height: about 1.5 m (5 ft) after 10 years, ultimately 30 m (100 ft), **Flowers and cones:** insignificant, **Foliage:** deep green, leathery and overlapping, sharply pointed; evergreen, **Position:** open and sunny, **Soil:** any moist, but well-drained soil, **Habit:** when mature it is dome shaped, **Propagation:** best raised from seed in garden frame. Or tip cuttings in mid-summer in sand and peat.
☐ Only recommended for large gardens.

Arenaria balearica
Caryophyllaceae Sandwort
ZONES 5–10   ROCK PLANT
Height: 2 cm (1 in), **Flowers:** starry white flowers in early spring – mid-summer, **Foliage:** medium-green, very small, evergreen, **Position:** shade; best on north side of rock garden, **Soil:** suits most well-drained soils, **Habit:** carpet forming, spreading to 45 cm (1½ ft), **Propagation:** by division in autumn or spring.
□Also useful for planting in paving, choosing a shady spot.

Arenaria montana
Caryophyllaceae Sandwort
ZONES 5–9   ROCK PLANT
Height: 15 cm (6 in), **Flowers:** bright white, late spring – early summer, **Foliage:** deepish green, evergreen, **Position:** sun or semi-shade, **Soil:** well-drained, **Habit:** forms a dense carpet, spreading to 30 cm (1 ft), **Propagation:** by division in autumn or spring; or by cuttings of basal shoots taken early – late summer, inserted in sand and peat mix in a garden frame.

Aristolochia macrophylla
Aristolochiaceae Dutchman's pipe
ZONES 4–10   CLIMBER
Height: up to 6 m (20 ft), **Flowers:** yellow and brown, pipe-shaped, often hidden by leaves, early summer, **Foliage:** green, large, up to 30 cm (1 ft) long, deciduous, **Position:** full sun or semi-shade, **Soil:** well drained and rich, **Habit:** a vigorous twiner, **Propagation:** by summer cuttings in a propagator, or by layering.
□Useful for covering unsightly walls or old tree stumps.

Armeria maritima
Plumbaginaceae Common thrift, Lady's pin cushion
ZONES 6–10   ROCK PLANT
Height: 20 cm (8 in), **Flowers:** globular pink flower heads produced late spring – mid-summer, **Foliage:** green, grass like, evergreen, **Position:** sunny position, **Soil:** well-drained; **Habit:** forms a dense mound of foliage, **Propagation:** by divison in early – mid-spring; or by seed sown in early – mid-spring in a garden frame.
□Useful for rock gardens and paving. Thrives by the sea.

Aronia melanocarpa
Rosaceae Black chokeberry
ZONES 4–9   SHRUB
Height: 1 m (3 ft), **Flowers:** white, late spring – early summer, **Foliage:** green, colouring brown-red in autumn, deciduous, **Position:** sun or partial shade, **Soil:** deep, well-drained, **Habit:** bushy, **Propagation:** seed, cuttings or division in autumn.
□Glossy black berries create additional interest. Pruning is unnecessary.

Artemisia abrotanum
Compositae Southernwood, old man, lad's love
ZONES 8–10   SHRUB
Height: 1 m (3 ft), **Flowers:** yellow, mid-summer – early autumn, **Foliage:** greyish below, sweetly fragrant, feathery, deciduous, **Position:** sun, **Soil:** not too rich, **Habit:** erect, bushy, **Propagation:** cuttings in mid-summer, division in mid-autumn.
□Shoots damaged by frost, or any over-long straggly growths, can be cut back early in the spring. Good shrub for cottage garden. Ideally grown with old roses.

Artemisia arborescens
Compositae

ZONES 8–10   SHRUB

Height: 1 m (3 ft), **Flowers:** yellow, early – mid-summer, **Foliage:** silver and feathery, deciduous semi-evergreen, **Position:** sun, **Soil:** tolerates most soils, **Habit:** round and bushy, **Propagation:** cuttings in mid-summer, division in mid-autumn.

☐ This shrub may be semi-evergreen in mild winters but could be killed by severe weather in cold parts of the country. Lovely plant for cottage garden, especially when grown with old roses.

Artemisia lactiflora
Compositae White mugwort

ZONES 4–10   HERBACEOUS PERENNIAL

Height: 1.2–1.5 m (4–5 ft). **Flowers:** creamy white, tiny, held in long plumes, fragrant, late summer – early autumn, **Foliage:** dark green, feathery, deciduous, **Position:** sun or semi-shade, **Soil:** well-drained, acid soil ideal, **Habit:** robust perennial, **Propagation:** by dividing clumps mid-autumn – early spring; by cuttings taken in summer and inserted in a garden frame; or by seeds sown outdoors in spring.

☐ Good for cottage gardens, in association with old roses.

Right: *Artemisia lactiflora*

Artemisia 'Silver Queen'
Compositae

ZONES 5–10   HERBACEOUS PERENNIAL

Height: 75 cm (2½ ft), **Flowers:** white, early – late summer, **Foliage:** silvery, finely cut, deciduous, **Position:** sun or semi-shade, **Soil:** tolerates most soils, **Habit:** loosely upright perennial, **Propagation:** by dividing clumps mid-autumn – early spring; or take cuttings in summer and insert in a garden frame.

☐ Attractive foliage plant, useful for flower arranging. Good for cottage gardens, especially in association with old roses.

Aruncus dioicus
  (syn. *A. sylvester*)
Rosaceae Goat's beard

ZONES 3–9   HERBACEOUS PERENNIAL

Height: 1.2–1.8 m (4–6 ft), **Flowers:** feathery heads of creamy white blooms, early summer, **Foliage:** pale green, formed of several leaflets; deciduous, **Position:** prefers dappled shade, **Soil:** moisture-retentive, **Habit:** vigorous and erect perennial, **Propagation:** by seeds sown in spring, or by division in autumn or spring.

☐ Most purchased plants are male with better flowers than female. Associates well with many ornamental shrubs.

Arundinaria japonica
Gramineae Bamboo

ZONES 5–10   SHRUB

Height: 3–5 m (10–16 ft), **Flowers:** insignificant, rarely produced, **Foliage:** deep green, shiny, more blue-green underneath, evergreen, **Position:** sunny, sheltered, **Soil:** suits most moisture-retentive soils, **Habit:** tall, upright and invasive, **Propagation:** division in spring.

☐ Imparts a sub-tropical touch to a planting scheme.

Arundinaria pumila

Gramineae Bamboo

ZONES 5–10 SHRUB

Height: 30–60 cm (1–2 ft), **Flowers:** rarely produced and detrimental to the health of the plant when they do occur, **Foliage:** green, pointed, lanceolate, on purple stems, evergreen, **Position:** sunny, sheltered, **Soil:** suits most moisture-retentive soils, **Habit:** a dwarf bamboo, spreads readily, **Propagation:** divide and replant in spring.

☐ Good ground cover for shrub borders and sheltered banks.

Arundinaria variegata

Gramineae Bamboo

ZONES 5–10 SHRUB

Height: 60 cm–1.2 m (2–4 ft), **Flowers:** insignificant, **Foliage:** green, striped white, evergreen, on deep green stems, **Position:** sunny, sheltered, **Soil:** suits most moisture-retentive soils, **Habit:** makes a dense thicket of canes, compact, **Propagation:** divide in spring.

☐ Imparts a sub-tropical touch to a planting scheme.

Asclepias incarnata

Asclepiadaceae Swamp milkweed

ZONES 8–10 HERBACEOUS PERENNIAL

Height: 60 cm–1.2 m (2–4 ft), **Flowers:** palest pink, in umbels, mid – late summer, **Foliage:** long, medium green, deciduous, **Position:** sunny spot, sheltered from wind, **Soil:** moist, lime-free, humus-rich with added peat or leafmould, **Habit:** vigorous perennial, erect stems, some support advisable, **Propagation:** by division in autumn or spring; or by seeds sown in spring in a warm propagator.

☐ A useful plant for the woodland garden or shrub border.

Aster alpinus

Compositae

ZONES 5–9 ROCK PLANT

Height: 15 cm (6 in), **Flowers:** violet, yellow-eyed daisies, mid-summer, **Foliage:** greyish green, deciduous, **Position:** full sun, **Soil:** any reasonably good soil, **Habit:** carpeting, **Propagation:** by seed sown outdoors or under glass in spring; or by division in autumn or spring.

☐ Forms in various other colours are available too. Useful for front of border, rock garden or for gaps in paving.

Aster amellus

Compositae

ZONES 6–9 HERBACEOUS PERENNIAL

Height: 45–60 cm (1½–2 ft), **Flowers:** blue or pink shades, late summer – early autumn, **Foliage:** greyish green, deciduous, **Position:** sunny and open, partial shade, **Soil:** any reasonably good soil, **Habit:** clump-forming, erect perennial, **Propagation:** by division of clumps in autumn or spring.

☐ Associates well with shrubs noted for autumn colour. Good for cutting.

Left: *Aster alpinus*, useful for the front of a border, rock garden or gaps in paving

Top left: *Aster linosyris*
Top right: *Aster novi-belgii* cultivar
Below: *Aster novae-angliae* 'Harrington's Pink'

Aster ericoides
Compositae Michaelmas daisy
ZONES 6–9   HERBACEOUS PERENNIAL
Height: 60 cm–1 m (2–3 ft), **Flowers:** white, flushed with pink, small but numerous, early – mid-autumn, **Foliage:** medium green, **Position:** sun or partial shade, **Soil:** any reasonably good soil, **Habit:** perennial with slender erect stems, **Propagation:** by seed sown outdoors or under glass in spring; or by division of clumps in autumn or spring.
☐ Flowers are good for cutting.

Aster × frikartii
Compositae Michaelmas daisy
ZONES 6–9   HERBACEOUS PERENNIAL
Height: 75 cm–1 m (2½–3 ft), **Flowers:** lavender-blue daisies, late summer – mid-autumn, **Foliage:** deep green, deciduous, **Position:** sun or partial shade, **Soil:** moist, but well drained and fertile chalk soil, **Habit:** erect stemed clump-forming perennial, **Propagation:** by division of clumps in autumn or spring.
☐ Excellent cut flower. Looks superb with shrubs grown for autumn leaf colour.

Aster linosyris
Compositae Goldilocks
ZONES 5–9   HERBACEOUS PERENNIAL
Height: 60 cm (2 ft), **Flowers:** yellow, late summer – early autumn, **Foliage:** matt green, lanceolate, deciduous, **Position:** sunny and open, partial shade, **Soil:** moist but well drained and fertile, **Habit:** upright perennial, **Propagation:** by seed sown outdoors or under glass in spring; or by division in autumn or spring.
☐ Excellent cut flower.

Aster novae-angliae
Compositae Michaelmas daisy
ZONES 5–9   HERBACEOUS PERENNIAL
Height: 1.2–1.5 m (4–5 ft), **Flowers:** early – mid-autumn, **Foliage:** matt green, lanceolate, deciduous, **Position:** sunny and open, partial shade, **Soil:** moist but well drained and fertile, **Habit:** upright perennial, needs some support, **Propagation:** by division in autumn or spring.
☐ Good for cutting. Cut back to ground level after flowering.
'Harrington's Pink' is a beautiful shade of pink, 'September Ruby' is rich crimson. Grow with autumn-colouring shrubs.

Aster novi-belgii
Compositae Michaelmas daisy
ZONES 4–9   HERBACEOUS PERENNIAL
Height: 90 cm–1.2 m (3–4 ft), **Flowers:** shades of blue and mauve, double or single, early – mid-autumn, **Foliage:** mid-green, glossy, narrow and pointed, deciduous, **Position:** sunny and open, partial shade, **Soil:** moist but well drained and fertile, **Habit:** erect, excellent cut flower, **Propagation:** by division of clumps mid-autumn – early spring.
☐ Cut back to ground level after flowering. There are many excellent cultivars including 'Ada Ballard', mauve-blue, double; 'Blandie', white, double; 'Chequers', deep purple-violet, single; 'Crimson Brocade', red, double; 'Fellowship', pink, semi-double; 'Marie Ballard', light blue, double.

Aster novi-belgii
Compositae Dwarf Michaelmas daisy
ZONES 4–9   HERBACEOUS PERENNIAL
Height: 30–45 cm (12–18 in), **Flowers:** white and shades of blue and pink, single or double; early – mid-autumn, **Foliage:** mid-green, narrow and pointed, deciduous, **Position:** sunny and open, partial shade, **Soil:** moist but well drained and fertile, **Habit:** compact and bushy, **Propagation:** by division of clumps mid-autumn – early spring.
☐ Cut back stems to ground level after flowering. 'Audrey', light blue, semi-double; 'Jenny', red, double; 'Little Pink Baby', pink single; 'Snowsprite', white.

Astilbe × arendsii

Saxifragaceae False goat's beard

ZONES 4–9 HERBACEOUS PERENNIAL

Height: 60 cm–1 m (2–3 ft), **Flowers:** shades of pink, red and white, in pyramidal plumes, early – late summer, **Foliage:** mid green, deeply divided, coppery tinted when young, deciduous, **Position:** sun or partial shade, excellent for pond-side planting, **Soil:** must be moist, mulch with peat or leafmould in mid-spring, **Habit:** graceful clump-forming perennial, **Propagation:** divide clumps in early – mid-spring.

☐ Cut to ground level in mid-autumn. Grow with other moisture loving plants like bog primulas and hostas.

'*Bressingham Pink*' is pure pink; '*Deutschland*' is white; '*Fanal*' is deep red; '*Granat*' is deep crimson-pink.

Right: *Astilbe × arendsii* cultivars, such as 'Fanal', are ideal for associating with other moisture-loving perennials like bog primulas and hostas

Astilbe chinensis var. pumila

Saxifragaceae False goat's beard

ZONES 4–9 ROCK PLANT

Height: 23 cm (9 in), **Flowers:** reddish-purple, in dense erect plumes, summer, **Foliage:** mid green, fern-like, deciduous, **Position:** sun or partial shade, **Soil:** suits most moist soils, **Habit:** dwarf, compact and clump-forming perennial, **Propagation:** divide clumps in early – mid-spring.

☐ Suitable for a rock garden.

Astrantia major

Umbelliferae Masterwort

ZONES 4–9 HERBACEOUS PERENNIAL

Height: 60 cm (2 ft), **Flowers:** green and pink, star-shaped, early – mid-summer, **Foliage:** medium green, formed of three leaflets, deciduous, **Position:** partial shade, or sun provided soil stays moist, **Soil:** moisture-retentive, **Habit:** clump-forming perennial, flowerheads raised above the foliage, **Propagation:** divide clumps mid-autumn – early spring; or by seed sown in early autumn and germinated in a garden frame.

☐ Cut down the stems in late summer.

Aubrieta deltoidea

Cruciferae Aubrieta, rock cress

ZONES 4–9 ROCK PLANT

Height: 15 cm (6 in), **Flowers:** purple, pink, red, or blue, early – late spring, **Foliage:** green or greyish green, evergreen, **Position:** sun, on rock garden, wall or bank, **Soil:** neutral or alkaline, **Habit:** trailing perennial, **Propagation:** by cuttings in sandy soil in a propagator during summer, or by division in spring.

☐ Seeds of cultivars will not come true. Cut back after flowering. Grow with yellow alyssum and white arabis.

Aubrieta deltoidea 'Variegata'
Cruciferae Variegated aubrieta
ZONES 4–9   ROCK PLANT
Height: 10 cm (4 in), **Flowers:** purple, early – late spring, **Foliage:** green with prominent white margins, evergreen, **Position:** sun, on rock garden, wall or in paving, **Soil:** neutral or alkaline, **Habit:** more compact than the species, **Propagation:** by cuttings in sandy soil in a propagator during summer, or by division in spring.
□Combines well with yellow alyssum.

Below: *Azalea* 'Blue Danube'

Aucuba japonica 'Variegata'
Cornaceae Spotted laurel, Gold Dust Plant
ZONES 7–10   SHRUB
Height: 3m (10ft), **Flowers:** greenish white, **Foliage:** green, speckled yellow, evergreen, **Position:** sun or shade, **Soil:** soil-tolerant, **Habit:** dense rounded bush, **Propagation:** by cuttings 10–15 cm (4–6 in) long in late summer – early autumn.
□This shrub will grow in any situation, but will hold its variegation best in an open position. It tolerates industrial pollution and thrives near the sea.

AZALEAS

In the strict botanical sense azaleas are included in the genus rhododendron. But I am keeping them separate in this book since most gardeners think of them as a separate group of shrubs.

Unfortunately, none of them tolerate any lime in the soil (or water), but where the garden soil does not suit them they can be grown in tubs filled with an ericaceous compost. They thrive in sheltered, semi-shaded situations.

The selection of azaleas here includes deciduous and evergreen kinds, belonging to different hybrid groups.

For more details on propagation see page 71.

Azaleas associate well with candelabra primulas, hostas and lilies.

The hybrid groups are:

Deciduous
Ghent hybrids
Knaphill hybrids
Mollis azaleas
Occidentale hybrids
Rustica hybrids

Evergreen
Gable hybrids
Glenn Dale hybrids
Indica hybrids
Kaempferi hybrids
Kurume hybrids
Oldhamii hybrids
Vuyk hybrids
Propagation: see page 71.

Azalea 'Annabelle'
Ericaceae Knaphill hybrid
ZONES 5–9   SHRUB
Height: 1.2–1.8 m (4–6 ft), **Flowers:** orange and yellow in bud opening to yellow, suffused with orange-rose, late spring – early summer, **Foliage:** green; good autumn colour, deciduous, **Position:** semi-shade, protect from winds, **Soil:** humus rich, acid, **Habit:** upright, bushy, **Propagation:** by layering, at any time of year.

Azalea 'Balzac'
Ericaceae Knaphill hybrid
ZONES 5–9   SHRUB
Height: 1.2–1.8 m (4–6 ft), **Flowers:** deep orange-red and orange, fragrant, late spring – early summer, **Foliage:** green, good autumn colour, deciduous, **Position:** semi-shade, protect from winds, **Soil:** humus-rich, acid, **Habit:** upright, bushy, **Propagation:** by layering at any time of year.

Above: *Azalea* 'Mother's Day'
Right: *Azalea* 'Gibraltar'
Below right: *Azalea* 'John Cairns'

Azalea 'Compte de Gomer'
Ericaceae Mollis azalea
ZONES 5–9   SHRUB
Height: 1.2–1.8 m (4–6 ft), **Flowers:** pink and orange, late spring, **Foliage:** green, good autumn colour, deciduous, **Position:** semi-shade, protect from winds, **Soil:** humus-rich, acid, **Habit:** upright, bushy, **Propagation:** by layering at any time of year.

Azalea 'Dracula'
Ericaceae Knaphill hybrid
ZONES 5–9   SHRUB
Height: 1.2–1.8 m (4–6 ft), **Flowers:** very dark red buds, opening to crimson-red, frilled edges, late spring – early summer, **Foliage:** opens bronzy, turning green, later good autumn colour, deciduous, **Position:** semi-shade, protect from winds, **Soil:** humus-rich, acid, **Habit:** upright, bushy, **Propagation:** by layering at any time of year.

Azalea 'Gibraltar'
Ericaceae Knaphill hybrid
ZONES 5–9   SHRUB
Height: 1.2–1.8 m (4–6 ft), **Flowers:** large orange-red, buds deep orange-crimson, late spring – early summer, **Foliage:** green, good autumn colour, deciduous, **Position:** semi-shade, protect from winds, **Soil:** humus-rich, acid, **Habit:** upright, bushy, **Propagation:** by layering at any time of year.

Azalea 'Hollandia'
Ericaceae Ghent hybrid
ZONES 5–9   SHRUB
Height: 1.5–2.5 m (5–8 ft), **Flowers:** yellow and orange, early summer, **Foliage:** green, deciduous, **Position:** semi-shade, protect from winds, **Soil:** humus-rich, acid, **Habit:** upright, bushy, **Propagation:** by layering at any time of year.

Azalea 'Orange Truffles'
Ericaceae Knaphill hybrid
ZONES 5–9   SHRUB
Height: 1.2–1.8 m (4–6 ft), **Flowers:** apricot with petals yellow inside flushed red outside, wavy margins, double, late spring – early summer, **Foliage:** young leaves coppery red, turning green, good autumn colour, deciduous, **Position:** semi-shade, protect from winds, **Soil:** humus-rich, acid, **Habit:** upright, bushy, **Propagation:** by layering at any time of year.

Azalea 'Raphael de Smet'
Ericaceae Ghent hybrid
ZONES 5–9   SHRUB
Height: 1.5–1.8 m (5–8 ft), **Flowers:** white, flushed pink, double, early summer, **Foliage:** green, good autumn colour, deciduous, **Position:** semi-shade, protect from winds, **Soil:** humus-rich, acid, **Habit:** upright, bushy, **Propagation:** by layering at any time of year.

Azalea 'Addy Wery'
Ericaceae Kurume hybrid
ZONES 5–9   SHRUB
Height: 60 cm–1.2 m (2–4 ft), **Flowers:** orange-scarlet, late spring, **Foliage:** green, evergreen, **Position:** semi-shade, **Soil:** humus-rich, acid, **Habit:** compact, bushy, **Propagation:** by cuttings taken from young growths from mid – late summer.

Azalea 'Blaauw's Pink'
Ericaceae Kurume hybrid
ZONES 5–9   SHRUB
Height: 60 cm–1.2 m (2–4 ft), **Flowers:** warm-pink, spring, **Foliage:** green, evergreen, **Position:** semi-shade, **Soil:** humus-rich, acid, **Habit:** compact, bushy, **Propagation:** by cuttings which are taken from young growths in mid – late summer.

Azalea 'Blue Danube'
Ericaceae Vuyk hybrid
ZONES 5–9   SHRUB
Height: 1.2 m (4 ft), **Flowers:** a most striking violet-blue, large, late spring, **Foliage:** green, evergreen, **Position:** semi-shade, **Soil:** humus-rich, acid, **Habit:** compact, bushy, **Propagation:** by cuttings taken from young growths, mid – late summer.

Right: *Azalea* 'Palestrina'

Azalea 'Hinodegiri'
Ericaceae   Kurume hybrid
ZONES 5–9   SHRUB
Height: 60 cm–1.2 m (2–4 ft), **Flowers:** crimson-red, late spring, **Foliage:** green, evergreen, **Position:** semi-shade, **Soil:** humus rich, acid, **Habit:** compact, bushy, **Propagation:** by cuttings which are taken from young growths in mid – late summer.

Azalea 'Hinomayo'
Ericaceae   Kurume hybrid
ZONES 5–9   SHRUB
Height: up to 1.5 m (5 ft), **Flowers:** soft pink, late spring, **Foliage:** green, evergreen, **Position:** semi-shade, **Soil:** humus-rich, acid, **Habit:** compact, bushy, **Propagation:** by cuttings taken from young growths, mid – late summer.

Azalea 'Johann Strauss'
Ericaceae   Vuyk hybrid
ZONES 5–9   SHRUB
Height: 60 cm–1.2 m (2–4 ft), **Flowers:** warm pink with deeper markings, large, late spring, **Foliage:** green, evergreen, **Position:** semi-shade, **Soil:** humus-rich, acid, **Habit:** compact, bushy, **Propagation:** by cuttings taken from young growths, mid – late summer.

Azalea 'John Cairns'
Ericaceae   Kaempferi hybrid
ZONES 5–9   SHRUB
Height: 1–1.2 m (3–4 ft), **Flowers:** deep reddish orange, late spring, **Foliage:** green, evergreen, **Position:** sun or partial shade, protect from cold winds, **Soil:** humus-rich, acid, **Habit:** compact, bushy, **Propagation:** by cuttings taken from young growths, mid – late summer.

Azalea 'Mother's Day'
Ericaceae   Kurume × Indica hybrid
ZONES 5–9   SHRUB
Height: up to 1 m (3 ft), **Flowers:** rose-red, late spring, **Foliage:** green, evergreen, **Position:** sun or partial shade, protect from cold winds, **Soil:** humus-rich, acid, **Habit:** compact, bushy, **Propagation:** by cuttings taken from young growths, mid – late summer.

Azalea 'Palestrina'
Ericaceae   Vuyk hybrid
ZONES 5–9   SHRUB
Height: 60 cm (2 ft), **Flowers:** white, spring, **Foliage:** green, evergreen, **Position:** sun or partial shade, protect from cold winds, **Soil:** humus-rich, acid, **Habit:** dwarf, compact and spreading, **Propagation:** by cuttings taken from young growths, mid – late summer.

Azara lanceolata
Flacourtiaceae
ZONES 7–10   SHRUB
Height: 6 m (20 ft), **Flowers:** showy yellow, fragrant, mid – late spring, **Foliage:** green, evergreen, **Position:** sun or partial shade, **Soil:** tolerates most soils, **Habit:** forms a round shrub in open ground or train against a wall, **Propagation:** cuttings in summer rooted in propagator.
☐ A very good shrub for south- or west-facing walls. Tolerates clipping which can be done after flowering.

Berberidopsis corallina
Flacourtiaceae   Coral plant
ZONES 4–9   CLIMBER
Height: 4.5–6 m (15–20 ft), **Flowers:** dark crimson on pendulous stalks in late summer, **Foliage:** dark green above, glaucous beneath, almost holly-like, evergreen, **Position:** shady and sheltered, **Soil:** open or sandy loam, preferably neutral or acid, **Habit:** climber, requires support, **Propagation:** sow seed in sandy compost in spring and germinate in propagator; insert cuttings in similar compost and temperature, or increase by layering.
☐ Ivies make good companions.

Above: *Berberis darwinii*
Right: *Berberis* × *stenophylla*

Berberis aggregata 'Barbarossa'
Berberidaceae Barberry
ZONES 5–9   SHRUB
Height: 2.5 m (8 ft), **Flowers:** pale yellow, mid-summer, **Foliage:** green, turning brilliant orange and red in autumn, **Position:** best in sun but tolerates partial shade, **Soil:** tolerates most soils, **Habit:** bushy, rounded, easily kept to shape by pruning, **Propagation:** cuttings in autumn.
☐ Produces heavy crops of red berries, plus excellent autumn foliage colour. Try associating it with Michalmas daisies – a stunning combination.

Berberis candidula
Berberidaceae Barberry
ZONES 5–9   SHRUB
Height: 60 cm (2 ft), **Flowers:** yellow, late spring – early summer; followed by black berries, **Foliage:** shiny deep green, evergreen, **Position:** sun or partial shade, **Soil:** soil-tolerant, **Habit:** compact and rounded, **Propagation:** seed or cuttings.
☐ A useful species for the larger rock garden; or for planting at the front of a border.

Berberis darwinii
Berberidaceae Barberry
ZONES 5–9   SHRUB
Height: 3 m (10 ft), **Flowers:** deep yellow, or orange-yellow, followed by blue-black berries; late spring, **Foliage:** dark-green, shiny, like miniature holly leaves, evergreen, **Position:** sun or partial shade, **Soil:** tolerates most soils, **Habit:** bushy, **Propagation:** seed or cuttings.
☐ This is one of the most popular barberries, excellent as a free-standing shrub or as a hedge which should be lightly trimmed back after flowering. Good for seaside planting.

Berberis gagnepainii 'Lancifolia'
Berberidaceae Barberry
ZONES 5–9   SHRUB
Height: 1.8 m (6 ft), **Flowers:** yellow, followed by blue-black berries; late spring, **Foliage:** dark green, evergreen, **Position:** sun or partial shade, **Soil:** soil-tolerant, **Habit:** forms a dense, upright bush, **Propagation:** seeds, cuttings or layering.
☐ A robust shrub making an excellent hedge in most situations, including seaside.

Berberis linearifolia 'Orange King'
Berberidaceae Barberry
ZONES 6–9   SHRUB
Height: 3 m (10 ft), **Flowers:** deep orange, mid-spring, followed by blue-black berries, **Foliage:** shiny green, evergreen, **Position:** sun or partial shade, **Soil:** tolerates most soils, **Habit:** erect, slow growing, **Propagation:** cuttings.
☐ A beautiful shrub. The flowers are more showy than those of any other berberis. Can be grown as an informal hedge.

Berberis × *rubrostilla*
Berberidaceae Barberry
ZONES 5–9   SHRUB
Height: 1 m (3 ft), **Flowers:** yellow, late spring, **Foliage:** greyish green, deciduous, bright red tints in autumn, **Position:** best in sun, tolerates partial shade, **Soil:** tolerates most soils, **Habit:** compact, **Propagation:** seed or cuttings.
☐ Profusion of bright red oval berries greatly enhance the beauty of the autumn foliage. Specially good in association with *Ceratostigma willmottianum*.

Berberis sargentiana
Berberidaceae Barberry
ZONES 5–9   SHRUB
Height: 1.8 m (6 ft), **Flowers:** yellow, spring, **Foliage:** dark green, evergreen, **Position:** sun or partial shade, **Soil:** tolerates most soils, **Habit:** forms a thicket of erect stems, **Propagation:** seed or cuttings.
☐ This berberis is armed with the longest spines in the entire genus. Black fruits in autumn.

Berberis × *stenophylla*
Berberidaceae Barberry
ZONES 5–10   SHRUB
Height: 3 m (10 ft), **Flowers:** yellow, mid-spring, followed by round purple-blue berries; **Foliage:** dark-green, evergreen, **Position:** sun or partial shade, **Soil:** tolerates most soils, **Habit:** forms a dense thicket of arching branches, **Propagation:** cuttings.
☐ Can be grown as a hedge when it should be lightly trimmed back after flowering, or used as a specimen plant.

Top: *Berberis thunbergii* 'Rose Glow'
Above: *Berberis × stenophylla* 'Corallina Compacta'
Right: *Berberis thunbergii* 'Aurea'

Berberis × stenophylla 'Corallina Compacta'

Berberidaceae Barberry

ZONES 7–10   SHRUB

Height: 30–45 cm (1–1½ ft), **Flowers:** open yellow from red buds, **Foliage:** dark green, evergreen, **Position:** sun or partial shade, **Soil:** tolerates most soils, **Habit:** bun shaped, compact, **Propagation:** cuttings.

☐ A useful pretty little dwarf shrub suitable for a rock garden.

Berberis thunbergii 'Atropurpurea Nana'

Berberidaceae Barberry

ZONES 5–9   SHRUB

Height: 30–45 cm (1–1½ ft), **Flowers:** yellow, spring, followed by red berries, **Foliage:** reddish purple in sunny positions, deciduous, **Position:** sun or partial shade, **Soil:** tolerates most soils, **Habit:** dwarf, compact, **Propagation:** cuttings.

☐ This pleasing little shrub makes an excellent low hedge which should be trimmed in late summer. It produces the best-coloured deep reddish purple foliage when planted in full sun. Also makes an excellent plant for the larger rock garden.

Berberis thunbergii 'Aurea'

Berberidaceae Barberry

ZONES 7–9   SHRUB

Height: 45–60 cm (1½–2 ft), **Flowers:** yellow, spring, **Foliage:** yellow, but eventually turns light green, deciduous, **Position:** sun, **Soil:** tolerates most soils, **Habit:** dwarf, compact, **Propagation:** cuttings.

☐ This dwarf shrub is grown primarily for its golden foliage. Scarlet berries follow on from the flowers. An excellent companion for purple-leaved barberries.

Berberis thunbergii 'Helmond Pillar'

Berberidaceae Barberry

ZONES 5–9   SHRUB

Height: 1.5 m (5 ft), **Flowers:** yellow, late spring, **Foliage:** deep red, deciduous, **Position:** sun or partial shade, **Soil:** tolerates most soils, **Habit:** fastigiate, **Propagation:** cuttings.

☐ Excellent for low hedges. Foliage colour is richest in full sun. Red berries follow on from the flowers.

Berberis thunbergii 'Red Chief'

Berberidaceae Barberry

ZONES 5–9   SHRUB

Height: 1.8 m (6 ft), **Flowers:** yellow, late spring, followed by red berries, **Foliage:** shiny deep crimson, deciduous, **Position:** sun or partial shade, **Soil:** tolerates most soils, **Habit:** densely branching, **Propagation:** cuttings.

☐ Good to associate with golden foliage. Best foliage colour in full sun.

Berberis thunbergii 'Rose Glow'

Berberidaceae Barberry

ZONES 5–9   SHRUB

Height: 1–1.5 m (3–5 ft), **Flowers:** yellow, late spring, followed by red berries, **Foliage:** purple when young, later splashed with silvery-pink, turning purplish-red before falling, **Position:** sun or partial shade, **Soil:** tolerates most soils, **Habit:** densely branching, **Propagation:** seed or cuttings.

☐ Associates well with *Spiraea japonica* 'Goldflame' and should also complement *Choisya ternata* 'Sundance'. Best foliage colour in full sun.

Berberis verruculosa
Berberidaceae Barberry
ZONES 5–9   SHRUB
Height: about 1.2 (4 ft), **Flowers:** yellow, late spring – early summer, **Foliage:** dark green, holly-like, evergreen, **Position:** sun or partial shade, **Soil:** tolerates most soils, **Habit:** compact and spiky, **Propagation:** seed or cuttings.
☐The yellow flowers are followed in autumn by blue-black berries.

Berberis wilsoniae
Berberidaceae Barberry
ZONES 5–9   SHRUB
Height: 1–1.5 m (3–5 ft), **Flowers:** yellow, mid-summer, **Foliage:** green, deciduous, excellent autumn colour, **Position:** sun for best autumn colour, **Soil:** tolerates most soils, **Habit:** low spreading, **Propagation:** seed or cuttings.
☐A profusion of pinkish-red berries is produced which complements the colourful autumn foliage. This species can be used for ground cover or as an informal hedge.

Bergenia 'Ballawley'
Saxifragaceae Elephant's ears, megasea
ZONES 4–9   HERBACEOUS PERENNIAL
Height: 30–60 cm (18–24 in), **Flowers:** pinkish-red, in loose heads raised above foliage, mid – late spring, **Foliage:** green, tinged red, turning brighter red in autumn, evergreen, **Position:** sun or partial shade, **Soil:** any moist garden soil, tolerates lime, **Habit:** large evergreen leaves, spreading, **Propagation:** by division in autumn or spring.
☐Overcrowded plants should be divided. Bergenia make good ground cover.

Bergenia cordifolia
Saxifragaceae Elephant's ears, megasea
ZONES 2–9   HERBACEOUS PERENNIAL
Height: 30 cm (1 ft), **Flowers:** mauve-pink, in loose heads raised above foliage, early – mid-spring, **Foliage:** green, glossy and leathery, evergreen, often reddish in the autumn, **Position:** sun or partial shade, **Soil:** any moist garden soil, tolerates lime, **Habit:** large evergreen leaves, spreading, **Propagation:** by division in autumn or spring.
☐Good for ground cover.

Bergenia × *schmidtii*
Saxifragaceae Elephant's ears, megasea
ZONES 4–9   HERBACEOUS PERENNIAL
Height: 37 cm (15 in), **Flowers:** rose-pink, late spring – early summer, **Foliage:** green, glossy and leathery, evergreen, **Position:** sun or partial shade, **Soil:** suits moist soils and tolerates chalk, **Habit:** large leaves, spreading, **Propagation:** by division in autumn or spring.
☐Good ground cover.

Betula pendula 'Youngii'
Betulaceae Young's weeping birch
ZONES 2–9   TREE
Height: 5–7.5 m (16–25 ft), **Flowers:** pale yellow catkins, spring, **Foliage:** mid-green, rhomboidal shaped leaves, deciduous, **Position:** sun or partial shade, **Soil:** any type, but best on slightly acid or neutral soils, **Habit:** ultimately a small pendulous mushroom-shaped tree, **Propagation:** by grafting on to young stock of *B. pendula*.
☐Perfect small specimen tree for a lawn.

Betula pendula
(syn. *B. verrucosa*)

Betulaceae Silver birch

ZONES 2–9   TREE

Height: 9–15 m (30–50 ft), **Flowers:** pale yellow catkins, spring, **Foliage:** mid green, almost diamond shaped, deciduous, **Position:** sunny and open or partial shade, **Soil:** any soil, acid or alkaline, but grows larger on slightly acid soils, **Habit:** elegant and dainty with silver bark, light canopy, **Propagation:** by seeds sown on the surface and gently pressed into sandy compost or a good seed compost in a garden frame. The numerous cultivars are grafted on to young stock of the type plant.
□ An excellent small tree for creating light woodland conditions, for rhododendrons, azaleas, camellias, etc.

Right: The spring catkins of the silver birch, *Betula pendula*

Left: *Buddleia davidii* 'Black Knight'
Above: *Buddleia davidii* 'White Bouquet'

Buddleia alternifolia

Loganiaceae

ZONES 5–10   SHRUB

Height: 4–6 m (13–20 ft), **Flowers:** mauve-blue, fragrant, summer, **Foliage:** green leaves arranged alternately, deciduous, **Position:** sun, **Soil:** light loamy soil, **Habit:** makes a graceful arching specimen, **Propagation:** by 12–15 cm (5–6 in) long cuttings of partially-ripe side shoots taken with a heel in mid – late summer.
□ Extremely beautiful in full flower, this shrub can be trained as a standard, making an excellent specimen plant in a lawn.

Buddleia davidii

Loganiaceae Butterfly bush

ZONES 5–10   SHRUB

Height: up to 3 m (10 ft), **Flowers:** vary in colour according to cultivar, often fragrant, held in long panicles, mid-summer early autumn, **Foliage:** narrow green leaves up to 30 cm (1 ft) long, white and downy beneath, deciduous, **Position:** sun, **Soil:** light loamy soil, tolerates lime, **Habit:** spreads widely, of open growth, **Propagation:** hardwood cuttings, 23–30 cm (10–12 in) long, taken in mid-autumn and inserted in the garden.
□ *B. davidii* cultivars and varieties are best pruned hard back in early spring to keep a shrub of manageable size. As common

name suggests, these plants attract butterflies.

Recommended cultivars of *Buddleia davidii*

'*Black Knight*' – violet-blue flowers.
'*Empire Blue*' – blue, each with an orange centre.
'*Harlequin*' – reddish purple flowers; only grows to 1.8 m (6 ft) white-variegated foliage.
'*Ile de France*' – violet-blue flowers.
'*Pink Pearl*' – pink flowers.
'*Royal Red*' – large reddish-purple blooms.
'*White Bouquet*' – white flowers.

Buddleia 'Lochinch'
Loganiaceae
ZONES 5–10   SHRUB
Height: 1.5–3 m (5–10 ft), **Flowers:** pale
violet-blue each with orange centre, held
in erect spikes, fragrant, mid-summer –
early autumn, **Foliage:** covered in white
hairs when young, later green above and
white below, deciduous, **Position:** sun,
Soil: light loamy soil, **Habit:** makes a
compact bushy specimen, **Propagation:**
hardwood cuttings as for *B. davidii*.
☐Probably a hybrid between *B. davidii*
and *B. fallowiana*.

Buxus microphylla
Buxaceae Small-leaved box
ZONES 5–10   SHRUB
Height: 1–1.2 m (3–4 ft), **Flowers:**
greeny yellow, scented, mid-spring, insignificant, **Foliage:** green, evergreen, **Position:** sun or shade, **Soil:** tolerates most
soils, **Habit:** slow-growing, compact,
Propagation: by cuttings 5–8 cm (2–3 in)
long, taken in late summer – early autumn.
☐Clip plants in spring and late summer.
Useful for the front of a shrub border and
for containers.

Buxus sempervirens
Buxaceae Common box
ZONES 5–10   SHRUB
Height: up to 2.4 m (8 ft), more if left
unclipped, **Flowers:** greeny yellow, scented, mid-spring, insignificant, **Foliage:**
green, 'Elegantissima' and 'Aureo-
Variegata' have foliage variegated with
cream, all are evergreen, **Position:** sun or
shade, **Soil:** tolerates most soils, **Habit:**
dense foliage, growth slow, **Propagation:**
by cuttings 5–8 cm (2–3 in) long taken in
late summer – early autumn.
☐Trim in spring and late summer. An
ideal shrub for topiary, low hedges and
edgings. 'Suffruticosa' is edging box.

Calceolaria integrifolia
Scrophulariaceae
ZONES 9–10   SHRUB
Height: 60 cm (2 ft), **Flowers:** bright
yellow, mid-summer – early autumn, **Foliage:** green, generally evergreen, **Position:** sun and maximum shelter, **Soil:**
tolerates most soils, **Habit:** dense, erect
growth, **Propagation:** seed or cuttings.
☐This half-hardy sub-shrub is not suitable for overwintering outside in cold
districts. But it is a delightfully colourful
plant for a long period. Cut back by half in
mid-spring.
    Its main use is for summer bedding.

Callicarpa bodinieri var. giraldii
Verbenaceae
ZONES 6–10   SHRUB
Height: 1.8 m (6 ft), **Flowers:** violet, mid
– late summer, **Foliage:** matt green, deciduous, colours yellow and red in
autumn, **Position:** full sun or partial
shade, **Soil:** suits most soils, **Habit:** upright, **Propagation:** cuttings early – mid-
summer.
☐The flowers are followed by showy
violet-blue berries. Best to grow two or
three plants together as then more berries
are produced.

Callistemon citrinus 'Splendens'
Myrtaceae Bottle brush
ZONES 8–10   SHRUB
Height: 1.5–1.8 m (5–6 ft), **Flowers:**
bright red stamens, mid-summer – early
autumn, **Foliage:** green, evergreen, **Position:** sun, **Soil:** suits most soils, **Habit:**
loose, arching, **Propagation:** seed or
cuttings.
☐This magnificent shrub thrives in mild
and protected places such as against a
south- or south-west facing wall, but is not
hardy enough for colder areas.

Calluna vulgaris

Ericaceae Ling, heather
ZONES 4–8 SHRUB
Height: 15–80 cm (6–33 in), **Flowers:** white, shades of pink, mauve and purple, late summer – early autumn, **Foliage:** green, gold or orange, evergreen, **Position:** best in full sun, tolerates some shade, **Soil:** light, lime-free with added peat, **Habit:;** dwarf, compact and bushy suitable for ground cover, **Propagation:** heeled cuttings summer/autumn.
□Trouble-free plants; lightly clip off straggly growth and dead flowers. Associates well with other members of the Ericaceae and small conifers.

Recommended cultivars of C. vulgaris

'*Alba Plena*' – double white flowers; 45 cm (18 in) high; compact.
'*Alportii Praecox*' – crimson; 45 cm (18 in) high; compact.
'*County Wicklow*' – double pale pink flowers; 23 cm (10 in) high; spreading.
'*Elsie Purnell*' – double silvery pink flowers, darker in bud; 60–80 cm (2–2¾ ft); upright.
'*Golden Feather*' – golden foliage turns a soft orange in autumn; 45 cm (18 in) high; mauve flowers of little value; compact.
'*Gold Haze*' – white flowers; brilliant yellow foliage; 60 cm (2 ft) high; compact.

'*Hammondii Rubrifolia*' – purple flowers; young foliage bright red turning green with age; 45 cm (1½ ft) high; compact.
'*H.E. Beale*' – double rose-pink flowers; dark green foliage; 60 cm (2 ft) high; compact.
'*Multicolor*' ('Prairie Fire') – purple flowers; foliage in shades of yellow, orange and red throughout the year, especially bright in winter; 15 cm (6 in) high; the best prostrate cultivar.
'*Orange Queen*' – pink flowers; young foliage golden, becoming orange; 60 cm (2 ft) high; compact.
'*Peter Sparkes*' – double deep pink flowers;

Above left: Winter foliage of *Calluna vulgaris* cultivars 'Gold Haze' and 'Robert Chapman'
Above right: *Calluna vulgaris* 'Alba Plena'

45 cm (18 in) high; compact.
'*Robert Chapman*' – purple flowers; golden summer foliage turns flame-red in winter; 45 cm (18 in) high; compact.
'*Silver Queen*' – mauve-pink flowers; woolly, silver foliage; 45 cm (1½ ft) high; upright.
'*Sister Anne*' ('Hirsuta Compressa') – purple flowers; downy greyish-green foliage; 15 cm (6 in); prostrate.

Calocedrus decurrens

Cupressaceae Incense cedar
ZONES 5–10 CONIFER
Height: up to 2.5 m (8 ft) after 10 years, ultimately 30 m (100 ft), **Flowers and cones:** of no particular merit, **Foliage:** rich-green all year round, aromatic, 'Aureovariegata' has irregularly occurring golden shoots, evergreen, **Position:** open and sunny, **Soil:** any normal well-drained garden soil, **Habit:** slow-growing, narrowly columnar, **Propagation:** best raised from seed; or cuttings.
□Makes a magnificent lawn specimen in the large garden.

Caltha palustris 'Flore Plena'

Ranunculaceae Marsh marigold, kingcup
ZONES 4–9 HERBACEOUS PERENNIAL
Height: 15 cm (6 in), **Flowers:** yellow, double, early – late spring, **Foliage:** dark green, shiny, deciduous, **Position:** sun or partial shade, **Soil:** moist, loamy, neutral or moderately acid; or in water 15 cm (6 in) or more deep, **Habit:** compact and spreading, **Propagation:** by division in late spring – early summer after flowering.
□Good marginal plant for ponds or for moist herbaceous borders.

Calycanthus occidentalis

Calycanthaceae Allspice
ZONES 4–9 SHRUB
Height: 4 m (13 ft), **Flowers:** purplish red, smells unpleasantly, early summer – early autumn, **Foliage:** dark green; deciduous, **Position:** full sun, **Soil:** suits most soils, but add some peat, **Habit:** loose and open, the wood is aromatic, **Propagation:** best by layers, as seed does not always ripen. Suckers sometimes make it possible to propagate by division.
□An unusual shrub normally grown in a shrub or mixed border: best suited to the larger garden.

CAMELLIAS

Camellias, so handsome in flower and foliage, deserve to be more popular than they are. Perhaps it is their exotic appearance that suggests they must be difficult to grow. In fact they are generally hardy and, given the right soil and situation, can be grown with success. They require a good, light but completely lime-free soil with plenty of added peat and leafmould. If your soil does not satisfy this requirement then camellias make ideal tub plants if an ericaceous compost is used to fill the container.

The best position for a camellia is one sheltered from cold winds and frosts and protected by other shrubs or a wall, preferably facing north or west. Although they will flower more freely in an open sunny situation the blooms will be damaged by early morning sun on frosted blossoms and by heavy rain.

Camellia 'Cornish Snow'
Theaceae Camellia
ZONES 7–10   SHRUB
Height: 2.5–3 m (8–10 ft), **Flowers:** profusion of small white flowers all along the stems, late winter – mid-spring, **Foliage:** dark green, shiny, evergreen, **Position:** sun or partial shade, protected from north and east winds, **Soil:** moisture-retentive, acid or neutral peaty soil, **Habit:** bushy, upright, **Propagation:** take cuttings of half-ripe side shoots, 8–10 cm (3–4 in) long early – late summer.
□Camellias thrive in a sunny position but bear in mind when planting that their flowers should be protected from early morning sun or frost damage will occur.

Camellia japonica
Theaceae Common camellia
ZONES 7–10   SHRUB
Height: 3–4 m (10–13 ft) or more, **Flowers:** single, semi-double or double, white or shades of red or pink, late winter – late spring, **Foliage:** deep green, shiny, evergreen, **Position:** sun or partial leafy shade, **Soil:** moisture-retentive acid or neutral soil with added peat, **Habit:** varies according to cultivar but generally pleasing, **Propagation:** by leaf-bud cuttings or semi-ripe side shoots 8–10 cm (3–4 in) long in early – late summer.
□Unfortunately, camellia blossoms are easily damaged by frost and rain.

Top left: *Camellia* 'Cornish Snow'
Top right: *Camellia japonica* 'Lady Clare'
Right: An example of a formal double flower of *Camellia japonica*

Recommended cultivars of C. japonica
'*Adolphe Audusson*' – big, semi-double flowers, rich-red with attractive stamens; vigorous yet restrained.
'*Contessa Lavinia Maggi*' – medium, formal double flowers, white with red-cerise flecks; bushy and upright.
'*Devonia*' – medium-sized, single cup-shaped, white flowers; upright, vigorous.
'*Donckelarii*' – large, semi-double flowers, red, maybe speckled white; bushy habit, slow-growing.
'*Elegans*' ('Chandleri Elegans') – large, anemone form flowers, pink flecked with white; compact, excellent for tub planting.
'*Lady Clare*' – big, deep pink, semi-double flowers; strong, wide grower.
'*Mathotiana*' – large, crimson, formal double flowers; vigorous, compact and erect.
'*Mathotiana Alba*' – large, white, formal double flowers; vigorous, compact and erect.

Camellia 'Leonard Messel'
Theaceae
ZONES 7–10   SHRUB
Height: 4 m (13 ft) or more, **Flowers:** big, rich pink, semi-double, early – mid-spring, **Foliage:** deep green, leathery, net-veined, evergreen, **Position:** sun or leafy, partial shade, **Soil:** moisture-retentive acid or neutral peaty soil, **Habit:** vigorous and tall growing, **Propagation:** by cuttings of half-ripe side shoots, 8–10 cm (3–4 in) long taken early – late summer.
□A very beautiful tall, hardy, evergreen shrub producing flowers up to 15 cm (6 in) in diameter.

Camellia × *williamsii* 'Donation'
Theaceae
ZONES 7–10   SHRUB
Height: 1.8–3 m (6–10 ft), **Flowers:**
large, soft-pink, semi-double, late autumn
– mid-spring, **Foliage:** dark green, glossy,
evergreen, **Position:** sun or leafy, partial
shade, **Soil:** moisture-retentive acid or
neutral peaty soil, **Habit:** upright vigorous grower, **Propagation:** take cuttings of
half-ripe side shoots 8–10 cm (3–4 in) long
in early – late summer.
☐ Possibly the most beautiful camellia,
and certainly among the most popular.

Camellia × *williamsii* 'Golden Spangles'
Theaceae
ZONES 7–10   SHRUB
Height: 1.8–3 m (6–10 ft), **Flowers:**
small, bright-pink, single, late autumn –
mid-spring, **Foliage:** dark green with a
central golden blotch, **Position:** sun or
leafy, partial shade, **Soil:** moisture-retentive acid or neutral peaty soil, **Habit:**
erect, **Propagation:** take cuttings of half-
ripe side shoots 8–10 cm (3–4 in) long in
early – late summer.

Right: *Camellia* × *williamsii* 'Golden
Spangles'

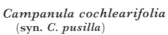

Campanula carpatica
Campanulaceae Bellflower
ZONES 5–9   ROCK PLANT
Height: 23–30 cm (9–12 in), **Flowers:**
shades of blue, but can be white, mid – late
summer, **Foliage:** green, deciduous, **Position:** semi-shade or full sun, **Soil:** well-
drained, fertile, **Habit:** forms a compact
clump, **Propagation:** sow seeds in mid-
autumn or early – mid-spring under glass;
or by cuttings of young basal shoots taken
in mid – late spring, inserted in sand and
peat in a garden frame.
☐ Suitable for rock garden, front of border
or paving.

Campanula cochlearifolia (syn. *C. pusilla*)
Campanulaceae Bellflower
ZONES 4–9   ROCK PLANT
Height: 10–15 cm (4–6 in), **Flowers:**
blue, bell-shaped on thin stems, mid-
summer – early autumn, **Foliage:**
medium green, rounded, deciduous; **Position:** full sun or semi-shade, **Soil:** well
drained, fertile, **Habit:** a tufted plant,
Propagation: by seed sown in sandy
compost in a garden frame or greenhouse,
or by division in autumn or spring.
☐ 'Alba' (above) is pure white. Suitable
for rock garden, front of border or paving.

Campanula garganica
Campanulaceae Bellflower
ZONES 4–9   ROCK PLANT
Height: 12–15 cm (5–6 in), **Flowers:**
blue, starry, profuse, in 15 cm (6 in) long
sprays, mid-summer – early autumn, **Foliage:** medium green, kidney-shaped, deciduous, **Position:** full sun or semi-shade,
Soil: well-drained, fertile, **Habit:** this
perennial forms a neatly rounded clump,
Propagation: by seed sown in sandy
compost in a garden frame or greenhouse;
or by division in autumn or spring.

Above left: *Campanula lactiflora*
Above centre: *Campanula lactiflora* 'Alba'
Above right: *Campanula persicifolia*
Right: *Campanula poscharskyana*

Campanula glomerata 'Superba'
Campanulaceae Bellflower
ZONES 5–10   HERBACEOUS PERENNIAL
Height: 60 cm (2 ft), **Flowers:** bell-shaped, purple, carried on upright stems, late spring – mid-autumn, **Foliage:** medium green, deciduous, **Position:** full sun or semi-shade, **Soil:** well-drained, fertile, **Habit:** upright, clump-forming perennial, **Propagation:** divide roots in autumn or spring, or sow seed in autumn or spring.
☐An excellent border plant, associating well with yellow achilleas.

Campanula lactiflora
Campanulaceae Bellflower
ZONES 5–10   HERBACEOUS PERENNIAL
Height: 1.2 m (4 ft), **Flowers:** blue, early – mid-summer, **Foliage:** pale green, deciduous, **Position:** full sun or semi-shade, **Soil:** well-drained, fertile, **Habit:** tall and erect, clump-forming, needs some support, **Propagation:** by division in autumn or spring.
☐'Loddon Anna' is an excellent cultivar with pinky flowers. 'Alba' has white flowers. 'Brantwood' is a good violet-purple. This campanula looks lovely planted with yellow achilleas.

Campanula lactiflora 'Pouffe'
Campanulaceae Bellflower
ZONES 6–10   HERBACEOUS PERENNIAL
Height: 30 cm (1 ft), **Flowers:** violet-blue, early – late summer, **Foliage:** green, deciduous, **Position:** full sun or semi-shade, **Soil:** tolerates most soils, **Habit:** low-growing and compact, clump-forming perennial, **Propagation:** divide in autumn or spring.
☐Plant in groups for best effect. Suitable for the front of a border.

Campanula persicifolia
Campanulaceae Peach-leaved bellflower
ZONES 4–10   HERBACEOUS PERENNIAL
Height: 60 cm–1 m (2–3 ft), **Flowers:** blue shades (sometimes white), cup-shaped, early – late summer, **Foliage:** medium green, rosettes, evergreen, **Position:** full sun or semi-shade, **Soil:** humus-rich, **Habit:** rigid stems, **Propagation:** by seed sown in seed compost in a garden frame or greenhouse; or by division, autumn or spring. Not true to type from seed.
☐The most popular campanula for border planting.

Campanula poscharskyana
Campanulaceae Bellflower
ZONES 4–9   ROCK PLANT
Height: 25 cm (10 in), **Flowers:** blue, starry flowers in long sprays, early summer – late autumn, **Foliage:** medium green, rounded, deciduous, **Position:** full sun, **Soil:** tolerates most soils, **Habit:** spreading and excessively vigorous, **Propagation:** by seed sown in spring or autumn in seed compost in a garden frame or greenhouse; or by division in autumn or spring.
☐A good ground cover plant.

Campsis radicans

Bignoniaceae Trumpet vine, trumpet creeper

ZONES 8–10 CLIMBER

Height: about 10 m (33 ft), **Flowers:** orange-scarlet, tubular, late summer and early autumn, **Foliage:** green, pinnate, formed of seven to nine leaflets, deciduous, **Position:** sheltered wall in full sun, **Soil:** any fertile soil, **Habit:** eventually climbing by aerial roots, but requires some tying initially, **Propagation:** cuttings, summer, in propagator; or layering.

☐*Campis grandiflora* has larger flowers but is not so hardy.

Campsis × tagliabuana 'Madame Galen'

Bignoniaceae Trumpet vine, trumpet creeper

ZONES 8–10 CLIMBER

Height: about 8 m (26 ft), **Flowers:** reddish salmon, tubular, **Foliage:** green, pinnate, with seven to nine leaflets, deciduous, **Position:** sheltered wall in full sun, **Soil:** any fertile soil, **Habit:** eventually self-clinging, but initially requires training, **Propagation:** cuttings of ripening shoots, summer, in propagator; or layering.

☐Cut back last year's shoots in late winter.

Carpenteria californica

Philadelphaceae

ZONES 9–10 SHRUB

Height: 3 m (10 ft), **Flowers:** large shining white, fragrant, early – mid-summer, **Foliage:** green, evergreen, **Position:** plenty of sun, shield from cold winds, **Soil:** tolerates most soils, **Habit:** bushy, **Propagation:** seed sown in early – mid-spring.

☐Pruning is unnecessary but untidy growth can be cut back when flowering is over. Good wall plant.

Caryopteris × clandonensis

Verbenaceae

ZONES 5–10 SHRUB

Height: 1 to 1.2 m (3–4 ft), **Flowers:** blue, early – mid-autumn, **Foliage:** green, deciduous, **Position:** best in full sun, **Soil:** well-drained, including chalk, **Habit:** bushy, **Propagation:** cuttings in late summer.

☐Prune back in early spring. This delightful shrub is attractive to bees.

Good as ground cover around autumn-colouring shrubs.

Cassiope 'Edinburgh'

Ericaceae

ZONES 6–10 SHRUB

Height: 18 cm (8 in), **Flower:** white, bell-like, red edge, mid – late spring, **Foliage:** green, evergreen, **Position:** light shade, open as possible, as it is a plant native to moorland, **Soil:** moist, acid, peaty, **Habit:** dwarf plant with thin deep green stems, **Propagation:** layers or cuttings in late summer.

☐Generally trouble-free and needs no pruning. Ideal subject for a peat garden, with dwarf rhododendrons, etc.

Catananche caerulea 'Major'

Compositae Cupid's dart

ZONES 6–10 HERBACEOUS PERENNIAL

Height: 60 cm (2 ft), **Flowers:** blue, daisy-like, early summer – early autumn, **Foliage:** green, deciduous, **Position:** sunny, **Soil:** tolerates almost any soil, even one that is sandy and dry, **Habit:** short-lived perennial, **Propagation:** by root cuttings in early spring inserted in seed compost in a garden frame. Seeds can be sown in mid – late spring but will not come true to type.

☐Suitable for the front of a border; good for cutting and drying.

Top: *Ceanothus* 'A.T. Johnson'
Above: *Ceanothus impressus*
Right: *Ceanothus thyrsiflorus* var. *repens*

Ceanothus 'A.T. Johnson'
Rhamnaceae   Californian lilac
ZONES 7–10   SHRUB
Height: 1.8–3 m (6–10 ft), **Flowers:** blue, summer and early autumn, **Foliage:** green, evergreen, **Position:** open, sunny in mild areas, but wall protection elsewhere, **Soil:** light, in good condition, well drained, **Habit:** branching, **Propagation:** cuttings of ripening side shoots in mid – late summer.
☐No regular pruning. Good companion plants on walls are climbing roses.

Other *Ceanothus* hybrids

All ceanothus make ideal wall shrubs with initial training.
EVERGREEN
'*Autumnal Blue*' – light blue flowers from late summer through autumn; branching. ZONES 7–10.
'*Burkwoodii*' – intense blue flowers mid – late summer and mid-autumn; branching. ZONES 7–10.
'*Delight*' – intense blue flowers from late spring to early summer; hardy and bushy, requiring no regular pruning. ZONES 7–10.
'*Southmead*' – intense blue flowers in late spring and early summer; small leaves, dense and bushy habit. ZONES 7–10.

DECIDUOUS
'*Gloire de Versailles*' – pale blue scented flowers, early summer to mid autumn; strong growing, open habit, cut back hard in mid-spring by reducing last year's growth to about 10 cm (4 in) above old wood. ZONES 5–10.
'*Topaz*' – bright blue flowers, early summer to mid autumn; rounded and bushy; prune as above. ZONES 7–10.

Ceanothus impressus
Rhamnaceae   Californian lilac
ZONES 7–10   SHRUB
Height: 3 m (10 ft), **Flowers:** dark blue, prolific, mid – late spring, **Foliage:** small, dark green, shiny, evergreen, **Position:** sun, sheltered by a sunny wall, **Soil:** light and well drained, **Habit:** bushy, **Propagation:** by cuttings 10 cm (4 in) long of ripening side shoots, preferably with a heel, taken in mid-summer.
☐No regular pruning needed. A good wall shrub. Climbing or rambler roses make attractive companions.

Ceanothus thyrsiflorus
   var. *repens*
Rhamnaceae   Californian lilac
ZONES 7–10   SHRUB
Height: 1.2 m (4 ft), **Flowers:** small, pale blue, late spring – early summer, **Foliage:** deep green and glossy, evergreen, **Position:** sun, **Soil:** light, well drained, **Habit:** low, spreading, **Propagation:** by cuttings of ripening side shoots preferably with a heel, taken in mid-summer.
☐No regular pruning is needed. Makes good ground cover for a largish area: can be used for clothing steep banks.

Cedrus atlantica 'Aurea'
Pinaceae Atlas cedar

ZONES 7–10   CONIFER

Height: about 2.5 m (8 ft) after 10 years, ultimately 5 m (16 ft), **Cones:** large brown, barrel-shaped on mature trees only, **Foliage:** rich yellow, evergreen, **Position:** sunny and open, **Soil:** well-drained, **Habit:** slow-growing and not very vigorous, initially conical, but flat topped with age, **Propagation:** by grafting.
☐ An attractive specimen tree for a lawn. Looks good with 'blue' conifers.

Cedrus atlantica var. glauca
Pinaceae Atlas cedar

ZONES 6–10   CONIFER

Height: about 4 m (13 ft) after 10 years, ultimately 30 m (100 ft), **Cones:** large, bluish, barrel-shaped, on mature trees only, **Foliage:** bluish-green or grey-green, evergreen, **Position:** sunny and open, suitable for seaside planting, **Soil:** suits most well-drained soils, **Habit:** loosely conical, **Propagation:** seed: select the bluest seedlings. Also by grafting.
☐ 'Glauca Pendula' is smaller with weeping branches down to ground. Makes a fine lawn specimen in large gardens.

Right: Cones of *Cedrus atlantica*

Cedrus deodara
Pinaceae Deodar

ZONES 6–10   CONIFER

Height: about 5 m (16 ft) after 10 years, ultimately 30 m (100 ft) or more, **Cones:** light brown, about 10 cm (4 in) long, on old trees only, **Foliage:** blue-green when young, changing to deep green, evergreen, **Position:** sunny and open, **Soil:** well-drained, **Habit:** drooping branches and wide spreading, **Propagation:** seed.
☐ Unsuitable for the smaller garden. 'Aurea' only grows to half the height of the species and has golden foliage in spring, turning green by autumn.

Cedrus libani
Pinaceae Cedar of Lebanon

ZONES 6–10   CONIFER

Height: about 2.5 m (8 ft) after 10 years, ultimately 30 m (100 ft) or more, **Cones:** light brown, barrel-shaped, on old trees only, **Foliage:** bright or deep green, evergreen, **Position:** sunny and open, **Soil:** well-drained, **Habit:** slow-growing, young specimens cone-shaped, older ones flat-topped, **Propagation:** best raised from seeds.
☐ Only suitable for very large gardens. 'Nana' is dwarf, forming a dense conical bush 1 m (3 ft) high, but eventually taller.

Celastrus orbiculatus
Celastraceae Bittersweet

ZONES 3–9   CLIMBER

Height: up to 12 m (40 ft), **Flowers:** insignificant, mid-summer, followed by very attractive, sparkling scarlet and gold fruits surrounded by yellow calyces, **Foliage:** green, turning yellow in autumn, deciduous, **Position:** sun or partial shade, **Soil:** suits most soils, **Habit:** shrubby twiner, **Propagation:** by layering of young shoots. Or by semi-ripe cuttings in summer, or hardwood cuttings in autumn.
☐ Train to grow through the branches of a mature tree or to cover an old stump.

Centaurea montana

Compositae   Perennial cornflower
ZONES 3–9   HERBACEOUS PERENNIAL
Height: 45–60 cm (1½–2 ft), **Flowers:** blue, freely produced, late spring – late summer, **Foliage:** green, with white hairs, lanceolate, deciduous, **Position:** sun or partial shade, **Soil:** rich, well-drained, **Habit:** floppy growth, clump-forming perennial, spreads rapidly in good conditions, **Propagation:** by division of clumps mid-autumn – early spring.
☐ Cut back stems after flowering to encourage possible further flowering in autumn.
A useful front-of-the-border plant.

Centranthus ruber

Valerianaceae   Red valerian
ZONES 6–10   HERBACEOUS PERENNIAL
Height: 60 cm–1 m (2–3 ft), **Flowers:** deep pink, in clusters on upright stems, early summer – early autumn, **Foliage:** blue-green, oval, deciduous, **Position:** sunny, **Soil:** dry, poor and chalky are all acceptable, **Habit:** short-lived perennial, informal, self-seeding, **Propagation:** sow seeds in the open ground during spring.
☐ Dead stems should be cut down mid-autumn onwards. Ideal perennial for those difficult hot dry spots.

Cephalotaxus harringtonia var. drupacea

Taxaceae   Cow's tail pine, Japanese plum yew
ZONES 5–9   CONIFER
Height: about 1 m (3 ft) after 10 years, ultimately 2.5 m (8 ft), **Flowers:** insignificant, but ovoid green fruits 2–3 cm (about 1 in) long are produced, **Foliage:** yew-like but longer and with two silvery bands beneath, evergreen, **Position:** very tolerant, grows well in shade, **Soil:** tolerates most soils, including chalk, **Habit:** similar to a large-leaved yew, dense and compact, **Propagation:** by seeds.
☐ Useful for shaded areas and chalk soils.

Cerastium biebersteinii

Caryophyllaceae   Snow in summer
ZONES 4–10   ROCK PLANT
Height: 10–15 cm (4–6 in), **Flowers:** white in profusion, late spring – early summer, **Foliage:** silvery and woolly, evergreen, **Position:** sunny, **Soil:** well drained, **Habit:** very invasive, **Propagation:** by seeds sown in spring, or by division in early – mid-spring.
☐ Good for covering banks.

Ceratostigma plumbaginoides

Plumbaginaceae   Hardy plumbago
ZONES 8–10   SHRUB
Height: 30 cm (1 ft), **Flowers:** blue, mid-summer – late autumn, **Foliage:** green, deciduous, colouring red in autumn, **Position:** preferably full sun, **Soil:** dry, well-drained, **Habit:** wider than high, spreading sub-shrub, **Propagation:** cuttings of ripening side shoots in mid-summer.
☐ Makes good ground cover among larger shrubs but not suitable for colder districts.

Ceratostigma willmottianum

Plumbaginaceaea   Hardy plumbago
ZONES 8–10   SHRUB
Height: 1–1.2 m (3–4 ft), **Flowers:** blue, mid-summer – mid-autumn, **Foliage:** green, deciduous, red-tinted in autumn, **Position:** preferably full sun, **Soil:** dry, well drained, **Habit:** bushy sub-shrub, **Propagation:** cuttings of ripening side shoots in mid-summer.
☐ Suitable for sheltered shrubberies or herbaceous borders. Michaelmas daisies make good companion plants.

Chaenomeles japonica

Rosaceae Maule's quince, Japanese quince

ZONES 4–9   SHRUB

Height: 2.5 m (8 ft), **Flowers:** bright orange-red, early – mid-spring, **Foliage:** green, deciduous, **Position:** sun or shade, **Soil:** tolerates most soils, **Habit:** wide spreading, **Propagation:** heeled cuttings of side shoots in mid – late summer.

☐ Edible fruits are produced that can be used in preserves. Can be trained against a wall, when plants should be pruned after flowering by cutting back last year's shoots.

Chaenomeles × *speciosa*

Rosaceae Japonica

ZONES 4–9   SHRUB

Height: 1.8 m (6 ft), **Flowers:** mostly shades of red, late winter – mid-spring, **Foliage:** green, deciduous, **Position:** open, or trained against shady or sunny walls, **Soil:** tolerates most soils, **Habit:** much branched and spreading, **Propagation:** heeled cuttings of side shoots in mid – late summer; or layer stems in early autumn. Ripe seeds can be sown in early – mid-autumn.

☐ 'Nivalis' has large white flowers, 'Rosea Plena', double pink and 'Simonii', bright red. Pruning as for *C. japonica*. Fragrant yellow fruits produced in autumn. Ideal for training against a wall.

Chaenomeles × *superba*

Rosaceae Ornamental quince

ZONES 4–9   SHRUB

Height: 1.8 m (6 ft), **Flowers:** mostly shades of red and orange, late winter – mid-spring, **Foliage:** green, deciduous, **Position:** sun or shade, good for wall training of any aspect, **Soil:** suits most soils, **Habit:** wide spreading with dense foliage, **Propagation:** heeled cuttings, 10 cm (4 in) long, of side shoots in mid – late summer.

☐ Impressive golden apple-like fruits are produced in late summer. These are edible but not tasty unless used for jams or jellies. 'Boule de Feu' has orange flowers, 'Crimson and Gold' rich crimson with yellow anthers, 'Pink Lady', pink. All are suitable for training against a wall.

Chamaecyparis lawsoniana

Cupressaceae Lawson cypress

ZONES 5–9   CONIFER

Height: about 3 m (10 ft) after 10 years, ultimately 30 m (100 ft), **Cones:** small and scaly in profusion but not specially attractive, **Foliage:** mid to dark green, evergreen, **Position:** sun or partial shade, **Soil:** tolerates most soils, **Habit:** cone shaped, **Propagation:** by seeds or cuttings taken with a heel (see p. 70).

☐ A good hedging plant. Never cut into old wood when trimming. There are many cultivars available and most are used as specimen plants in lawns, or the dwarf cultivars can be grown in heather beds or on rock gardens.

Left: *Chamaecyparis lawsoniana* 'Lutea' (back) and *C. l.* 'Blue Nantais' (front).

Recommended cultivars of *Chamaecyparis lawsoniana*

Heights given are approximate, after 10 to 15 year's growth. Many of the taller growing cultivars will eventually reach well over 6 m (20 ft).

'*Albovariegata*' – 1.2–4.5 m (4–15 ft); foliage tipped with creamy white; dense, rounded bush. ZONES 6–9.

'*Allumii*' – 1.8–4.5 m (6–15 ft); pinkish or red male strobili in spring; soft bluish-grey foliage; columnar. ZONES 5–9.

'*Blue Nantais*' – 1.5–2.2 m (5–7 ft); red male strobili in spring; blue-green foliage, bluish white beneath; broadly conical. ZONES 5–9.

'*Chilworth Silver*' – 1.2–3 m (4–10 ft); silvery blue young foliage; densely columnar. ZONES 6–9.

'*Columnaris Aurea*' – 1.5–2.2 m (5–7 ft); pinkish to red male strobili in spring; greeny yellow foliage, brighter in full sun; broadly columnar. ZONES 6–9.

'*Columnaris Glauca*' – 1.8–4.5 m (6–15 ft); pinkish to red male strobili in spring; blue-grey foliage; forms a narrow pointed tipped pillar. ZONES 6–9.

'*Ellwoodii*' – 1.5–3 m (5–10 ft); dark grey-green foliage, turning bluish in winter; dense feathery sprays form a slow-growing column. ZONES 5–9.

'*Ellwood's Gold*' – 1.2–4.5 m (4–15 ft); yellow-tinted foliage; ZONES 6–9.

'*Ellwood's Pillar*' – 1.5–4.5 m (5–15 ft); grey-green foliage, bluish in winter; slow-growing column. ZONES 5–9.

'*Ellwood's White*' – 1.5–4.5 m (5–15 ft); dark grey-green foliage, some white tipped; slow growing column. ZONES 6–9.

'*Erecta Aurea*' – 1.8–2.5 m (6–8 ft); golden green foliage, tends to scorch in hot sun; dense and very erect. ZONES 6–9.

'*Erecta Viridis*' – 1.8–2.5 m (6–8 ft); bright shiny dark green foliage; compact, dense, very erect and pointed; can suffer damage in snow. ZONES 6–9.

'*Filiformis Compacta*' – 60–75 cm (2–2½ ft); dark green foliage on drooping thread-like branchlets; rounded bush. ZONES 5–9.

'*Fletcheri*' – 1.8–2.5 m (6–8 ft); pinkish to red male strobili; greyish-green foliage; several main stems. ZONES 5–9.

'*Gimbornii*' – 30–75 cm (1–2½ ft); blue-green leaves; slow growing, dwarf rounded bush. ZONES 5–9.

'*Green Pillar*' – 1.5–4.5 m (5–15 ft); pinkish to red male strobili; bright green foliage; dense compact and very erect similar to 'Erecta Viridis' but hardier. ZONES 5–9.

'*Lanei*' – 1.8–2.2 m (6–7 ft); golden-green foliage with bright gold tips; loosely conical. ZONES 6–9.

'*Lutea*' – 1.8–2.2 m (6–7 ft); pinkish to red male strobili; gold-tipped foliage, colours better in sunny position; broadly columnar. ZONES 6–9.

'*Maas*' – 2.5–3 m (8–10 ft), pinkish to red male strobili; yellowish-green foliage; broad cone. ZONES 5–9.

'*Minima Aurea*' – 25–75 cm (10–30 in); dense, brilliant yellow foliage; slow-growing, pyramid shape. Outstanding for a small garden, rock garden or heather bed. ZONES 6–9.

'*Minima Glauca*' – 30–75 cm (12–30 in); grey-green; slow grower; compact dome-shaped bush. ZONES 5–9.

'*Nana*' – 45–75 cm (1½–2½ ft); bright grey-green; broadly conical, similar to 'Minima Glauca'. ZONES 6–9.

'*Nana Albospica*' – 45–75 cm (1½–2½ ft); green foliage with white tips gives an overall appearance of a cream coloured bush; broadly conical; protect from cold winds. ZONES 7–9.

'*Pembury Blue*' – 1.8–6 m (6–20 ft) pinkish to red male strobili; rich blue foliage; conical. ZONES 6–9.

'*Pottenii*' – 1.8–4.5 m (6–15 ft); pinkish to red male strobili; pale green, soft feathery foliage; protect from cold winter winds; very bushy. ZONES 6–9.

'*Pygmaea Argentea*' – 20–60 cm (8–24 in); pinkish red male strobili; blue-green leaves tipped white; slow growing, round and bushy. ZONES 6–9.

Top left: *Chamaecyparis lawsoniana* 'Minima Aurea'.
Top right: *C. l.* 'Lanei'. **Above left:** *C. l.* 'Pembury Blue'. **Above right:** *C. l.* 'Ellwoodii'

'*Spek*' – 1.8–2.5 m (6–8 ft); male strobili pinkish to red; foliage deeper blue than 'Pembury Blue'; conical. ZONES 6–9.

'*Stewartii*' – 2.5–4 m (8–13 ft); pinkish to red male strobili; rich gold foliage turning yellowish-green in winter, best colour in a sunny position; conical, upright with narrow sprays. ZONES 6–9.

'*Tamariscifolia*' – 1–1.5 m (3–5 ft), pinkish to red male strobili; bright grey green foliage; spreading, semi-prostrate when young, mushroom-shaped when more mature. Slow growing. Associates well with golden-foliage conifers. ZONES 5–9

'*Westermanni*' – 2.5–3 m (8–10 ft); foliage light yellow held in pendulous sprays when young, turning green with age; loosely conical. ZONES 5–9.

'*Winston Churchill*' – 1.5–1.8 m (5–6 ft); pinkish to red male strobili; deep gold foliage throughout the year; broadly conical. ZONES 6–9.

'*Wisselii*' – 2.5–3 m (8–10 ft); profusion of red male strobili in spring; foliage blue-green; upright and distinctive. ZONES 5–9.

Chamaecyparis nootkatensis 'Compacta'

Cupressaceae Nootka Cypress
ZONES 4–9 CONIFER
Height: 75 cm–1 m (2½–3 ft) after 10 years, ultimately 3 m (10 ft), **Flowers:** yellow male strobili in spring, **Foliage:** matt green, evergreen, **Position:** sun or partial shade, **Soil:** humus-rich, **Habit:** bushy, conical, **Propagation:** by cuttings (see p. 70).
□Useful for the heather garden. 'Lutea' ('Aurea') is conical with golden yellow foliage. Best in full sun.

Chamaecyparis nootkatensis 'Pendula'

Cupressaceae Nootka cypress
ZONES 4–9 CONIFER
Height: about 3 m (10 ft) after 10 years, ultimately 24 m (80 ft), **Flowers:** yellow male strobili in spring, dull blue cones, **Foliage:** matt green, rough feeling, evergreen, **Position:** sun or partial shade, **Soil:** humus-rich, **Habit:** pendulous, cone shaped, **Propagation:** by cuttings (see p. 70).
□Train leading shoot vertically. Good as a lawn specimen.

Chamaecyparis obtusa 'Crippsii'

Cupressaceae
ZONES 5–9 CONIFER
Height: about 1.8 m (6 ft) after 10 years, ultimately 7.5 m (25 ft), **Flowers and cones:** insignificant, **Foliage:** deep yellow, evergreen, **Position:** sun or partial shade, best in an open, sunny position, **Soil:** suits most humus-rich soils, **Habit:** cone-shaped, growth slow, **Propagation:** by cuttings (see p. 70).
□Occasional light pruning to maintain a thickness of growth.
Good as a lawn specimen, especially with 'blue' conifers.

Other recommended cultivars of *Chamaecyparis obtusa* ZONES 5–9

'*Nana*' – about 23 cm (10 in) after 10 years; dark green foliage held in layers of concave, densly packed fans; small flat-topped bush.
'*Nana Gracilis*' – about 60 cm (2 ft) after 10 years; shiny deep green foliage; similar to but larger than 'Nana'.
'*Nana Lutea*' – about 30 cm (1 ft) after 10 years, can reach 75 cm (2½ ft) or more; leaves yellow and white; best in full sun; compact and bushy.
'*Pygmaea*' – about 23 cm (10 in) but can reach 75 cm (2½ ft) or more; leaves green, bronze-flushed in winter; slow growing, globular bush.

Chamaecyparis pisifera 'Boulevard'

Cupressaceae
ZONES 5–9 CONIFER
Height: about 1 m (3 ft) after 10 years, ultimately 2.5 m (8 ft), **Flowers and cones:** insignificant, **Foliage:** silver blue, evergreen, **Position:** sun or partial shade, best colour in partial shade, **Soil:** moisture-retentive but well-drained, preferably lime-free, **Habit:** dense and conical, **Propagation:** by cuttings (see p. 70).
□Excellent conifer for heather gardens.

Other recommended cultivars of *Chaemaecyparis pisifera*

Sawara cypress
'*Filifera Aurea*' – 1.2–3 m (4–10 ft); bright yellow, cord-like foliage; slow growing, rounded bush. ZONES 5–9.
'*Filifera Nana*' – about 1.3 m (4½ ft) or more; green foliage on long cord-like branchlets; rounded bush. ZONES 5–9.
'*Plumosa Aurea*' – 1–3 m (3–10 ft) or more; soft feathery foliage, yellow in summer, but it becomes more green in winter; slow growing, broadly conical. ZONES 5–9.

Top left: *Chamaecyparis obtusa* 'Pygmaea'
Top right: *Chamaecyparis obtusa* 'Nana'
Left: *Chamaecyparis pisifera* 'Filifera Aurea'

'Plumosa Aurea Nana' – 45–75 cm (1½–2½ ft); similar to 'Plumosa Aurea' but slower growing and more compact. ZONES 6–9.

'Plumosa Rogersii' – 30–75 cm (1–2½ ft); rich yellow foliage in full sun, dulls in winter; rounded compact cone; protect from cold winds. ZONES 6–9.

'Pygmaea' – 30–75 cm (1–2½ ft); fine, dense green young foliage; slow-growing compact cone. ZONES 5–9.

'Squarrosa Sulphurea' – 1–1.5 m (3–5 ft); foliage sulphur-yellow in full sun, turns pale bluish green in winter; feathery appearance, broadly conical. ZONES 5–9.

Chamaecyparis thyoides
'Andelyensis'
Cupressaceae White cypress
ZONES 5–9 CONIFER
Height: 75 cm–1 m (2½–3 ft) after 8 years, ultimately 5 m (16 ft), **Cones:** small with a bloom, **Foliage:** bluish green, bronze tinged in winter, evergreen, **Position:** sun or partial shade, **Soil:** best in moist, humus-rich, lime-free soils, **Habit:** slow-growing, pillar-shaped, **Propagation:** by cuttings (see p. 70).
☐Useful for the heather garden.

Chamaecyparis thyoides
'Ericoides'
Cupressaceae White cypress
ZONES 5–9 CONIFER
Height: about 60 cm (2 ft) after 10 years, ultimately 1.5 m (5 ft), **Flowers and cones:** insignificant, **Foliage:** dark bronze green in summer, purplish in winter, evergreen, soft feeling, **Position:** sun and shelter from winds and frosts, **Soil:** best on moist, humus-rich, lime-free soils, **Habit:** compact and conical, **Propagation:** by cuttings (see p. 70).
☐Excellent conifer for heather gardens.

Chamaedaphne calyculata 'Nana'
Ericaceae Leather leaf
ZONES 6–9 SHRUB
Height: 30 cm (1 ft), **Flowers:** white, pendulous, mid – late spring, **Foliage:** green, evergreen, **Position:** open, sunny, **Soil:** lime-free, humus-rich, **Habit:** small, dense, wiry shrub with horizontal branches, **Propagation:** by seed or cuttings.
☐A good shrub to associate with heathers and Japanese azaleas, which like the same conditions. Not always easy to obtain.

Chimonanthus praecox
(syn. *C. fragrans*)
Calycanthaceae Winter sweet
ZONES 5–9 SHRUB
Height: 3 m (10 ft), **Flowers:** pale yellow marked purple at centre, not showy but very fragrant, winter, **Foliage:** green, deciduous, **Position:** sunny and sheltered, **Soil:** deep, rich and well-drained, will succeed on chalk, **Habit:** bushy, of dense growth, **Propagation:** ripe seeds sown in early – mid-autumn; or layer stems in early autumn.
☐Can be wall-trained. Prune wall-trained shrubs in early spring; cut flowered shoots to within 10 cm (4 in) of their base.

A lovely shrub to have near the house where its scent can be easily savoured. Plant winter heathers around it.

Left: *Chimonanthus praecox*

Chionanthus virginicus

Oleaceae Fringe tree

ZONES 4–10   SHRUB

Height: 5 m (16 ft) or more, **Flowers:** white, in profusion in early – mid-summer, slight scent, **Foliage:** green, deciduous, **Position:** full sun, preferably protected by south- or west-facing wall, **Soil:** fertile loamy soil, **Habit:** erect, **Propagation:** cuttings of firm young wood in late summer or autumn.

☐ Unusual but easy subject for the shrub border.

Choisya ternata

Rutaceae   Mexican orange blossom

ZONES 7–9   SHRUB

Height: 3 m (10 ft), **Flowers:** white, scented, mid-spring, then at intervals until late autumn, **Foliage:** green, shiny, evergreen, aromatic, **Position:** plants for sun, or semi-shade, **Soil:** well-drained, lime tolerant, **Habit:** forms a rounded bush, **Propagation:** cuttings of semi-ripe side shoots in late summer.

☐ An excellent shrub for seaside gardens.

  In cold areas it is best grown against a warm south- or west-facing wall.

Choisya ternata 'Sundance'

Rutaceae

ZONES 7–9   SHRUB

Height: 1.2–1.5 m (4–5 ft), **Flowers:** white, scented, mid-spring, then at intervals 'till late autumn, **Foliage:** bright yellow young foliage, holding colour throughout the year, **Position:** sunny and sheltered, **Soil:** well-drained, lime-tolerant, **Habit:** forms a rounded bush, **Propagation:** cuttings of semi-ripe side shoots in late summer.

☐ This recent development is a winner. Smaller growing than the species and complementary to most other shrubs.

Chrysanthemum maximum 'Wirral Supreme'

Compositae   Shasta daisy

ZONES 5–10   HERBACEOUS PERENNIAL

Height: 1 m (3 ft); **Flowers:** white, double, early – late summer, **Foliage:** green, longish with toothed edges, deciduous, **Position:** sunny, **Soil:** good drainage, fairly rich, ideally alkaline, **Habit:** erect-stemmed perennial, **Propagation:** cuttings of basal shoots in early spring in a garden frame; or by division of clumps in early spring.

☐ Good cut flower. Grow with spire-like perennials, such as delphiniums.

Left: *Chrysanthemum maximum* 'Wirral Supreme'

Chrysanthemum rubellum 'Clara Curtis'

Compositae

ZONES 7–10　　HERBACEOUS PERENNIAL
Height: 45–75 cm (1½–2½ ft), **Flowers:** rose-pink daisies, fragrant, mid-summer – mid-autumn, **Foliage:** medium-green, **Position:** sunny, **Soil:** good drainage, fairly rich, ideally alkaline, **Habit:** bushy and free-flowering perennial, **Propagation:** basal cuttings in early spring in a garden frame; or division in spring.
☐ Good cut flower.

Cimicifuga foetida 'White Pearl'

Ranunculaceae　Bugbane

ZONES 4–9　　HERBACEOUS PERENNIAL
Height: 1.2 m (4 ft), **Flowers:** white racemes, early – mid-autumn, **Foliage:** green and deciduous, **Position:** preferably partial shade but tolerates sun, **Soil:** moist, humus-rich, **Habit:** a graceful perennial with erect flower stems, **Propagation:** by division of clumps mid-autumn – early spring.
☐ Particularly recommended for the shrub border or woodland garden.

Cistus × *aguilari* 'Maculatus'

Cistaceae　Sun rose

ZONES 8–10　　　　　　　　SHRUB
Height: 1.2–1.5 m (4–5 ft), **Flowers:** large white with deep purple basal blotches, early – mid-summer, **Foliage:** pale green, evergreen, **Position:** full sun essential, **Soil:** well-drained, poor, **Habit:** erect bush, **Propagation:** heeled cuttings 10 cm (4 in) long of semi-ripe side shoots in mid – late summer.
☐ Good for mild coastal gardens.

Cistus × *corbariensis*

Cistaceae　Sun rose

ZONES 8–10　　　　　　　　SHRUB
Height: 1–1.2 m (3–4 ft), **Flowers:** white, yellow at base, red buds, late spring – early summer, **Foliage:** matt green, evergreen, **Position:** full-sun essential, **Soil:** well drained, poor, **Habit:** forms a low bush, **Propagation:** cuttings of semi-ripe side shoots in mid – late summer.
☐ Hardier than most sun roses, but like all of them is an ideal plant for hot, dry places, and for coastal gardens.

Cistus × *purpureus*

Cistaceae　Sun rose

ZONES 8–10　　　　　　　　SHRUB
Height: 1.2–1.5 m (4–5 ft), **Flowers:** deep purplish pink with chocolate basal blotches, late spring – mid-summer, **Foliage:** greyish green, evergreen, **Position:** full sun essential, **Soil:** well-drained, poor, **Habit:** erect bush, **Propagation:** cuttings of semi-ripe side shoots in mid – late summer.
☐ Ideal for hot dry places and coastal gardens.

Cistus 'Silver Pink'

Cistaceae　Sun rose

ZONES 8–10　　　　　　　　SHRUB
Height: 1 m (3 ft), **Flowers:** pink with a prominent cluster of yellow stamens, early – mid-summer, **Foliage:** green above, grey below, evergreen, **Position:** full sun, **Soil:** well-drained, poor, **Habit:** compact and bushy, **Propagation:** cuttings of semi-ripe, side shoots in mid – late summer.
☐ This hybrid has flowers borne on up-right stems well clear of the leaves. Ideal for hot dry places and coastal gardens.

CLEMATIS

These cause confusion in the matter of pruning. This is because there are basically three groups of clematis, each requiring different treatment, according to their time and habit of flowering.

Group A These flower between winter and spring. Flowers carried directly on the previous season's growth. In this group are included all the *C. montana* cultivars, *C. armandii* and *C. chrysocoma*. These need no regular pruning, but, where space is restricted, all flowering shoots may be removed immediately after flowering, and young shoots will break from lower down the stems. These may then be trained into position to flower the following year.

Group B Flowering in late spring and early summer and in most cases again in autumn. Flowers are produced on short growths from the previous season's wood. In this group are included many of the large-flowered cultivars such as 'Barbara Dibley', 'Nelly Moser', the improved sport, double-flowered 'Vyvyan Pennell' and 'Duchess of Edinburgh'.

In spring, as soon as the buds start to show, all weak and dead wood must be cut out, and strong shoots re-tied into flowering position. In order that bushy growth is established during the formative years, it pays in the long run to cut all growth right down to about 23 cm (9 in) from ground level in the second year after planting.

On a wall where space is restricted, the new strong young shoots may be shortened, but never by more than a third or many early flowers will be lost. If the clematis is growing through trees, then no great amount of pruning is necessary which is a blessing because it could be difficult. Occasional thinning out old and dead wood is all that is required.

Group C Flowering from mid-summer onwards. The flowers carried on terminal shoots or from leaf axils of the summer growth. In this group are included the popular Jackmanii hybrids, many species, and cultivars such as 'Ernest Markham' and 'Hagley Hybrid'.

This group of clematis may be pruned down to about 30 cm (1 ft) of the ground level in spring. On a wall, it is a good idea to train two shoots horizontally at about 30 cm (1 ft) high, one each side of the planting position, to form permanent wood from which flowering stems will grow vertically each year. Every spring thereafter, pruning consists of cutting back all the previous season's flowering stems to just above a pair of plump buds near their bases.

Clematis 'Duchess of Edinburgh'

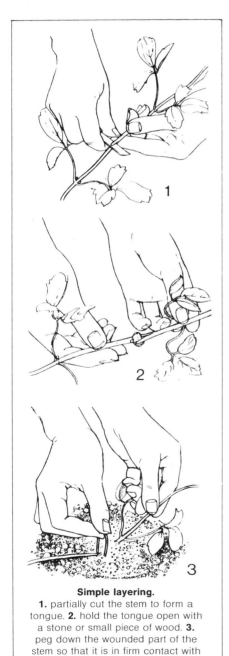

Simple layering.
1. partially cut the stem to form a tongue. **2.** hold the tongue open with a stone or small piece of wood. **3.** peg down the wounded part of the stem so that it is in firm contact with the soil.

Clematis armandii

Ranunculaceae   Virgin's bower
ZONES 8–10   CLIMBER
Height: 5–6 m (16–20 ft), **Flowers:** cream-white, very fragrant, borne in clusters, mid – late spring, **Foliage:** deep green, comprising three shiny leathery deeply veined leaflets, evergreen, **Position:** full sun and shelter, shade its roots, **Soil:** must be fertile, cool, moist, alkaline or neutral, **Habit:** climbs and twines by means of its leaf stalks, but requires some training, **Propagation:** cuttings very difficult, so increase from seeds when available. These can be sown when ripe or in the spring.
□ Prune as for group A (see p. 113).

Clematis cirrhosa

Ranunculaceae   Virgin's bower
ZONES 7–10   CLIMBER
Height: up to 3 m (10 ft), **Flowers:** cream-white, mid-winter – early spring, followed by fluffy seed heads, **Foliage:** green, variable, simple to compound, evergreen, **Position:** sunny and sheltered, shade its roots, **Soil:** cool, moist but well-drained, fertile, alkaline or neutral, **Habit:** climbs and twines but needs initial training, **Propagation:** by cuttings 10–12 cm (4–5 in) long of semi-ripe growth taken in summer and rooted in peat/sand mix in propagator; or by seeds sown in sandy compost in spring.
□ Prune as for group A (see p. 113).

Clematis cirrhosa var. balearica

Ranunculaceae   Fern-leaved clematis
ZONES 7–10   CLIMBER
Height: up to 3.6–4.5 m (12–15 ft), **Flowers:** pale yellow flecked with reddish spots inside, throughout winter, **Foliage:** green, segmented, bronzy-tinted during winter, evergreen, **Position:** sun and shelter, **Soil:** cool, moist but well drained, fertile, alkaline or neutral, **Habit:** climbs and twines but needs initial training, **Propagation:** by cuttings, see *C. cirrhosa* above.
□ Prune as for group A (see p. 113).

Clematis flammula

Ranunculaceae   Virgin's bower
ZONES 5–9   CLIMBER
Height: 3 m (10 ft), **Flowers:** scented, white, late summer – mid-autumn, followed by fluffy seed heads, **Foliage:** bright green, formed of three leaflets, deciduous, **Position:** sunny situation preferred, shade roots, **Soil:** cool, moist but well drained, fertile, alkaline or neutral, **Habit:** vigorous, producing a dense profusion of growth, **Propagation:** by cuttings or seed (see *C. cirrhosa* above).
□ Can prune back last year's growth in spring to restrict size.

Clematis florida 'Sieboldii' (syn. C. florida 'Bicolor')

Ranunculaceae   Virgin's bower
ZONES 5–9   CLIMBER
Height: about 3 m (10 ft), **Flowers:** white with a central ring of purple petal-like stamens, early – mid-summer, **Foliage:** glossy green, compound, comprising nine leaflets, deciduous, **Position:** sunny situation preferred, shade roots, **Soil:** cool, moist but well drained, fertile, alkaline or neutral, **Habit:** self-supporting by its twining leaf stalks, **Propagation:** by cuttings. See *C. cirrhosa* above.
□ Prune as for group A (see p. 113).

Clematis heracleifolia

Ranunculaceae   Herbaceous clematis
ZONES 5–9   HERBACEOUS PERENNIAL
Height: 1–1.2 m (3–4 ft), **Flowers:** light blue, curled back petals, late summer – early autumn, **Foliage:** dark green, trifoliate, deciduous, **Position:** sunny, **Soil:** any moist, but well drained neutral or alkaline soil, **Habit:** a sub-shrub, lax habit, **Propagation:** by basal cuttings in spring in-

Top left: *Clematis armandii*
Top right: *Clematis cirrhosa* var. *balearica*
Above: *Clematis heracleifolia*

serted in sand and peat in a garden frame.
□ Suitable for herbaceous or mixed borders. Cut down stems to 15 cm (6 in) in autumn.

Clematis integrifolia 'Hendersonii'

Ranunculaceae   Herbaceous clematis
ZONES 5–9   HERBACEOUS PERENNIAL
Height: 60 cm (2 ft), **Flowers:** deep blue, 5 cm (2 in) across, early summer – early autumn, **Foliage:** mid-green, prominently veined, deciduous, **Position:** sunny, **Soil:** any alkaline or neutral garden soil, **Habit:** requires support with twiggy sticks, **Propagation:** by basal cuttings taken in mid – late spring and inserted in sandy peaty compost in a garden frame.
□ Suitable for herbaceous or mixed borders. Cut down stems to ground level in autumn.

Clematis × jackmanii

Ranunculaceae   Virgin's bower

ZONES 5–9   CLIMBER

Height: up to 4 m (13 ft), **Flowers:** deep purple, mid-summer – mid-autumn, **Foliage:** green, pinnate and twining, deciduous, **Position:** sun preferred, though more tolerant of some shade than most, shade roots, **Soil:** cool, moist but well drained, fertile, alkaline or neutral, **Habit:** climbs by its twining leaf stalks, **Propagation:** by layering or taking cuttings. See *C. cirrhosa* p. 114.

□ Prune as for group C (see p. 113).

Clematis macropetala

Ranunculaceae

ZONES 5–9   CLIMBER

Height: up to 2.4 m (8 ft), **Flowers:** violet-blue with paler blue; hanging and bell-like; late spring – early summer onwards; fluffy seed heads, **Foliage:** green, attractively divided, deciduous, **Position:** sunny situation preferred, shade roots, **Soil:** cool, moist but well drained, fertile, alkaline or neutral, **Habit:** climbs by its twining leaf stalks, **Propagation:** by seed or cuttings. See *C. cirrhosa* p. 114.

□ 'Maidwell Hall' is a deeper blue cultivar. Prune as for group A (see p. 113).

Clematis macropetala
'Markham's Pink'

Ranunculaceae

ZONES 5–9   CLIMBER

Height: up to 2.4 m (8 ft), **Flowers:** attractive deep-pink, hanging and bell-like; late spring – early summer onwards; seedheads fluffy, **Foliage:** green, prettily divided, deciduous, **Position:** sunny situation preferred, shade roots, **Soil:** cool, moist but well drained, fertile, alkaline or neutral, **Habit:** climbs by its twining leaf stalks, **Propagation:** by layering or cuttings. See *C. cirrhosa* p. 114.

□ Prune as for group A (see p. 113).

Clematis montana

Ranunculaceae   Virgin's bower

ZONES 5–9   CLIMBER

Height: up to 9 m (30 ft), **Flowers:** white, profuse, late spring, **Foliage:** deep green, three leaflets, twining leaf stalks, deciduous, **Position:** sun or partial shade, shade roots, **Soil:** cool, moist but well drained, fertile, alkaline or neutral, **Habit:** vigorous, even rampant, climbs by twining leaf stalks, **Propagation:** by layers or cuttings. See *C. cirrhosa* p. 114.

□ Vigorous and curtain forming, suitable for covering pergolas or verandas. 'Tetrarose' has mauve-pink flowers.

Prune as for group A (see p. 113).

Clematis orientalis

Ranunculaceae   Virgin's bower

ZONES 5–9   CLIMBER

Height: 6 m (20 ft), **Flowers:** yellow, pendulous, fragrant; late summer – mid-autumn; fluffy silvery seedheads, very decorative, **Foliage:** pale green, feathery, deeply cut, deciduous, **Position:** sunny

Top left: *Clematis* × *jackmanii*
Above: *Clematis macropetala*

situation preferred, shade roots, **Soil:** cool, moist but well drained, fertile, alkaline or neutral, **Habit:** strong grower, fairly dense growth, **Propagation:** by cuttings. See *C. cirrhosa* p. 114.

□ Prune as for group C (see p. 113).

Clematis montana var. rubens

Ranunculaceae   Virgin's bower

ZONES 5–9   CLIMBER

Height: 9 m (30 ft), **Flowers:** light pink, profuse, late spring, **Foliage:** flushed with bronze, three leaflets, twining leaf stalks, deciduous, **Position:** sun or partial shade, shade roots, **Soil:** cool, moist but well drained, fertile, alkaline or neutral, **Habit:** vigorous, rampant, climbs by its twining leaf stalks, **Propagation:** by layers of cuttings. See *C. cirrhosa* p. 114.

□ Prune as for group A (see p. 113).

Clematis tangutica

Ranunculaceae   Virgin's bower

ZONES 5–9   CLIMBER

Height: up to 6 m (20 ft), **Flowers:** yellow, lantern-shaped; late summer – mid-autumn; followed by fluffy seed heads, **Foliage:** greyish green, divided, deciduous, **Position:** prefers sunny situation, shade its roots, **Soil:** cool, moist but well drained, fertile, alkaline or neutral, **Habit:** strong grower, but slim in habit, **Propagation:** by cuttings. See *C. cirrhosa* p. 114.

☐ Best when left to run free, either up trees, on fences or over banks.

Prune as for group C (see p. 113).

Clematis viticella 'Abundance'

Ranunculaceae   Virgin's bower

ZONES 5–9   CLIMBER

Height: up to 3.5 m (12 ft), **Flowers:** soft purple, bell-shaped and hanging, mid-summer – early autumn, **Foliage:** deep green, several leaflets, deciduous, **Position:** sun and shelter, shade its roots, **Soil:** cool, moist but well drained, fertile, alkaline or neutral, **Habit:** has a slim habit of growth, **Propagation:** by cuttings. See *C. cirrhosa* p. 114.

Prune as for group C (see p. 113).

Clematis 'Barbara Dibley' (large-flowered hybrid)

Ranunculaceae   Virgin's bower

ZONES 5–9   CLIMBER

Height: up to 4 m (13 ft), **Flowers:** pink with darker bars, single, 15 cm (6 in) across; early summer – mid-autumn, **Foliage:** green, three leaflets, with twining leaf stalks, deciduous, **Position:** prefers sunny situation, **Soil:** cool, moist but well drained, fertile and alkaline, **Habit:** climbing by its twining leaf stalks, **Propagation:** by layers or cuttings. See *C. cirrhosa* p. 114.

☐ Prune as for group B (see p. 113). Many large-flowered hybrids will grow against east- or north-facing walls.

Other recommended large-flowered hybrids

ZONES 5–9

'*Duchess of Edinburgh*' – up to 4 m (13 ft); white, double, scented, late spring – early summer and late summer; prune as for group B (see p. 113).

'*Ernest Markham*' – up to 4 m (13 ft); single red, early summer–early autumn; cut back to 30 cm (12 in) from ground in late winter–early spring; prune as for group C (see p. 113).

'*Hagley Hybrid*' – up to 2.5 m (8 ft); single deep pink, early summer – early-autumn; cut back to 30 cm (1 ft) from ground in late winter – early spring; prune as for group C.

'*Jackmanii Superba*' – up to 3 m (10 ft); large rich purple; mid summer – mid autumn; cut back to 30 cm (12 in) from ground in late winter; prune as for group C.

'*Mrs Cholmondeley*' – up to 3 m (10 ft); large light blue, late spring – late summer; cut back to 30 cm (1 ft) from ground in late winter – early spring; prune as for group B.

'*Nelly Moser*' – up to 4 m (13 ft); pale pinky mauve with deeper bars, late spring – early summer and late summer – early autumn; trim back dead flower head immediately after flowering; prune as for group B.

'*The President*' – up to 4 m (13 ft); large single bluish-purple, early summer – early autumn; trim back old flowering growth immediatly after flowering; prune as for group B.

'*Vyvyan Pennell*' – up to 4 m (13 ft); double violet-blue, late spring – mid-summer; prune back old flowering shoots immediately after flowering; prune as for group B.

'*William Kennett*' – up to 4 m (13 ft); crinkle-edged medium-blue with dark stamens, early – late summer; trim back old flowering growth immediately after flowering; prune as for group B.

Top left: *Clematis tangutica*
Top right: *Clematis* 'Nelly Moser'
Left: *Clematis* 'William Kennett'

Clerodendrum bungei
Verbenaceae
ZONES 6–10   SHRUB
Height: 1.8–2.5 m (6–8 ft), **Flowers:** starry, deep pink, scented, late summer – early autumn, **Foliage:** large, rounded, deep green, deciduous, **Position:** full sun, sheltered from wind, **Soil:** rich, well drained, **Habit:** upright thin stems, produces suckers, **Propagation:** remove rooted suckers in early – mid-autumn or early spring. Heeled cutting 12 cm (5 in) long, of side shoots in late summer or early autumn.
☐ It can be pruned almost to ground level each spring. Can be grown against a warm sunny wall.

Right: *Clerodendrum bungei*

Clerodendrum trichotomum
Verbenaceae
ZONES 5–10   SHRUB
Height: 5 m (16 ft), **Flowers:** white, flushed pink, starry, fragrant, late summer, **Foliage:** medium green, deciduous, unpleasant scent when crushed, **Position:** full sun, sheltered from wind, **Soil:** rich, well drained, **Habit:** large and bushy, **Propagation:** cuttings as for *C. bungei*.
☐ The late flowers are followed by bright blue berries surrounded by very attractive red calyces. An outstanding large shrub for late summer and autumn.

Clethra alnifolia
Clethraceae Sweet pepper bush
ZONES 3–9   SHRUB
Height: 1.8 m (6 ft), **Flowers:** scented, white, bell-shaped, late summer – mid-autumn, **Foliage:** green, deciduous, bright yellow in autumn, **Position:** open, sunny, **Soil:** lime-free loam, moist, high in humus, **Habit:** upright, bushy, **Propagation:** heeled cuttings of side shoots, 10 cm (4 in) long, mid – late summer.
☐ Good for seaside planting.

Clethra barbinervis
Clethraceae
ZONES 5–9   SHRUB
Height: 4 m (13 ft), **Flowers:** white in long racemes, fragrant, mid-summer – early autumn, **Foliage:** green, deciduous, turning red and yellow in autumn, **Position:** sunny and open, **Soil:** lime-free loam, moist, high in humus, **Habit:** wide spreading, **Propagation:** heeled cuttings 10 cm (4 in) long of side shoots, mid – late summer.
☐ Remove some of the oldest stems each winter. A good shrub for seaside planting.

Colutea arborescens
Leguminosae Bladder senna
ZONES 5–10   SHRUB
Height: 2.5 m (8 ft), **Flowers:** yellow, similar to those of the pea, early summer – early autumn, **Foliage:** ferny, pale green, deciduous, **Position:** sun or partial shade, suitable for hot, dry situations, **Soil:** tolerates most soils, **Habit:** bushy but airy habit, **Propagation:** sow seeds outdoors in early spring; or take heeled cuttings of side shoots in early autumn.
□The main attraction of this shrub is its 8 cm (3 in) long inflated light green pods, liberally tinted with red or bronzy-gold. Last year's growth cut back in mid spring.

Convolvulus cneorum
Convolvulaceae
ZONES 9–10   SHRUB
Height: 1 m (3 ft) at most, **Flowers:** creamy-white, buds pink, late spring – early autumn, **Foliage:** long and narrow, covered with shiny silver hairs; evergreen, **Position:** sun and sheltered from wind, **Soil:** tolerates most soils, **Habit:** low bushy habit, **Propagation:** cuttings 8 cm (3 in) long with a heel from basal or side shoots, early – late summer.
□Not completely hardy but certainly deserves a home with those who garden in warmer areas. An attractive shrub for the larger rock garden.

Cordyline australis
Agavaceae Cabbage tree
ZONES 8–10   SHRUB
Height: 4 m (13 ft) as a shrub, **Flowers:** creamy white, scented, mid-summer, **Foliage:** greyish green, sword-like, evergreen, **Position:** full sun, mild districts only, **Soil:** well-drained, moderately rich, **Habit:** single erect trunk until flowering age then erect branching, **Propagation:** remove suckers in early – mid-spring, or sow seeds in mid-spring.
□An exotic addition to the garden, can be grown in a container. Thrives in seaside gardens.

Coreopsis grandiflora
Compositae Tickseed
ZONES 3–9   HERBACEOUS PERENNIAL
Height: 45 cm (1½ft), **Flowers:** rich yellow, daisy-like on long slender stems, early summer – mid-autumn, **Foliage:** green, narrow, deciduous, **Position:** sunny and open, **Soil:** moist but well drained, alkaline, **Habit:** bushy and erect, can be rather short-lived, **Propagation:** by division in autumn or spring; or by seed sown outdoors or under glass in early spring.
□Taller cultivars include 'Badengold', 1 m (3 ft), 'Mayfield Giant', 75 cm (2½ft), and 'Sunburst' 75 cm (2½ ft).

Coreopsis verticillata
Compositae Tickseed
ZONES 3–9   HERBACEOUS PERENNIAL
Height: 45–60 cm (1½–2 ft), **Flowers:** yellow, star-shaped, small but prolific, **Foliage:** green, divided into thin segments, **Position:** sunny and open, **Soil:** alkaline and not too heavy, **Habit:** upright, compact and bushy, **Propagation:** by division in spring; by softwood cuttings taken in mid – late summer; or by seed sown outdoors or under glass in early spring.
□A good cultivar is 'Grandiflora'. Excellent for cutting.

Coriaria japonica
Coriariaceae
ZONES 9–10   SHRUB
Height: 60 cm (2 ft), **Flowers:** green at first, becoming bright red then purplish black, **Foliage:** green, ferny, deciduous, **Position:** warm and sheltered, **Soil:** rich, loamy soil, **Habit:** low-growing, renewing itself by strong shoots from the base, **Propagation:** this is not a long-lived shrub, so should be renewed occasionally from seeds or cuttings.
□Not suitable for cold districts. Red fruits and autumn tints are additional bonuses.

Cornus alba
Cornaceae   Red-stemmed dogwood
ZONES 2–9   SHRUB
Height: 3 m (10 ft), **Flowers:** small, yellowish, late spring – early summer, **Foliage:** green above, grey below, sometimes turning red in autumn, deciduous, **Position:** sun or partial shade, **Soil:** moist, **Habit:** upright and suckering, **Propagation:** 15 cm (6 in) hardwood cuttings in late autumn; or remove and replant suckers in late autumn.
☐ This shrub's main attraction is its thicket of bright red young shoots which come into their own in winter. To maintain these cut hard back in mid-spring. Cultivar 'Sibirica' has brilliant crimson shoots.

Cornus alba 'Elegantissima'
Cornaceae   Dogwood, cornel
ZONES 2–9   SHRUB
Height: 1.8–2.5 m (6–8 ft), **Flowers:** small, yellowish , late spring – early summer, **Foliage:** white variegated, deciduous, **Position:** sun or partial shade, **Soil:** moist, **Habit:** suckering, forming a thicket of stems, brilliant red when young, **Propagation:** hardwood cuttings or replanting suckers removed with roots in late autumn.
☐ Young stems are brilliant red. Cut back in mid-spring to maintain stem colour.

Cornus alba 'Spaethii'
Cornaceae   Dogwood, cornel
ZONES 2–9   SHRUB
Height: 1.8–2.5 m (6–8 ft), **Flowers:** small, yellowish, late spring – early summer, **Foliage:** variegated gold, very eye-catching, deciduous, **Position:** sun or partial shade, **Soil:** moist, **Habit:** suckering, forming a thicket of stems, brilliant red when young, **Propagation:** hardwood cuttings, or replanting rooted suckers removed in late autumn.
☐ Young stems brilliant red. Cut back in mid-spring to maintain stem colour.

Top: *Cornus canadensis*
Left: *Cornus alba*
Above: *Cornus alternifolia* 'Argentea'

Cornus alternifolia 'Argentea'
Cornaceae   Dogwood, cornel
ZONES 5–9   SHRUB
Height: 2.5–3 m (8–10 ft), **Flowers:** white, late spring, **Foliage:** small, creamy-white edges, deciduous, **Position:** sun or partial shade, **Soil:** moist, **Habit:** horizontally spreading branches, **Propagation:** cuttings of firm shoots in summer.
☐ One of the best of all deciduous shrubs with variegated foliage. Particularly attractive with purple-leaved shrubs such as cotinus varieties.

Cornus amomum
Cornaceae   Dogwood, cornel
ZONES 5–9   SHRUB
Height: 3 m (10 ft), **Flowers:** small, yellow-white, late spring – early summer, **Foliage:** dark green above, silky reddish down beneath, deciduous, **Position:** sunny, **Soil:** moist, **Habit:** more or less compact, **Propagation:** cuttings of firm shoots in summer.
☐ Thrives well in moist situations in all areas. Its distinctive features are its purple young stems and blue berries.

Cornus canadensis
Cornaceae   Creeping dogwood
ZONES 5–9   SHRUB
Height: 10–20 cm (4–8 in), **Flowers:** white, early summer, **Foliage:** green, deciduous, **Position:** partial shade, **Soil:** peaty or rich in leafmould, slightly acid, **Habit:** low and creeping, **Propagation:** semi-ripe cuttings in mid – late summer.
☐ Edible red fruits are produced after the white flowers. An attractive groundcover plant for the shrub border or woodland garden.

Cornus controversa
Cornaceae Dogwood, cornel
ZONES 5–9 SHRUB
Height: 6 m (20 ft), **Flowers:** masses of white flowers in early – mid-summer followed by black fruits, **Foliage:** medium green, deciduous, some leaves may turn red in autumn, **Position:** sun or half shade, **Soil:** moist, humus-rich, **Habit:** branches form horizontal layers, **Propagation:** semi-ripe heel cuttings, in mid – late summer.
□'Variegata' is an exquisite and most unusual shrub with silver variegated foliage. A fine feature plant.

Cornus florida var. rubra
Cornaceae Flowering dogwood
ZONES 4–9 SHRUB
Height: 5 m (16 ft), **Flowers:** insignificant, green, surrounded by four large deep pink bracts, late spring, **Foliage:** young leaves reddish, turning green, then autumn tinted, **Position:** sun or partial shade, **Soil:** humus-rich, moist, **Habit:** dense and bushy, **Propagation:** heeled semi-ripe cuttings, mid – late summer.
□Round red fruits late summer and autumn.

Cornus kousa
Cornaceae Dogwood, cornel
ZONES 5–9 SHRUB
Height: 3 m (10 ft), **Flowers:** the white bracts are very showy, early summer, **Foliage:** medium to deep green, deciduous, **Position:** sun or partial shade, **Soil:** humus-rich, **Habit:** wide spreading, **Propagation:** heeled semi-ripe cuttings, mid – late summer.
□Round red fruits in early autumn.

Cornus mas
Cornaceae Cornelian cherry
ZONES 4–9 SHRUB
Height: 4 m (13 ft), **Flowers:** yellow, on leafless stems in late winter – early spring, **Foliage:** green, deciduous, colouring well in autumn, **Position:** sun or partial shade, **Soil:** moist humus-rich, **Habit:** wide spreading, rather open, **Propagation:** seeds when ripe in late summer – early autumn; or by heeled, semi-ripe cuttings, 10 cm (4 in) long, in mid – late summer.
□Red berries sometimes produced. Try an under planting of winter-flowering heathers.

Top left: *Cornus florida* var. *rubra*
Top right: *Cornus kousa*
Right: *Cornus stolonifera* 'Flaviramea'

Cornus nuttallii
Cornaceae Dogwood, cornel
ZONES 6–9 SHRUB
Height: 6 m (20 ft), **Flowers:** conspicuous white bracts, late spring, followed by red fruits, **Foliage:** green, deciduous, beautiful autumn colouring, **Position:** sun or partial shade, **Soil:** moist, humus-rich, not for chalk soils, **Habit:** upright and bushy, **Propagation:** seeds when ripe in late summer – early autumn; or by heeled semi-ripe cuttings 10 cm (4 in) long.
□Not suitable for colder districts.

Cornus stolonifera 'Flaviramea'
Cornaceae Dogwood, cornel
ZONES 2–9 SHRUB
Height: 2.5 m (8 ft), **Flowers:** white, late spring – early summer, **Foliage:** green, deciduous, **Position:** sun or partial shade, **Soil:** moist, humus-rich, **Habit:** suckering, dense thickets of stems, **Propagation:** remove and replant rooted suckers in late autumn; or layer long shoots in early autumn and sever in the mid-autumn of following year; or hardwood cuttings late autumn.
□Yellow winter bark associates well with the red stems of *C. alba*. Prune as for *C. alba*.

Coronilla emerus var. *emeroides*
Leguminosae
ZONES 6–10   SHRUB
Height: 1 m (3 ft), **Flowers:** pea-shaped, yellow, late spring – early summer, **Foliage:** green, ferny, deciduous, **Position:** sun or partial shade, warm and sheltered, **Soil:** fertile and well drained, **Habit:** dense and bushy, **Propagation:** cuttings in summer or nearly autumn or seeds sown in spring. Germination is improved if hot water, about 88°C (284°F) is poured over the seeds first.
□A useful shrub for underplanting trees and taller shrubs.

Coronilla glauca
Leguminosae
ZONES 7–10   SHRUB
Height: 3 m (10 ft), **Flowers:** pea-shaped, yellow, late spring – early summer, fragrant in daytime, **Foliage:** blue-green, pinnate, evergreen, **Position:** sun or partial shade, **Soil:** fertile, light and loamy, well drained, **Habit:** dense and bushy, rounded form, **Propagation:** cuttings in summer or early autumn.
□Best grown against a warm sheltered wall in most districts.

Right: *Coronilla glauca*

Cortaderia selloana
(**syn. *C. argentea, Gynerium argenteum***)
Gramineae Pampas grass
ZONES 7–10   HERBACEOUS PERENNIAL
Height: 1.8–3 m (6–10 ft), **Flowers:** silvery-white fluffy plumes, autumn, **Foliage:** green, narrow and arching, evergreen, **Position:** sunny and open, protected from wind, **Soil:** deep and well drained, rich, light and sandy, **Habit:** large perennial grass, **Propagation:** by seed sown in sandy compost in spring in a propagator; or by division in spring.

Left: *Cortaderia* selloana
Above: *C. selloana* 'Pumila'

□'Pumila' is a dwarfer cultivar 1.2–1.5 m (4–5 ft) high. Plumes can be cut in autumn for house decoration.

A spectacular specimen plant, particularly set against a dark background.

Corylopsis pauciflora
Hamamelidaceae
ZONES 5–9   SHRUB
Height: 1.8 m (6 ft), **Flowers:** light yellow, early – mid-spring, highly fragrant, **Foliage:** green, deciduous, **Position:** full sun or semi-shade, sheltered, **Soil:** humus-rich, ideally acid, **Habit:** wide bushy shrub, **Propagation:** heeled cuttings of side shoots, in mid – late summer, or layer shoots in mid-autumn and sever from the parent plant a year or two later.

Corylus avellana 'Contorta'
Corylaceae Corkscrew hazel

ZONES 4–9   SHRUB

Height: 3 m (10 ft), **Flowers:** yellow 'lamb's tail' catkins, late winter – early spring, **Foliage:** green, deciduous, yellow in autumn, **Position:** open, full sun, or partial shade, but sheltered from cold winds, **Soil:** well-drained, **Habit:** slow-growing, twisted branches, **Propagation:** by layers in summer or autumn and severed when rooted after one year, or by cuttings of ripe wood in mid – late summer.

☐ Though nuts are produced, the main interest is this shrub's twisted stems. An unusual specimen plant for a lawn, conspicuous in winter.

Corylus avellana 'Pendula'
Corylaceae Weeping hazel

ZONES 4–9   SHRUB

Height: 5 m (16 ft), **Flowers:** pendulous yellow catkins, late winter – early spring, **Foliage:** green, deciduous, yellow in autumn, **Position:** open, full sun or partial shade, sheltered, **Soil:** well-drained, **Habit:** arching, weeping branches, **Propagation:** by layers or cuttings.

☐ Clusters each of four or five hazelnuts are produced and ripen in early – mid-autumn.

Corylus maxima 'Purpurea'
Corylaceae Purple-leaf filbert

ZONES 5–9   SHRUB

Height: 4–5 m (13–16 ft), **Flowers:** long purplish catkins, late winter – early spring, **Foliage:** intense purple, deciduous, **Position:** sun or partial shade, **Soil:** well-drained, **Habit:** robust and bushy, **Propagation:** by layers and cuttings.

☐ Nuts, longer than the hazel's and sheathed in cup-like bracts, are produced singly or in pairs. This shrub with its deep purple foliage associates well with golden-foliage shrubs.

Cotinus coggygria
Anacardiaceae Smoke tree

ZONES 4–9   SHRUB

Height: 3 m (10 ft), **Flowers:** buff-pink, fluffy-feathery, early – mid-summer, **Foliage:** green, smooth and rounded, deciduous, very good autumn colour, **Position:** sunny, **Soil:** well-drained, **Habit:** dense, bushy, wide-spreading shrub, **Propagation:** layer long shoots in early autumn, or take heeled cuttings, 10 to 12 cm (4–5 in) long, in late summer – early autumn.

☐ This shrub's flowers hang on, turning grey in late summer, creating a smoky effect which earns it its common name. One of the best shrubs for autumn foliage colour; good plant associations are pampas grass and Michaelmas daisies.

Left: *Cotinus coggygria*

Cotinus coggygria 'Royal Purple'
Anacardiaceae Smoke tree

ZONES 4–9   SHRUB

Height: 3 m (10 ft), **Flowers:** buff-pink, fluffy-feathery flowers, early – mid-summer, **Foliage:** deep purple, turning reddish in autumn, deciduous, **Position:** sunny, **Soil:** well-drained, **Habit:** rounded, **Propagation:** layers or cuttings.

☐ Plant this shrub where the sun can shine through its foliage and you will see it light up as no other shrub can. Good companion plants are red or pink shrub roses.

Cotinus obovatus
Anacardiaceae

ZONES 4–9   SHRUB

Height: 5 m (16 ft), **Flowers:** buff, fluffy-feathery, early – mid-summer, **Foliage:** green, deciduous, magnificent autumn colouring in shades of red, **Position:** sunny, **Soil:** well-drained, **Habit:** tree-like with red branches, **Propagation:** layers or cuttings.

☐ Deserves to be better known as it is one of the finest for autumn colour.

Right: *Cotinus obovatus*

Cotoneaster conspicuus 'Decorus'
Rosaceae

ZONES 4–9   SHRUB

Height: up to 1 m (3 ft), **Flowers:** white, early summer, followed by numerous red berries, **Foliage:** small, dark green, evergreen, **Position:** sun or partial shade, **Soil:** tolerates most soils, **Habit:** low-growing, compact, **Propagation:** heeled cuttings 10 cm (4 in) long of ripening wood in mid – late summer, or layering in late autumn.

☐ This is very free-berrying. Useful for covering banks and areas between tall shrubs.

Cotoneaster dammeri
Rosaceae

ZONES 4–9   SHRUB

Height: 20 cm (8 in), **Flowers:** white, late spring, **Foliage:** deep green, evergreen, **Position:** sun, partial or even full shade, **Soil:** tolerates most soils, **Habit:** quite prostrate with long spreading branches, **Propagation:** well adapted for layering in late autumn, usually rooting well within a year. Alternatively take cuttings of ripening wood, 10 cm (4 in) long, in mid – late summer.

☐ Useful for covering banks or as ground cover under trees. Coral-red berries.

Cotoneaster horizontalis
Rosaceae Herringbone cotoneaster

ZONES 4–9   SHRUB

Height: roughly 1 m (3 ft), **Flowers:** white, late spring – early summer, **Foliage:** small deep green shiny leaves, with red autumn tints, deciduous, **Position:** sun, partial or full shade, **Soil:** tolerates most soils, **Habit:** branches of flat, herringbone pattern, **Propagation:** layering in late autumn or cuttings in mid – late summer.

☐ Red berries follow flowers. An invaluable shrub for north- or east-facing walls or for covering banks.

Above left: *Cotoneaster microphyllus*
Above centre: *Cotoneaster* 'Rothschildianus'
Above right: *Cotoneaster salicifolius*
Below right: *Cotoneaster salicifolius*

Cotoneaster horizontalis
'Variegatus'
Rosaceae
ZONES 5–9   SHRUB
Height: about 1 m (3 ft), **Flowers:** white, late spring – early summer, **Foliage:** cream variegated, flushed with red in autumn, deciduous, **Position:** sun or partial shade, **Soil:** tolerates most soils, **Habit:** densely spreading shrub with herringbone branch arrangement, **Propagation:** by layering in late autumn or cuttings in mid – late summer.
☐ Bright red berries follow flowers. Leaves colour in autumn. Ideal for planting against a wall.

Cotoneaster microphyllus
Rosaceae
ZONES 5–9   SHRUB
Height: 15 cm (6 in), **Flowers:** white, late spring – early summer, **Foliage:** small, deep green shiny leaves, evergreen, **Position:** sun or partial shade, **Soil:** suits most soils, **Habit:** very prostrate and spreading to 2.5 m (8 ft), **Propagation:** by layering in late autumn, or cuttings taken in mid-summer or mid-autumn.
☐ A very useful shrub for clothing banks, walls and manholes. The red berries are extra large.

Cotoneaster 'Rothschildianus'
Rosaceae
ZONES 6–9   SHRUB
Height: 1.8–3 m (6–10 ft), **Flowers:** white, late spring – early summer, followed by pale yellow berries, **Foliage:** medium green, semi-evergreen, **Position:** sun or partial shade, **Soil:** tolerates most soils, **Habit:** distinctive, spreading habit, **Propagation:** by layering in late autumn, or cuttings taken mid – late summer.
☐ The cultivar 'Exburiensis' is similar in producing large clusters of yellow berries. Both excellent alongside autumn-foliage shrubs and tolerates the seaside.

Cotoneaster salicifolius
Rosaceae
ZONES 6–9   SHRUB
Height: 4.5 m (15 ft), **Flowers:** white, early summer, **Foliage:** dark-green, evergreen, **Position:** sun or partial shade, **Soil:** tolerates most soils, **Habit:** tall and graceful, **Propagation:** by layering in late autumn, or cuttings taken during mid – late summer.
☐ Bright red fruits. Suitable for a large shrub border. Grows well in seaside gardens.

Cotoneaster simonsii
Rosaceae
ZONES 5–9   SHRUB
Height: 1.8–2.5 m (6–8 ft), **Flowers:** white, early – mid-summer, **Foliage:** deep green, ovate, semi-evergreen, **Position:** sun or partial shade, **Soil:** tolerates most soils, **Habit:** upright growing, **Propagation:** by heeled cuttings 10 cm (4 in) long in mid – late summer.
☐ Makes an attractive hedge. Large crops of red-orange fruits and upright habit. Suitable for seaside gardens.

Crambe cordifolia

Cruciferae Seakale

ZONES 7–9   HERBACEOUS PERENNIAL
Height: 1.2–1.5 m (4–5 ft), **Flowers:** white, in massive panicles, early – midsummer, **Foliage:** greyish green, very large heart-shaped, deciduous, **Position:** sunny and open. **Soil:** alkaline, fertile, **Habit:** robust perennial with thick roots, needs considerable space, **Propagation:** by seed sown outdoors in spring, or by division in spring.

□ Ideal foliage plant for seaside gardens.

Crataegus oxyacantha 'Coccinea Plena'

(syn. 'Paul's Scarlet')

Rosaceae Double scarlet hawthorn

ZONES 4–9   SHRUB
Height: 5–7.5 m (16–25 ft), **Flowers:** double scarlet, produced in profusion in late spring, followed in autumn by small red fruits, **Foliage:** mid green, deciduous, **Position:** full sun, open position but tolerates semi-shade, **Soil:** tolerates most soils, **Habit:** round headed, good for both town and seaside planting, **Propagation:** by grafting on to *C. monogyna* stocks in spring.

Crepis incana

Compositae Hawksbeard

ZONES 5–9   ROCK PLANT
Height: 23–30 cm (9–12 in), **Flowers:** pale pink, mid – late summer, **Foliage:** greyish-green, ovate, deciduous, **Position:** sunny borders, banks or rock gardens, **Soil:** well-drained, **Habit:** forms a compact clump, **Propagation:** by seed sown in spring, or division in spring.

Crinodendron hookeranum

Elaeocarpaceae Lantern tree

ZONES 8–10   SHRUB
Height: 3–5 m (10–16 ft), **Flowers:** deep red, lantern-shaped, pendulous, spring, **Foliage:** glossy green, evergreen, **Position:** semi-shade, sheltered from winds, **Soil:** acid, moisture retentive, fertile, **Habit:** densely branched, **Propagation:** heeled cuttings 10 cm (4 in) long of ripening shoots in mid – late summer.

□ A gem, but for mild districts only. Best grown against a warm sheltered wall.

Cryptomeria japonica 'Elegans'

Taxodiaceae Japanese cedar

ZONES 5–9   CONIFER
Height: about 1.8 m (6 ft) after 10 years, ultimately 6 m (20 ft), **Flowers and cones:** strobili orange or reddish in early spring, roundish cones, not particularly noticeable, **Foliage:** rusty green in summer, copper coloured in winter, evergreen, **Position:** sun or partial shade, **Soil:** moisture retentive, acid or neutral, **Habit:** broadly conical or pyramidal, **Propagation:** by seed or cuttings (see p. 70).

□ Attractive fine-textured conifer. Good specimen tree for the larger lawn.

Above: *Cryptomeria japonica* 'Lobbii Nana'
Above right: *C. japonica* 'Vilminiana'

Other recommended cultivars of *Cryptomeria japonica*

ZONES 5–9

Heights given are after approximately 10 years growth. All are ideal for planting in heather beds or in rock gardens.
'Globosa' – 30–75 cm (1–2½ ft) high; foliage in summer yellow-green; reddish in winter; broad rounded bush.
'Lobbii Nana' ('Compacta') – 45–75 cm (1½–2½ ft) high; summer foliage pale green turning rusty; elegantly rounded bush.
'Pygmaea' – 30–75 cm (1–2½ ft) high; lime green foliage turning bronze in winter; slow-growing compact rounded bush.
'Vilmoriniana' (above) – 30–75 cm (1–2½ ft); summer foliage green-bronze turning reddish purple; forms packed ball.

x *Cupressocyparis leylandii*

Cupressaceae   Leyland cypress

ZONES 5–9   CONIFER

Height: about 10 m (33 ft) after 10 years if unrestricted, ultimate height 20 m (65 ft), **Cones:** round and brown, but of no decorative merit, **Foliage:** mid-green, evergreen, **Position:** sun or partial shade, suits maritime gardens, **Soil:** deep, well-drained, **Habit:** broad cone, very fast growing, **Propagation:** by cuttings (see p. 70).

□A specimen tree or excellent hedging plant. As a hedge plants should be spaced 1 m (3 ft) apart. It can be pruned hard.

'Castlewellan' has green-gold foliage, at its brightest in full sun. Makes a fine hedge.

Cupressus glabra 'Conica' (**syn. *C. arizonica* 'Conica'**)

Cupressaceae   Smooth Arizona cypress

ZONES 7–10   CONIFER

Height: about 4 m (13 ft) after 10 years, ultimately 15 m (50 ft), **Cones:** brown and rounded, noticeable but not of great decorative merit, **Foliage:** bluish-grey, aromatic, evergreen, **Position:** sun or partial shade, **Soil:** any type, well-drained, **Habit:** broadly cone or pyramid shaped, **Propagation:** by cuttings, as seed will not come true to type. (see p. 70).

Cupressus macrocarpa

Cupressaceae   Monterey cypress

ZONES 6–10   CONIFER

Height: about 6 m (20 ft) after 10 years, ultimately 20 m (65 ft), **Cones:** brown and rounded, numerous, **Foliage:** mid-green, becoming darker with age, aromatic, evergreen, **Position:** sun or part shade, excellent for seaside planting, **Soil:** any type, well drained, **Habit:** columnar with conical top when young, broadening with age, when lower growths tend to die off, **Propagation:** by seed (see p. 68).

□Now largely superseded by x *Cupressocyparis leylandii* which is faster growing, hardier and does not become bare at the bottom.

Good hedging conifer, or can be used as a specimen in a large lawn.

Cupressus macrocarpa 'Goldcrest'

Cupressaceae   Monterey cypress

ZONES 7–10   CONIFER

Height: 3 m (10 ft) after 10 years, ultimately 7.5 m (25 ft), **Flowers and cones:** insignificant, **Foliage:** brilliant yellow, very intense in winter, aromatic, evergreen, **Position:** open and sunny, protect from cold winds, **Soil:** any type, well-drained, **Habit:** neat, upright and conical, **Propagation:** by cuttings (see p. 70).

□Good companions are 'blue' or grey conifers of similar stature.

Cupressus sempervirens 'Stricta'

Cupressaceae   Italian cypress

ZONES 8–10   CONIFER

Height: about 3 m (10 ft) after 10 years, ultimately 20 m (65 ft), **Flowers and cones:** insignificant, **Foliage:** deep green, aromatic, evergreen, **Position:** sunny, shelter from cold winds, **Soil:** dry type, well-drained, **Habit:** very narrow column, **Propagation:** by cuttings (see p. 70).

□Excellent as a focal point in larger garden.

Left: *Cupressus macrocarpa* 'Goldcrest'

Cytisus ardoinii

Leguminosae Broom

ZONES 5–10   SHRUB

Height: 20 cm (8 in), **Flowers:** yellow, mid – late spring, **Foliage:** green, deciduous, **Position:** very sunny, **Soil:** does best in neutral or slightly acid soils, **Habit:** miniature, forms a carpet, **Propagation:** seeds or heeled cuttings of sideshoots, 10 cm (4 in) long in late summer – early autumn.

☐ Recommended for rock gardens and ground cover (particularly on dry banks).

Cytisus battandieri

Leguminosae Algerian broom

ZONES 7–10   SHRUB

Height: 4 m (13 ft), **Flowers:** bright yellow, fruity scent, late spring – early summer, **Foliage:** silvery, deciduous, **Position:** very sunny, **Soil:** best in neutral or slightly acid soil, **Habit:** upright, **Propagation:** heeled cuttings of side shoots, in late summer – early autumn.

☐ Very sheltered spot needed in cold areas – excellent against a warm sunny wall where it looks good with climbing roses of all colours.

Cytisus × beanii

Leguminosae Broom

ZONES 6–10   SHRUB

Height: 60 cm (2 ft), **Flowers:** yellow, late spring, **Foliage:** green, deciduous, **Position:** sunny, **Soil:** best in neutral or slightly acid soil, **Habit:** dwarf, compact, **Propagation:** heeled cuttings of side shoots in late summer.

☐ Suitable for the rock garden or planting on dry sunny banks.

Cytisus decumbens

Leguminosae Broom

ZONES 5–10   SHRUB

Height: 1 m (3 ft), **Flowers:** yellow, late spring – early summer, **Foliage:** green, deciduous, **Position:** sunny, **Soil:** best in neutral or slightly acid soil, **Habit:** a prostrate shrub, wide spreading, **Propagation:** heeled cuttings 10 cm (4 in) long of side shoots, taken in late summer – early autumn.

☐ Makes good ground cover on a dry sunny bank.

Cytisus × kewensis

Leguminosae Broom

ZONES 6–10   SHRUB

Height: 60 cm (2 ft), **Flowers:** creamy yellow, late spring, **Foliage:** green, deciduous, **Position:** sunny, **Soil:** lime-tolerant, but best in neutral or slightly acid soil, **Habit:** a low-growing shrub of pros-

trate habit, **Propagation:** seed or cuttings.

☐ A very attractive little shrub, suitable for the rock garden, dry bank or front of a sunny border.

Cytisus nigricans

Leguminosae Broom

ZONES 5–10   SHRUB

Height: 1.5 m (5 ft), **Flowers:** yellow, held in long sprays, early summer – early autumn, **Foliage:** green, deciduous, **Position:** sunny, **Soil:** lime-tolerant, but best in neutral or slightly acid soil, **Habit:** erect, **Propagation:** seed or cuttings.

☐ A very useful shrub due to its exceptionally long flowering period.

Above left: *Cytisus battandieri*
Above: *Cytisus × beanii*

Cytisus × praecox

Leguminosae Warminster broom

ZONES 5–10   SHRUB

Height: 1.5 m (5 ft), **Flowers:** rich cream, mid – late spring, **Foliage:** green, insignificant, deciduous, **Position:** sunny, **Soil:** tolerates most soils, even dry, poor and stony, but not too acid or too limy, **Habit:** erect and bushy, with arching branches, **Propagation:** by cuttings taken in mid-summer.

☐ To stop this shrub becoming leggy, cut back immediately after flowering, but not into old, hard wood. 'Albus' has white flowers, 'Allgold', bright yellow.

Cytisus purpureus
Leguminosae   Purple broom
ZONES 5–10   SHRUB
Height: 60 cm (2 ft) or a little more, **Flowers:** purple, late spring – early summer, **Foliage:** deep-green, deciduous, **Position:** sunny, **Soil:** dry, normal garden soil, even poor and stony, but not too acid or alkaline, **Habit:** dwarf and compact, **Propagation:** by cuttings taken in midsummer.
☐A good little shrub for the front of a sunny border or for the rock garden. Prune young flowering stems after flowering. Suitable for seaside gardens.

Cytisus scoparius 'Andreanus'
Leguminosae   Common broom
ZONES 5–10   SHRUB
Height: 2.5 m (8 ft), **Flowers:** yellow and red, late spring – early summer, **Foliage:** green, trifoliate, deciduous, **Position:** sunny, **Soil:** tolerates most soils, even if dry, poor or stony, but not too acid or too limy, **Habit:** upright to arching branches, **Propagation:** by cuttings taken in midsummer.
☐Induce bushy growth by lightly cutting back young stems immediately after flowering. Good companion plants are cistus. Suitable for seaside gardens.

Cytisus scoparius 'Burkwoodii'

Other recommended cultivars of *Cytisus scoparius*
ZONES 5–10
'*Burkwoodii*' – 1.8 m (6 ft); deep-red flowers.
'*Firefly*' – 1.8 m (6 ft); yellow and deep red.
'*Golden Sunlight*' – 1.8 m (6 ft); bright golden yellow flowers.
'*Goldfinch*' – 1.8 m (6 ft); purple, red and yellow.
'*Lena*' – 1–1.5 m (3–5 ft); red and yellow flowers; keep bushy and compact by lightly cutting back flowering stems.

Daboecia cantabrica
   'Atropurpurea'
Ericaceae   Connemara heath, St Dabeoc's heath
ZONES 5–9   SHRUB
Height: up to 60 cm (2 ft), **Flowers:** purple-pink, pitcher-shaped in long racemes, early summer – late autumn, **Foliage:** deep green, silvery underneath, evergreen, **Position:** sun or partial shade, **Soil:** lime-free, sandy peat or loam, **Habit:** bushy and compact, **Propagation:** by cuttings taken in mid – late summer, or by layering shoots in autumn.

Above left: *Daboecia cantabrica*
Above: *Daboecia cantabrica* 'Alba'

☐Clip over in spring with shears. 'Alba' has white flowers, 'Bicolor' has purple-pink and white flowers.
   Ideal subject for heather beds.

Danae racemosa
   (syn. *Ruscus racemous*)
Ruscaceae   Alexandrian laurel
ZONES 6–10   SHRUB
Height: 1 m (3 ft), **Flowers:** greenish white, summer, **Foliage:** glossy, bright green leaf-like stems, evergreen, **Position:** partial or full shade, **Soil:** most moist soils, **Habit:** bamboo-like, **Propagation:** seeds sown outdoors in early – mid-autumn, or by division in spring.
☐Orange-red fruits are sometimes produced after mild summers. Good for cutting for flower arranging. Useful shrub for woodland conditions.